THE BLOODLESS REVOLUTION

STUART E. PRALL was a Fulbright scholar at the University of Manchester, England, 1953–54, and received his Ph.D. in 1960 from Columbia University. He is at present a professor of History at Queens College of the City University of New York and is the author of *The Agitation for Law Reform During the Puritan Revolution, 1640–1660*, the editor of *The Puritan Revolution: A Documentary History*, and the co-author of A *History of England*, 3d edition (with D. H. Willson).

THE
BLOODLESS
REVOLUTION

England, 1688

STUART E. PRALL

THE UNIVERSITY OF WISCONSIN PRESS

ACKNOWLEDGMENTS

*I want to express my gratitude to the doctoral faculty of the
City University of New York for their financial assistance; the
libraries of Columbia University for the liberty to use their
facilities; the staff of the Manuscripts Room of the British
Museum for their kind co-operation; Miss Ronnie Shushan,
who edited the manuscript; Mrs. Kay Scheuer, formerly of
Doubleday Anchor Books, for her interest and encouragement;
and most of all to my wife, Naomi, without whose help and
understanding this book would never have been written.*

Published 1985

The University of Wisconsin Press
114 North Murray Street
Madison, Wisconsin 53715

The University of Wisconsin Press, Ltd.
1 Gower Street
London WC1E 6HA, England

First Wisconsin printing
Published by arrangement with Doubleday & Company, Inc.

Printed in the United States of America

For LC CIP information see p. 344

ISBN 0-299-10294-7
LC 85-40377

The photographs in this book are reproduced by permission of the
National Portrait Gallery, London

Contents

LIST OF ILLUSTRATIONS

Preface

Since G. M. Trevelyan wrote *The English Revolution, 1688–1689*, in 1938, there has been a slow but steady increase in interest in this "glorious" or "sensible" or "necessary" or "bloodless" revolution. Until recent years, however, this interest was largely a by-product of the much greater concern with the Puritan Revolution of 1640–60, which was in turn a reflection of the general scholarly interest in all the great revolutionary movements of the modern era. With the world being in the midst of almost perpetual revolution since World War II, it is only natural that historians, political scientists, and sociologists have sought to come to grips with the present by plunging themselves into the history of seventeenth-century England, eighteenth-century France, nineteenth- and twentieth-century Russia, and twentieth-century China. All these studies have led to the new discipline of the study of comparative revolutions. It is in this context that the Puritan Revolution has come to be called "the English Revolution."

The Glorious Revolution has not so far evoked the same intense interest as these other revolutions, largely because it was bloodless, short, and, given its limited goals, highly successful. Even though Englishmen thought of it as "the Revolution" throughout the eighteenth and nineteenth centuries, it has come to be regarded as little more than a *coup d'état* by many twentieth-century scholars. What modern

scholars of revolution are looking for is a massive social upheaval, not a political or constitutional change
however profound. The revolution of 1688 has,
rather, largely been of interest only to scholars in the
English-speaking world who have not devoted their
lives to the study of the other revolutions. In other
words, it has been treated in isolation as far as revolutionary historiography goes. This seems to me a
fundamental error. In fact, it is my contention that the
Glorious Revolution is understandable only when it is
put into the context of the Puritan Revolution, and
thus of revolution in general.

In a more particular sense, it seems essential to link
the study of these two seventeenth-century English
revolutions, since the one is not really completely
understandable without the other. Although there is
still great controversy as to what caused the Puritan
Revolution, there is little dispute over the causes of
the Restoration, in 1660. However, the Restoration of
1660 cannot be looked upon as writing finis to the
score of years that preceded it. It is precisely because
the Restoration failed to solve the problems that
brought on revolution in 1642 that it was necessary
for England to experience the events of 1688–89.
When the two revolutions are thus linked together, a
brighter light may well be brought to bear upon the
actual causes of the Puritan Revolution. It is thus my
contention that the study of either of the seventeenth-
century English revolutions in isolation is misleading
and thus self-defeating. The great divide between
early and modern England is not 1640 or 1660 or
even 1688. The divide is the half century from 1640–
89. It was during this half century that the foundations were laid for the constitutional, political, religious, and socioeconomic structures of modern England, structures that were stable until the great
reforms of the nineteenth century, and structures that
in fact were changed less by these nineteenth-century
reforms than the earlier structures had been changed

by the revolutions of the seventeenth century. In the
words of Christopher Hill, seventeenth-century England was indeed a "century of revolution." A new
England was born, and it was to be an England still
recognizable today in its fundamental forms and attitudes.

If the views briefly presented above are valid, the
question then arises as to how the already existing lit-
erature on the revolution of 1688–89 may be seen as
giving an incomplete or inadequate picture of the
Glorious Revolution. The classic history of England
in the late-seventeenth century is of course the mag-
isterial work of Thomas Babington Macaulay. His
*History of England from the Accession of James the
Second*—originally published in five volumes between 1849 and 1865—continues to stand up well,
not only because of its magnificent style and classic
narrative form, which make it readily accessible to the
layman as well as the scholar, but also because he was
aware that the crucial events of 1688–89 had to be
put into the context of the entire seventeenth century.
In fact, one fifth of the entire work is devoted to events
prior to James's accession. The thought does come to
mind, though, that when Macaulay devoted so much
space to these earlier years, he was not so much influenced by awareness that this was necessary to a truer
understanding of James's reign as he was by the clas-
sical tradition of narrative history, which required the
author to start with the "beginning." And, true to this
tradition, Macaulay does start with the "beginning" of
the Saxon invasions of the British Isles. If there is a
serious fault to be found in Macaulay's work, it is that
in it he presents the classic Whig view that liberal England was the best of all possible worlds and that this
best of liberal worlds grew inevitably and inexorably
out of the whole course of English history, the Glorious Revolution merely being the coming of age of
all the virtues of liberal England which had been
spawned in the forests of Saxon England by its con-

version to Christianity. Many modern scholars find
this implication of an English "manifest destiny" distasteful, as they do Macaulay's tendency to take sides
and to paint his portraits of the major characters in
black and white terms. Nonetheless, Macaulay remains fine reading and good narrative history.

George Macaulay Trevelyan's classic essay has,
since its publication in 1938, continued to hold the
field as the modern statement of the Whig interpretation of the events and the significance of 1688–89.
While he does trace the origins of the Glorious Revolution from the time of the Restoration, and thus
puts it into the context of the effects of the earlier revolution, he does carry on the Macaulay tradition of
the seeming manifest destiny of the development of
liberal democratic institutions and a basic consensus
in English public life. In his view, the old England
had been divided by interests of class, economic function, religion, and region. The post-1869 England
was to have the liberal nineteenth-century characteristics of common sense, a spirit of compromise, and a
fundamental conviction that by peaceful evolution
England would move steadily forward on its preor-
dained path to the stable, democratic, united nation
he saw in the twentieth century. While many historians, again, do find this nationalistic and Whiggish interpretation distasteful, there is no question that Trevelyan's work, both because of this appeal to popular
prejudice and because of its readability and scholarship, is the standard against which the more-recent
scholarly work has been directed. One may try to refute or revise Trevelyan, but one cannot ignore him.

The works that have come closest to supplanting
Macaulay's as the standard history of the post-
Restoration era are David Ogg's two-volume *England
in the Reign of Charles II* (published four years before
Trevelyan's work) and his volume *England in the
Reigns of James II and William III* (which appeared in
1955). To the extent that Ogg goes beyond description

and narrative, his work is essentially in the Whig tradition. His volumes have become the new standard because of their immense scholarship, the breadth of their coverage of all facets of English life, and the solid bases for his interpretations. Like Trevelyan, he places the events of the post-Restoration in the long historical context of English institutional life. As with Trevelyan, one cannot work in this period of English history without relying heavily upon the work of David Ogg, both for an insight into what was important, and for reasoned, scholarly analysis. Ogg's work does not have the overtones of "manifest destiny" about it, and it is aware that all of England's problems for the future were not solved, nor were they on the way to being solved, because of the Glorious Revolution.

But the reasoned and scholarly work of David Ogg has not ended the interest in reinterpreting the Macaulay-Trevelyan traditions.

J. R. Jones has contributed a most interesting reinterpretation of James's policies and goals in *The Revolution of 1688 in England*. He stresses that James sought to establish an absolute monarchy, not necessarily a Catholic state. In the process of creating this absolutism, he tried to pack a new parliament, not to eliminate parliament. The packing was to be accomplished by an alliance with the urban business (and dissenting) classes. The result is that Jones offers us a paradox: a Whig king brought on a Tory Revolution. Whether or not this was the case, Jones's book is the best account available of the king's efforts to pack parliament and to achieve his goals by statutory means.

Since World War II, several scholars have attempted, in whole or in part, to supplant the Whig interpretation with what can be called a Tory interpretation. Some of this work can be called Tory for no other reason than that the authors sympathize with James II and his goals, or with the Jacobites, who refused to accept the Revolution as an accomplished fact that could not be undone. The scholars of this persuasion have either shown James II to be a statesman of high moral principle who truly and honorably sought religious toleration, or they have stressed the role of William of Orange and the conspiratorial nature of his descent on England, or they have even ignored the period of the Revolution itself and have concentrated on Tory politics, religion, and philosophy in subsequent years. The most thorough and complete reversal of the Whig view is to be found in Lucile Pinkham, *William III and the Respectable Revolution*. Mrs. Pinkham doesn't merely sympathize with James II, but considers that he and England were in fact the victims of a foreign conquest that was the fulfillment of William's lifelong ambition.

While there is undoubtedly a great deal of merit in Mrs. Pinkham's thesis, it is still *in toto* quite unacceptable. She does not bring herself to consider that there must have been circumstances in England that made William's venture a successful one. That William desired the conquest of England may be true, but why did England acquiesce in this conquest? The trouble, then, with her book is not that she is willing to look outside of England for the key to the problem of the Glorious Revolution, but that she ignores England in the process.

Mr. Maurice Ashley's *The Glorious Revolution of 1688* was planned as a corrective to both the Whig and the Pinkham theses. While he does devote a good deal of attention to the events in England itself in the reign of James II, he does not really place the revolution in an English historical context beyond a brief survey of the exclusion crisis of 1678–81. He, too, devotes at least equal treatment to the role of William and the general influence on both William and James of the European diplomatic and military situation of the 1680s. The result is a highly readable and informative essay, but the reader is still left with the problem of trying to understand how it was that a foreign intervention, aided and abetted by certain groups in England, came to be so readily and peacefully accepted by the great bulk of the established leaders in the English Church and state, and by the mass of ordinary Englishmen.

Both Mrs. Pinkham and Mr. Ashley represent something other than a Tory reaction, however. They both are rebelling against the insular nationalism of the Macaulay-Trevelyan genre. Their work is part of the post-World War II trend that insists that England is now and has always been part of general European history and that its own development cannot be studied meaningfully except in that European context. Without question, this has been a necessary and highly welcome corrective to the older, Whig interpretation, but it can in its turn be overdone. Mrs. Pinkham's work cannot be allowed to stand on its own, and Mr. Ashley's revision, while a long step in the direction of balancing the old with the new, still tends to lean too far in the direction of Mrs. Pinkham.

In addition to supplying a European corrective to the Whig interpretation, Mrs. Pinkham and Mr. Ashley also have shown themselves to be a part of the post-World War II school that accepts the modern pluralistic and secular state as the only acceptable democratic ideal. Thus James II himself is seen as a monarch who is in the modern tradition of religious toleration, contending with forces in the Church of England and among Dissenters who stood for one form or another of Protestant ascendency. But it is one thing to accept their views as to what makes for a truly democratic society in the twentieth century and quite another thing to assume that James II shared their goals in the seventeenth century. Where the Whig writers looked upon James as being essentially the bigot trying to foist an alien religion upon the unwilling mass of the English people, Pinkham and Ashley portray him as being truly modern in the sincerity with which he sought nothing more than a pluralistic

and tolerant society. In their attempt to redeem the
reputation of James II, they have surely gone too far.

John Carswell, in *The Descent on England*, also
portrays James II as well-meaning but stupid. He was
a patriot, unlike his brother Charles II, and sought an
efficient, tolerant, and independent nation under the
guidance of the crown. The book, in fact, is a newer
version of Mrs. Pinkham's thesis, except that it goes
into greater detail. Even when he recounts the background of the fall of James II, the reader is never made
to feel that the events in England and the attitudes
that Englishmen had to those events were really all
that important. As his title suggests, the Glorious Revolution was essentially William's invation of England.

In a more strictly Tory vein is Gerald Straka's *Anglican Reaction to the Revolution of 1688*. Mr. Straka
has attempted to avoid direct involvement by presenting the bestowal of the English crown upon William
and Mary in the light in which it was seen by contemporaries. What he has actually done is to challenge
the whole Whig interpretation by showing that there
was in fact a greater continuity in political and constitutional theory than the Whig historians have ever allowed. Straka shows how the Anglican Church in particular was able to accept the Revolution without
drastically modifying its historic views on the divine
nature of the English monrchy. But Straka is not so
concerned with what brought about the Revolution;
he is interested only in how traditional elements in
society were able to accept it. In the process, he ignores the Jacobites, those traditional Tories who were
not able to accept the Revolution or the settlement
that followed.

The historiography of the Glorious Revolution has
now reached the point at which a new effort must be
made to present the story of 1688–89 in a new context, one that takes full acount of the work not only of
the traditional Whig interpretation but also of the valuable correctives to that tradition which the post-

World War II generation of scholars has provided. It is my hope that this book will accomplish with some modicum of success this necessary goal. In pursuit of this goal I intend to develop the background in essentially chronological order, starting with the Restoration and continuing through the Act of Settlement of 1701. Within this essentially chronological order, narrative will be combined with analysis and commentary on the views of those historians concerned with each of the subjects under discussion.

It is hoped that this approach will show that the Glorious Revolution was indeed the culminating episode in the long crisis in English affairs begun back in 1640, and that the Revolution Settlement was in fact a settlement of those problems which the Puritan Revolution and the Restoration had left unsolved. To this extent, the Whig interpretation has been accepted, in that I do assume that the England that followed the Glorious Revolution was to have a constitutional and political structure different from that in the earlier-seventeenth century. It will also be seen, however, that even though the end result of the Revolution may be much like that described by the Whig historians, the role played by the Whig leaders in the later-seventeenth century was no more important—and possibly was even less important—than that played by the Tories. The real glory of the Revolution may indeed be that it was a Whig revolution effected by the Tories. The fundamental urge on the part of leaders of both parties in 1688 and 1689 to effect a revolution without reviving the horrors of the Civil War of the 1640s may well be seen to be a compromise by which Whig goals are achieved by means of Tory principles and leaders.

It is also hoped that the role and ambitions of William of Orange will be seen in a realistic context. The really important question is not what William's ambitions may have been but why England was willing to accept him and his ambitions. England will be seen as part of European history without losing sight of the fact that England's geographical insularity was a determining factor in the minds of many influential figures, and that in the seventeenth century, if not in the twentieth, the impact of outside influences upon England's domestic affairs was obviously far less than the impact of purely domestic considerations. The Glorious Revolution had a greater influence on Europe than Europe had upon the Glorious Revolution.

PART I

England Restored

CHAPTER 1

The Civil War Legacy

As Charles II made his triumphal progress from Dover to Westminster, amid the cheers of his loving and loyal subjects, Cavaliers and Roundheads were both thinking hard about how to turn this happy occasion into victory for the one and the avoidance of defeat for the other. Ever since the death of Oliver Cromwell, in September of 1658, the return to England of the ancient monarchy took on the air of inevitability. It was almost amazing the way all parties and factions assumed its inevitability. Even the Regicides appeared to be resigned to it. During the next twenty months leading up to Charles II's arrival, there was much coming and going, jockeying for position, and some little caviling; but no agreement was to emerge as to what conditions might or could be exacted from an obviously eager royal party awaiting the call from exile in Holland. The character, personality, and experiences in exile of the young king undoubtedly had much to do with the creation of this atmosphere in England. Few seriously expected that a bloody revenge would be enacted, as could logically be expected from a prince less politically astute or easygoing than Charles II. Of course, knowledge of Charles's astuteness was less important than the hints that had gone out from his court that he sought nothing more than the reinstatement of the ancient constitution coupled with the prompt holding of free elections to a Parliament held under the old franchise. Many were to suspect, and correctly, that such elections would return not a few from the old Parliamentarian fold.

It was undoubtedly a matter both of policy and of instinct that the declaration Charles issued from Breda seven weeks before he embarked for Dover should call for national reconciliation and a free pardon for all his and his father's enemies. It also confirmed his willingness to call for a free Parliament, and the fact that this free Parliament was to take the initiative in determining the form of the restoration of the nation's unity. If there was to be revenge, then Parliament would provide the specifics. By thus placing himself in the role of mediator and upholder of the national unity, Charles II succeeded in establishing a national basis for the institution of monarchy; but he also succeeded in arousing suspicions in the hearts of true Royalists, suspicions that were to lead eventually to the Glorious Revolution. By refusing, wisely, to return to England in the role of a mere leader of the Cavalier party, he forced the Cavaliers to look unto themselves for the leadership and the means by which to further their own interests. And it made them aware that their interests were not necessarily identical to, or even compatible with, those of the king.

That Charles was not to be the mere leader of a Cavalier interest is evidenced by his willingness to keep in being the Convention Parliament called by General George Monck in April 1660, a Convention called on the proviso that those who had fought on the Royalist side, or their sons, were not to be returned. Since this ban was not completely enforceable, at least one hundred Presbyterians were elected; that this was a disappointment to the Presbyterians should not hide from us the fact that the Cavaliers hoped to exclude them altogether. Charles returned at the end of May, and it was not until the end of December that the Convention was dissolved and new elections called. The spirit of reconciliation expressed in the Declaration of Breda was thus to be given some substance by a body in which the Cavaliers had less than full sway.

Even more remarkable, and disconcerting to the Cavaliers, was Charles's willingness to let the Convention Parliament determine the land settlement. Nothing, not even the nature of the constitution or the structure and doctrines of the Church, was to rank as high in the estimation of the aristocracy and gentry as the sanctity of private property, and of landed property especially. During the Civil War, crown lands, church lands, and the lands of many Royalists had been confiscated. Many other supporters of the king had been forced to sell land in order to secure the sums to pay their fines to the victorious Parliament. Still other Royalists had voluntarily disposed of their lands in order to contribute cash to the royal cause. A true restoration, then, meant the restoration of their lands, a restoration that in the name of national unity and reconciliation was not to be accomplished. The Act of Oblivion did restore the crown lands and the Church lands, but ordinary subjects were to have their lands returned only in those instances in which the lands had been subject to direct confiscation. All those lands that had been sold voluntarily or under the necessity to raise money with which to pay fines were not to be restored. Great numbers of gentry and nobles were to go to their graves feeling cheated of the fruits of victory. The king's willingness to forgive his father's murderers was one thing; his willingness to let his loyal Cavaliers pay the price of his Restoration was another. The Act of Oblivion probably did more than any other single act to keep the Royalists, or Cavaliers, from becoming just a party in the service of the crown. It was to make of them a Tory party, with both court and country elements. In return, however, the crown was to be rewarded with the support of many former Parliamentarians and moderate Puritans.

The new king's sense of moderation was also to be seen in the general area of the constitution or structure

of the government. In a strictly technical sense his
reign had begun the moment his father's head was
chopped off, and thus every act of government since
that point was legally null and void. Also, all the
actions of the Parliamentary government since the
Militia Bill of 1642 were legally null and void, since
Charles I had not sanctioned them. Thus the crown
that Charles II put on in May of 1660 was legally
the crown that his father had worn on the eve of
hostilities in 1642, a crown that had undergone many
significant reforms during the first two years of the
Long Parliament. Neither the king nor the Convention
was to seek to undo those reforms. The essential question is, how far had the reforms enacted during 1640
and 1641 gone toward eliminating those fundamental
political and constitutional grievances that had played
such a large role in precipitating the Civil War in the
first place?

Throughout the reigns of James I and Charles I the
unity of the Elizabethan state was slowly but surely
crumbling. England was faced with a most unhappy
concurrence of events. On the one hand there was the
accession to the throne of the Scottish house of Stuart,
represented in the first instance by a king who little
understood England and was basically unwilling to
learn about it, and represented in the second instance
by a king who may have understood the technical workings of the English government and society, but who
chose, perhaps because of this knowledge, to change
it in many important respects. On the other hand there
was emerging within the landed classes, and to a much
lesser extent within the commercial classes, a vocal,
experienced, and ambitious nucleus of men who
sought to preserve the fundamental forms of English
government and society by making use of their ability
to create a following in Parliament. The early Stuart
kings thus sought to perfect what they considered to be
the logic of "Tudor despotism" in an England that
was in fact going through a social, religious, and eco-

nomic transformation which in turn was to bring Parliament and the "country" elements within it to strive mightily to seize the initiative.[1] Unless some form of compromise could be found between these two opposing impulses, a resort to arms was not to be unexpected. It is necessary at this point to outline briefly the two opposing views as to the "fundamental" structure of the English state. These views would eventually be reconcilable only after a civil war, a republican experiment followed by military dictatorship, a restoration of the old monarchy on an increasingly shaky foundation, and the final conscious and deliberate compromise of the Glorious Revolution and its settlement.

As seen by James I and Charles I, England was a true monarchy. The king was the symbol of the sovereign state in both its temporal and its spiritual aspects. The king swore at his coronation to rule in both Church and state according to the laws, both written and unwritten, but at the base of this body of law was the all-important fact of the royal prerogative. This prerogative was claimed to include not merely the direct control of foreign and military policy, the power to call or not to call Parliament, the right to veto legislation, the right to coin money, the right to appoint the officers in Church and state who would administer the kingdom under his over-all direction, the responsibility for the administration of justice, and the power to bestow honors and titles of nobility; no one really was to question these powers of the crown. What was to be seriously questioned was the additional claim on

[1] The terms "court" and "country" came into increasing use during the seventeenth century, especially after the Restoration. Prior to the Exclusion Crisis they distinguished between the supporters and the opponents of crown policy. During and after the Exclusion Crisis the terms also took on more specific meanings, designating the specific groups who either constituted the administration or led the opposition in Parliament. Until after the accession of William and Mary the terms can often be replaced by the newer party names of "Tory" and "Whig."

the part of both James I and Charles I that over and above these traditional and formal rights of the crown, was the natural or God-given right of the king to set aside any or all of the prescriptive or customary laws that were designed to limit the exercise of the prerogative on behalf of the interests of the ordinary English subject. The heart of the controversy, put very simply, was whether the fundamental laws of English monarchy were to protect the king in the arbitrary use of his powers (if he wished to be arbitrary) or whether these fundamental laws were to provide a shield by which the English subject could protect himself, and his institutions, from the actions of an arbitrary king. Had the ancient prerogative of kingly rule been created to serve the interests of the king or the people? The mere stating of the question itself brings into the open the awareness on the part of both the king and the opposition to him that there was in fact no longer a oneness between the monarchy and the nation. The Stuarts continued to assume that the king was England in an era when increasing numbers of his subjects were coming to think of the king as one among many Englishmen, with special interests of his own that were not necessarily identical with the interests of particular subjects or with the interests of the nation as a whole.

There were several areas of policy, foreign and domestic, that were to manifest the divergence in interests between all the seventeenth-century kings and the interests of the nation, from 1603 until 1688. Before 1688 there was no institutional means by which these divergences could be reconciled. Government by king, Lords, and Commons is, after all, viable only when all three are basically in agreement. If they are not, a system of checks and balances is in effect and it is possible to prevent action, but not to take it. The importance of the Glorious Revolution is that these means were to be found in 1689 itself, or soon thereafter. In the area of foreign policy, the crown was rarely at one with the opinion of the country. James I made peace with Spain at the beginning of his reign, while the mass of public opinion still assumed that Spain was the deadly enemy. James continued to opt for a policy of peace after 1618, when most of his subjects thought that it was necessary for England to enter the Thirty Years' War in defense of Protestantism. Throughout the century up to 1688 the classes represented in Parliament looked upon foreign affairs with a simple and unsophisticated eye. There is little question that before 1640 the royal foreign policy was ineptly explained at home but was based upon realistic assumptions that Spain was no longer sufficiently powerful to threaten English interests and that the Thirty Years' War, to the extent to which it was in fact a struggle between Catholics and Protestants, was not a war in which England should get involved, since no party to the conflict was capable of doing serious harm to a neutral England or to England's Church. James I quite wisely sought a role as mediator and pacifier. To the gentry and commercial interests in Parliament, foreign policy was still looked upon as little more than the extension into foreign fields of the efforts at home either to reform or to uphold the Elizabethan structure in the Church. Where James sought to avoid involvement in the war in his own and the national interest, many in Parliament saw his policy as at best a willful refusal to come to the aid of the co-religionists fighting for their existence in the Germanies, or even as a covert attempt by James to encourage the triumph of the Catholic interest. During the reign of Charles I war did come, but against France not Spain. Where it might be possible to commend the prescience of Charles and his cohort Buckingham for their ability to divine the true nature of the emergence of French power into a commanding position in European affairs, his subjects saw war with France as an attack upon the one Catholic power that did have within it a large Protestant minority and was standing with the Protestant forces against the combined might of Spain and

the Austrian Hapsburgs. Where the crown still thought
of foreign policy as either the defense of the nation
or of the dynasty's interests, the opposition in Parliament had barely moved beyond the simplistic view of
foreign affairs evinced by so many in Elizabeth's reign.
The difference was that in Elizabeth's reign the dread
of Spain could be based upon fear of her military and
naval might as well as her religion. Elizabeth was lucky
that the national enemy was also the religious enemy.
The decline in the relative importance of Spain after
1588 was not a fact that the ordinary Englishman
could understand. (As has been observed by many students of the relationship between foreign policy and
public opinion, the latter is usually two generations
behind the realities of the former.) Thus it was that
the early Stuart kings faced a public that looked upon
foreign affairs through religious eyes, and these eyes
had been set in focus by the international and religious
realities of the latter third of the sixteenth century. It
is quite natural that seventeenth-century kings still assumed that foreign affairs were too arcane for any but
kings to comprehend.

As we noticed above, foreign policy was inextricably
entwined in the intricacies of religious controversy. For
this reason, if for no other, religion was perhaps the
crucial area of conflict between the crown's interest and
the interests of many powerful groups within the English society. The early Stuart kings, at least, considered
the Church to be the crucial test of their ability to
preserve the royal prerogative. One reason for the inability of the Stuart kings and the Puritans to understand each other is precisely that the Puritans were
unable to look upon the Church as merely being part
of the structure of monarchy. For them, religion was
more a matter of combining the will of God with individual conscience. Thus Puritan demands for reform
that were devoid of political implications as the Puritans saw them, aroused the dread fear of an attack
upon the whole structure of monarchical government

as the kings saw them. Since each side looked upon the purpose and role of religion from a vantage point directly opposite the other, it is not surprising that dialogue was almost totally out of the question. There is also little question but that the king's view of the Church as a chief prop for the security of the monarchy and its prerogatives was closer to reality than the Puritans' view that any number of radical reforms in that Church were of religious significance only, and had no bearing on the broader political, constitutional, and social structure of England. James I's famous aphorism —"no bishop, no king"—may have been an oversimplification of the implications of Presbyterianism, but it was a realistic awareness that the structure of the Church could not be changed without significant repercussions in the whole power structure of the state.

The Henrician church settlement of the 1530s and 1540s, and then the Elizabethan settlement of 1559, had, from the monarch's point of view, provided the means by which to satisfy the legitimate demands of God as found in the Bible and in the Christian tradition of England, with the earthly need to preserve the seamless fabric of English society. Since the royal prerogatives themselves were grounded on the obligation of preserving this same fabric, the Church and the state were merely two sides of the coin of monarchy. James I's experiences with Presbyterianism in Scotland could only strengthen his belief in this dual nature of English monarchy. Charles I, as the first king who truly believed in the Church of England as God's true church, and who also firmly believed in the divinity of kingly authority, obviously could not contemplate anything other than a rigid upholding of the royal prerogative in the Church. For both James I and Charles I, then, an attack upon any aspect of the Church—its doctrines, ritual, or administrative structure—was tantamount to attacking the Lord's Anointed and the commonweal.

The irony of the situation was, however, that those

who sought reforms in the Church were to be driven
eventually into seeking political power as a means of
achieving their religious goals. The crown itself must
share a large part of the credit for turning what began
as a purely religious movement into a political and
even a constitutional one. As early as Elizabeth's reign,
the Puritans were beginning to ally with or to be
represented by members of the House of Commons,
and even had powerful voices in the Privy Council and
at court. Thus, in Elizabethan England we see in
embryo the forerunner of the seventeenth-century alliance between Puritanism and Parliamentarianism.
The alliance was to be strengthened after 1603 by the
assumption that this alliance was necessary to restore
God's Church, uphold the fundamental laws, and defend England from her and God's enemies abroad. The
monarchy was to be seen as the opponent of God's
(Protestant) will, a destroyer of the fundamental laws,
and a sympathizer with God's and England's foreign
enemies. At the best of times, and with the most skill-
ful of monarchs, the reconciliation of these disparate
interests and the maintenance of national unity would
have been difficult enough. And in fact James I had
just enough of these qualities to succeed in maintaining
the fabric of the state. But his son, Charles I, was so
totally lacking in these qualities that civil war and revolution were the result. Whether or not this was inevitable is not the point. It is just a simple fact.

The divergent interests between the crown and the
court on the one hand and what can only be called the
"country" party on the other resulted in each construct-
ing an elaborate stereotype of the other. To the
country, the crown and the court were pictured as will-
fully destroying the fundamental laws of England in
a desire to see England restored to the Roman Catholic
fold as a vassal of both the Papacy and the Catholic
powers of Spain and France. For the king and the
court, the country was composed of ambitious, ruthless, and petty men who were able and willing to de-

stroy the painfully constructed fabric of English society in both Church and state in order to foist upon an unwilling people their own narrow and petty beliefs. The result would be the destruction of the monarchy and with it the rights of all Englishmen, high and low, Catholic, Anglican, and Puritan.

But this combination of divergent constitutional, religious, and international interests was to be complicated by the presence of another issue—money. In spite of all these other conflicts, civil war and revolution might have been avoidable if the crown had been able to secure adequate finances from the traditional sources. It was the failure of the traditional sources of royal revenue to meet the growing needs of the crown that brought all these other issues to a head. The rubric that "the king must live of his own" was devised in an earlier era, when the revenues from crown lands, customs duties, feudal incidents, and certain court fees had, at least in peacetime, been adequate to maintain the dignity of the crown and court, for the maintenance of law and order, and for modest preparation of naval and military defense. During the sixteenth century these revenues were to fall short, and with the passage of time, increasingly short, of what was needed. The reasons were both simple and complex. Few in the country had any real grasp of the problem. And no amount of explaining was to make the country understand what it either would not or could not understand.

Among the many causes of the crown's acute financial embarrassment were some that were the result of long-range cyclical trends that were not in themselves charged with a political content, such as the great increase in prices that had afflicted all of Western Europe since the early-sixteenth century. Even if the English crown made no changes whatsoever in its spending habits, inflation alone would have required a quadrupling of income by 1640. But inflation was far from being the only reason for the increased expenditures of the crown. Since the reign of Henry

VIII, the English government had added greatly to its normal peacetime activities in both the social and the economic spheres. By Elizabeth's reign the Privy Council was devoting a great part of its time, and spending a good deal of money, regulating conditions of life and labor on the local as well as the national level. Not only did these activities add to the cost of government, but in the reigns of the early Stuarts this centrally directed activity was to become a grievance felt deeply, and increasingly deeply, by many of the gentry and aristocracy. It was to be one of the factors responsible for the emergence of the country party.

Of even greater significance, however, was the simple fact that from the death of Henry VII England was no longer normally at peace. When there wasn't an actual war to be fought, there was always the possibility of one. So a royal income that traditionally was adequate to meet normal peacetime expenditures could not possibly be expected to meet the needs of a government perpetually facing the prospect of war. And just as the newly acquired economic and social activities of the crown caused an increase in expenditures and were highly controversial politically, so with the constant expenditures on naval and military defense. For many in the country, as was noted above, a minimum naval preparation was one thing, but a vast increase in expenditures on arms used to advance a foreign policy that meant one thing to the court and another to the country, was quite a different matter. Since foreign policy itself was a highly controversial political and religious issue, any increase in expenditures necessitated by that foreign policy would itself provide a new controversy.

Most controversial of all, at least in the reign of James I, was the great increase in expenditures on what the country could only view as a corrupt and dissolute court. Where Elizabeth had spent lavishly on her court, at least it was no more lavish than the great royal courts on the continent and it was seen by all to be a responsible court, spending no more than was necessary to maintain the dignity of the queen and through her of the nation itself. The court of James I was to be seen in a totally different light. The tales of corruption and immorality, the "squandering" of large sums upon Scottish favorites, and the draining off of even larger sums to enhance and then maintain the avaricious Buckingham and his clan, proved to be almost more than the country could bear. Even though the court of Charles I could not be accused of the same kind of degree of waste, the unpopularity of Buckingham and of Queen Henrietta Maria worked to preserve much of the hatred and contempt with which his father's court had been viewed.

A solution to the financial problems might have been found if there had been any real rapport between the court and its policies and the country and its expectations. The basic rapport that did exist in Elizabeth's reign might have been sufficient to find a solution, but in her reign few yet understood either the magnitude or the permanence of the problem. Certainly the queen herself was too unaware of the permanence of the situation to even contemplate the compromises with the parliamentary classes that would have been necessary to effect a solution. In James's reign both the Earl of Salisbury and, later, the Earl of Middlesex seemed to grasp the true extent of the problem, but neither was capable of putting together a package that the mutually distrustful king and Parliament could accept. The failure of Salisbury's Great Contract[2] might well be seen as the single most important cause of the revolutions of the seventeenth century. The failure to agree

[2] Salisbury concocted a scheme whereby the king would renounce any further resort to extralegal or feudal revenues in return for a guaranteed annual grant of tax revenue from Parliament. Each party to the contract expected prior compliance from the other party before fulfilling its own side of the bargain. Since neither trusted the other to respond to the first move, the scheme collapsed. James had been dubious about the whole thing anyway.

upon a solution to the crown's financial plight forced the crown to resort to extraordinary means of securing an income, and the combination of extraordinary (nay, illegal) sources of revenue coupled with highly controversial and costly expenditures could lead only to a political and even a constitutional crisis.

In addition to all the preceding controversies that bedeviled the early Stuart reigns, there was one that manifested itself only periodically prior to the convention of the Long Parliament but was as much at the heart of the whole struggle between king and Parliament as any other. It was the final, unconscious solution of this problem that was to end the century of revolution. This issue put simply was: who is to exercise the powers of the crown—the king himself with the aid of his chosen advisers, or Parliament either by choosing the king's advisers for him or by limiting the king's choice of advisers? In other words, was the government to be responsible to the king alone or to Parliament? This was too deep and fundamental a constitutional problem to be clearly understood by very many, and yet it was the most persistent constitutional problem throughout English history, at least from the reign of King John. The final elimination of all the other controversies from the realm of constitutional significance would not come until this question had been answered. And the answer to this question came in the generation after the Glorious Revolution. It was to take generations to solve, because it was to take generations before the full meaning of the question was understood by all the parties involved. As with all the other issues that have been discussed, so with this one. The problem was there in Elizabeth's reign, but was submerged through the queen's genius for compromise and the basic identity of interest between court and country. The accession of James I was to open a new era, and an era that did not end until the Hanoverian succession. In Elizabeth's reign the chief privy councilors also had seats in one or the other of the Houses of

Parliament. The peers were obviously in the House of Lords and the commoners always managed to get themselves elected to the House of Commons. Since Elizabeth's principal councilors were generally highly competent and relatively honest men with a significant popular following, it is not surprising that they sought and were given the roles of leadership in both Houses. Through great political skill they were thus able to combine the roles of being the chief agents of both the crown and Parliament. Whether the queen's basic success in handling her Parliaments can be attributed to this role played by her councilors, or whether it was due to her own political skills and her ability to identify her interests with those of her subjects is a moot point. The combination of the two certainly succeeded in delaying, if not preventing, the ultimate renewal of the great medieval controversy as to where the ultimate power of decision making lay.

The way in which James I and Charles I handled their relationships with Parliament was quite a different story. Of course those in the Privy Council or simply at court who were peers were members of the House of Lords, but in these two reigns they were not to play the essential role that their Elizabethan predecessors had played. Few of the councilors were commoners, if for no other reason than that the Stuarts were far more generous in bestowing titles upon their supporters and favorites than the great queen had been. Thus, even if the Stuarts had wanted to maintain the Elizbethan links with Parliament, the personnel were just not available for the task. But in fact neither James nor Charles was really that interested in using Parliament. For them, Parliament was barely accepted as a part of the fundamental constitution. Also, the type of person whom James chose to advise him would not have been acceptable to many of the country element in any case. The favorite, Scottish or English, was an object of resentment not respect. Charles's chief advisers, Laud and Strafford, could not be called "favorites," but their view of the constitution was not one conducive to creating an amicable relationship with either House.

This growing estrangement of king and Parliament in the early Stuart reigns and, especially, the growing atmosphere of resentment of the country toward the court represented something far deeper and more significant than the personal differences just referred to. Underlying this estrangement was the growing antagonism between the country and a crown that was seen to be taking into its own hands more and more of the responsibilities that had traditionally lain with the ruling circles in the provinces and localities. The centralization of the decision-making process and even the administrative process of so many social and economic matters which had begun in the reign of Henry VIII was bound to lead to a reaction in favor of decentralization. With the rapid expansion of these centralizing tendencies, especially during the personal rule of Charles I (1629–40), and the centralizing of authority in the hands of a court that did not have parliamentary support and did not even seek it, was to inflame feelings all around.

To what extent had the Civil War, the Commonwealth, and the Protectorate succeeded in solving all or any of these many crises in the English body politic? Obviously no final solutions had been found or there would not have been a universally accepted Restoration in 1660. However, some progress had been made, and some light was to be brought to bear on other solutions which pointed out possible grounds for hope in the future. The fundamental failure was in the inability to devise any new constitution that both the Cromwellian executive and a Parliament could live with. This failure, perhaps more than any other, caused the collapse first of the Commonwealth and then of the Protectorate. But this inability of Cromwell to work with any of his Parliaments, no matter how they were chosen or of whom they were composed, was largely due to a struggle for political power, since in the area of foreign policy there was a good deal of agreement, as there was in the area of finance and taxation. If the era of the Puritan Revolution can claim success in any area, it is in the area of taxation. Taxes were levied and *collected* in amounts far exceeding anything ever seen or even dreamed of before. Providing that there was agreement on expenditures, there would no longer be any real question as to the fact that the nation could support a far higher level of annual taxation than had been even faintly guessed at prior to the Long Parliament. This was to be one contribution, of sorts, of the Puritan Revolution.

Behind the inability of the executive to work with Parliament during the Commonwealth and the Protectorate lay the issue of centralization of government. Cromwell not only adopted the centralizing tendencies of his predecessors, but even furthered the cause. The union of England, Wales, Scotland, and Ireland was but the most obvious step in this direction. Only in the realm of religion was Cromwell a decentralizer. But here he flew in the face of the prevailing Erastian wind. Cromwell's Independent congregations could not win acceptance in a society still hoping for the official establishment of the one true faith, which the vast majority of Englishmen still assumed the Church of England to be.

As for public acceptance and respect for Cromwell's Council of State and the principal officers of state, the Elizabethan amity was not to be rediscovered. Cromwell officially relied on Parliament for advice on appointments, but in fact he depended more and more on subordinate army officers, and relatives, in-laws, and friends who held no official position at all. There was no effective accountability to anyone but Oliver Cromwell himself, and these men hardly had national reputations of such magnitude as to silence all criticism of this continuing centralization.

Thus the Restoration found the ancient monarchy

and Parliament resuming their respective roles as of 1641, with almost no institutional changes that could prevent the resumption of all or almost all those crises in religion, politics, economic and social policy, and foreign policy that had been building up to the crisis of the Long Parliament. The only significant change, however, was a crucial one. There was to be an unwritten, and perhaps unconscious, realization that things must never again be allowed to come to the pass that only civil war could provide a solution. The Tudors benefited for one hundred eighteen years from the national fear of a revival of the Wars of the Roses. The later Stuarts were to benefit from the same national fear of a revival of civil war. This fear fortunately was to last until the necessary institutional changes had been accomplished that would make civil war outdated as a possible solver of national problems. But if the foregoing conclusions are valid, how was it that in 1688–89 there was to be a Glorious Revolution? How can we characterize, much less explain, this new revolution? In the chapters to follow it will be seen that 1688–89 did see a revolution, a revolution made necessary by the failure of the earlier one, a revolution that had to succeed both in order to avoid civil war and *by* avoiding civil war.

CHAPTER 2

The Restoration Settlement

The Convention Parliament was dissolved at the end of 1660, and the new year witnessed the first unquestionably constitutional parliamentary election in twenty-one years. In the eyes of contemporaries, a "revolution" had truly occurred, for to the seventeenth-century mind "revolution" merely meant traveling in a circle and returning to the starting point. The new Parliament has been known by many names—Long, Cavalier, Pension. I choose to use the designation "Cavalier" both because it is an accurate description of its composition and its past loyalties and because it helps to underscore the contention made earlier that the post-Restoration era was to see the emergence of a Cavalier, or Tory, party with interests of its own, quite distinct from those of the crown, to which it supposedly owed such unquestioning loyalty. The Cavaliers of this Parliament were to play a role not unlike that played twenty years earlier by the emergent Parliamentarian party. Charles II and his brother, James II, both liked to think, and consistently hoped, that what was called the Cavalier, or Tory, interest would more consistently return to the principles and practices of its Royalist antecedents of the 1640s. This was not to be. The new Cavaliers were to prove to be as thoroughly "country" as their Parliamentarian and Puritan opposition had been in the reign of Charles I.

The Restoration was barely accomplished, then, before there emerged to the forefront of politics the fact that king and Parliament had represented and continued to represent divergent and potentially conflicting interests. Charles II, for all his genuine feelings of good will, a sense of compromise, and a fear of another civil war, and with all the national euphoria that had accompanied the Restoration, could not maintain for more than a few months that national unity and identity of interests that had been at the root of the maintenance of the Elizabethan state and had been so sorely lacking in the reigns of his father and grandfather. The constitution as it functioned prior to 1640 lacked machinery by which the conflicting interests of court and and country or crown and Parliament could be peacefully reconciled. Civil war and attempted revolution had been the result. With the old constitution now restored, with the reforms of the first years of the Long Parliament appended, a new test was to come. Given that crown and Parliament continued to reflect differing interests, could the constitution restored in 1660 meet the test of providing the necessary machinery to resolve peacefully the inevitable conflicts? For a few years, until the fall of Clarendon, the signs were hopeful. Later, with the rise of Danby, a new solution appeared to be in sight. But it, too, failed. The Exclusion Crisis seemed to suggest to Charles that his own and the national interest could best be served by relying on his own prerogatives and ruling without Parliament altogether, just as his father had done. Whether this new era of "personal rule" would have been successful is doubtful. In any case Charles was to die within four years. James II was to find that he could rule neither with a Parliament nor without one.

All forms of government are always dependent in the last analysis upon the characters and personalities of the men who work them, but when the success or failure of a system depends almost solely upon this personal factor there is something seriously, even fatally, wrong with the system. Perhaps no constitution can ever guarantee absolute stability and permanence, but sixteenth-century England had been relatively successful, and the eighteenth was to re-create that stability on a new foundation. All through the seventeenth century men knew that something was amiss. The answer was found in the two generations after 1688. And the conflicting interests that led to the revolution of 1688 were present, if not always in full view, in the Cavalier Parliament of 1661. The interests in conflict were once again to include religion, foreign policy, finance, the armed forces, and the respective roles and relative importance of central and local organs of government. The mixture was to differ from that of the pre-Civil War era, and the participants were also to differ, but, deep down, the struggle was not all that different from the old.

The new Parliament was far more decidedly Cavalier in composition than the Convention had been. Less than sixty of its over five hundred members were "Presbyterian," the Anglicans being presented with a fine opportunity to create a church settlement to their own liking. About half the members had sat in the Convention Parliament and were aware of the great benefit to their cause secured by the decision of the Convention to postpone the religious settlement until the election of a true Parliament. Another powerful element of Cavalier continuity was the fact that about one hundred members had sat in the 1640 Long Parliament. This Cavalier Parliament was, then, not entirely a group of new or untried men. They may have been Royalists, but many were also to know and respect the role and traditions of Parliaments. Except for land, the Restoration settlement was to be in their hands. And because of the Convention's land settlement, there was an even stronger urge to get revenge on the Puritan enemy in the religious and political spheres. Charles's hopes for toleration were to go by default.

The new king, of course, had no intention of serving as his own chief minister. Throughout his reign he always managed to shield his own position by appearing at least to work through a "ministry" headed by one or more leading figures, who took charge of day-to-day administration and also served as lightning rods to keep popular or parliamentary attacks from striking him directly. The king sought to secure his own indispensability by surrounding himself with those who were dispensable. Thus the new administration was headed by the Earl of Clarendon, who, as Sir Edward Hyde, had been an original leader of the opposition to Charles I in the first days of the Long Parliament. Clarendon was a Royalist and an Anglican in the old tradition. This old tradition dated from the reforms enacted in the first two years of the Long Parliament, and was grounded upon the need for a mixed government of king, Lords, and Commons in governmental matters and the need for a comprehensive Anglican Church in the religious sector. Clarendon quite accurately mirrored Charles II's own views of moderation in both Church and state. The failure of Clarendon's ministry to control Parliament and to make moderation work and take hold was due to the fact that mixed government was not yet a part of the constitution, but was in fact merely a party program. He failed to secure an all-embracing, comprehensive church, because this, too, was a party program and not the interest of the nation as such. One of the cruel ironies of history is that Clarendon's name was to become permanently fixed in the popular mind with a program almost directly the opposite of what he sought—the Clarendon Code.

The acts that constituted this code were neither the work of Clarendon himself nor in fact enacted as a package. Each was designed to be a further nail in the coffin of Puritanism as a force in local government, religion, and society. The impulse behind these acts came less from the members of Commons themselves than from their constituents. The first was the Corporation Act of 1661, which called upon all municipal government officers to renounce the Solemn League and Covenant (which had bound the Long Parliament to Scottish-style Presbyterianism), to uphold the principle of non-resistance to the king and his government, and to take the sacrament of Communion according to the rites of the Church of England. By this act, Presbyterians, republicans, Roman Catholics, and in fact all who were not Anglicans and Royalists, were barred from participation in municipal government. Since many of the more than four hundred borough representatives in Commons were elected by these municipal officers, not only was municipal government itself reserved for the upholders of king and Church, but Commons was guaranteed as well. Since the possibility of the Puritan, republican, or Catholic forces' winning a county election was so remote, no legislation affecting county government was deemed necessary, for the time being at any rate.

Having driven the opposition from municipal government, and in effect from the House of Commons, Parliament now turned its attention to the Church itself. The rigors of the Corporation Act could have been ameliorated by making some move in the direction of broadening the Church to include within its ranks those old Puritans who after 1660 were thoroughly loyal to the crown and did sincerely wish to participate in a truly national church, if such could be created. Even though the Act of Uniformity of 1662 reaffirmed the essentials of the Elizabethan settlement, it was a far cry from that settlement in spirit. The Elizabethan settlement had quite successfully constructed a Church that comprehended nearly all the then religious modes, excepting of course the devout Catholic. During the century that had passed since that settlement, Englishmen had fractured that national religious unity. Whether it was now possible to re-create that national religious comprehension is certainly questionable. But in fact no serious effort was made. Such an effort may

have been impossible of achievement, regardless of the
will to succeed, for various reasons. In the century since
the Elizabethan settlement, the Anglican Church had
become more than a conscious and deliberate compromise. It had, in the hearts of its loyal sons, become a
distinct denomination in its own right, with all the ac-
couterments of theology, ritual, and administrative ap-
paratus. Its followers had come to identify it not only
with the king and nation, but with God. It seemed to
be forgotten that the national Church had originally
been just that. And second, it would perhaps have been
too much to expect that loyal Anglicans could totally
forgive and forget all that had happened to them, to
their Church, and to their country during the Commonwealth and Protectorate. Thus the Act of Uniformity sought not comprehension, but a national Church
founded by legislative fiat. Englishmen were to be loyal
to the Church or they would pay the penalty of political and religious ostracism. The effect was the tacit
admission that the people of England belonged to
many religions, only one of which was legal. In the long
run this weakened the Church, because it kept in its
fold many men who used its protective covering to
pursue political policies out of step with the highest
interests of the faith and of the nation as well. And of
course it led to a deadening complacency among those
who were believers.

The Act of Uniformity barred any but a properly
ordained Anglican minister from holding a benefice,
and demanded total adherence to every last item of
the Book of Common Prayer. The old unofficial, uneasy, but real, tolerance was ended. A further buttress
for the future of Anglicanism was the provision that
anyone involved in any form of education, as teacher,
tutor, professor, etc., must first be licensed by the
bishop of the diocese. Considering that the printing
presses were still required to be licensed, this meant
that all media of information, knowledge, and propa-

ganda were controlled by either the crown, the Church, or both.[1]

These first two of the four parts that made up the so-called Clarendon Code had secured an Anglican triumph within both the Church itself and municipal government. The remaining acts were really more punitive than structural in nature. The Conventicle Act of 1664 forbade clergy expelled by the Act of Uniformity from preaching to groups of more than five persons, and it also prescribed punishments for anyone over sixteen years of age who attended such "conventicles." The Five-Mile Act of 1665 prohibited these expelled clergy from traveling within five miles of any place where they had once preached, either in a church or a conventicle. The act also strengthened the ban on teaching which was first established by the Act of Uniformity. The Convention Parliament may have been successful in compromising the claims of Royalists and Parliamentarians over the issue of the land settlement, thus assisting the king in his efforts to heal the wounds of civil war and unite the country. But the Cavalier Parliament had managed both to get revenge and to secure future political power for itself by its ability to dominate the Church, and through the Church to dominate the political life of England on the local, and hopefully on the national, levels. To the extent to which land was to be the dominant force in politics, the results would be mixed. To the extent that religion was to be the dominant force, the victory would lie with the Anglican establishment. Both the emerging Whig and Tory parties had their roots and their defense in the soil, but the Tories had the additional and decisive ability and need to fall back on the Church. James II was to discover, to his ruin, that the Tories were to become more wedded to the Church than to the monarch. The latter had failed them in what they considered their hour of

[1] See Robert S. Bosher, *The Making of the Restoration Settlement: The Influence of the Laudians, 1649–1662*, New York, 1951, pp. 281–83.

need. The former could provide the foundation for their continued hegemony. And when the threat to that hegemony came, it was to have a Catholic, not a Puritan, source.

Prior to Parliament's success in the first civil war, in 1646, England had never experienced a standing army. Since the reign of Henry VIII the county militia and the trained bands had been under the jurisdiction of the lords lieutenants of the shires, who, even though royal appointees, considered themselves as practically laws unto themselves in their bailiwicks. In the first years of his reign Charles I had raised a storm of protest when troops gathered for an expedition abroad had been quartered on the citizenry without a by-your-leave. But the Petition of Right of 1628 had outlawed quartering of troops in peacetime without parliamentary authorization. The commonwealth and the Protectorate inaugurated a new era. Cromwell had based his own personal power and that of the regime on the maintenance of a large standing army. The king in exile learned the lesson that Cromwell was teaching and sought to perpetuate a standing army for his own use after the Restoration. The Militia Act of 1662 was designed to reconcile several conflicting interests. On the one hand there was the fact that the immediate cause of the civil war in 1642 was the Militia Bill, which had taken control of the nationalized militias away from the king, giving it to Parliament. The Cavaliers of 1662 naturally had to repudiate this by restoring to the king his sole right to command the militia. At the same time, the militia was again put under the effective day-to-day command of the lords lieutenants in the counties. The leaders of the country once again commanded the armed forces as in pre-Civil War days. On the other hand, however, was the more significant question, not of control of the militia, but of a permanent, national, standing army under the immediate control of the monarch himself. The Cavalier Parliament had no interest whatsoever in bestowing this favor upon Charles

II, nor upon his successor. While in law the king was
free to raise troops if he wished, Parliament would
never give him the money he needed to do so. The
standing army, under the eye of the Mutiny Act, was
to be a result of the Glorious Revolution. What could
be vouchsafed to William III after 1688 was not to be
freely granted to either Charles II or James II in the
years before. The Cavaliers thus added control of the
militia to that of the Church.

In the realm of finances the king was to achieve what
at first appeared to be a remarkable success. Charles I
had thought to perpetuate his personal power on the
securing of an adequate personal income, and had
failed. Charles II was to receive from the Parliament
a guaranteed income that his father would have thought
beyond his fondest dreams. But this financial settlement was more the work of the Convention than of
the Cavalier Parliament. Just as Charles II seemed willing to forgive his and his father's enemies, so the Convention seemed willing to remove from contention the
financial want that had led Charles I to take such drastic, extralegal, and divisive measures to raise his revenue. But in the process of moving to secure an adequate income for the king, the Commons in fact
secured at last the implementation of Cecil's Great
Contract, which had failed of achievement in the
reign of James I. The result was an even greater victory
for the landholding class than for the crown.

Tunnage and poundage were granted to the king for
life, thus ending one of the controversies from the previous reign. This figure was calculated at £400,000
per year by the parliamentary committee. If the crown
had not been so lax in its control over the collection
of the customs, this figure could have grown greatly
because of the tremendous increase in trade during the
next generation. The old feudal dues were abolished,
as had been called for in Cecil's Great Contract. In
any case, the court of wards that had collected them
had been abolished during the Civil War. This con-

firmation of the abolition of the court of wards and of all feudal dues meant that feudalism was in fact dead. (The 1660 Act for the Abolition of Military Tenures did convert all military tenures into socage tenures, which remained in effect, as did sergeanty tenures.) Along with the abolition of feudal dues went the forced loans and the benevolences of the past. In their place the king had to rely strictly upon parliamentary grants such as the new excise taxes on domestic trade, the hearth tax, the customs, and of course his crown lands. The latter were expected to bring in only £100,000 per year. So out of an income of £1,200,000 per annum, which the Convention bestowed upon Charles II, all but £100,000 was dependent solely upon parliamentary grant. But this immense sum of 1.2 million pounds was based on what the Commons committee assumed were the normal peacetime expenses of the crown in 1640. Twenty years of inflation were to take their toll, however, and the financial problems of the crown had by no means been solved in reality. The feudal dues had been abolished, but the king was still going to be dependent upon parliamentary grants even in peacetime unless he could secure sums elsewhere. As in the reign of Charles I, the financial plight of the crown was to be both a cause of further conflict and the result of the king's conflicts with Parliament.

Before 1640 the nation could never accept that the king could not live on his own income ("his own" meaning his traditional, not his extraordinary, income). In 1660 Parliament recognized that the crown desperately needed vast financial aid on an annual basis, but this recognition was based on the budget of 1640, not 1660. Therefore, while Parliament may have come around to the crown's view that regular assistance was necessary, it so far failed to provide the necessary sums as really to have left the problem unsolved. Charles II's devices for raising the needed sums were to prove just as unsettling and unsavory as had those of Charles I. And once again a revolution was one of the results.

Ever since James I had ended the war with Spain in 1604, the monarch and nation had rarely agreed on matters of foreign policy, except during the rule of the Protector, Cromwell. During the first years of Charles II's reign there did appear to be a convergence of views on foreign policy, but there was in fact more appearance than substance, and this largely because the maneuverings of Louis XIV tended to hide from English eyes the true extent to which England's policy was actually pro-French. But Charles's policy was favorable to the French only in the long term; in the short and long term it was also decidedly pro-English in that it contributed to the defeat of Dutch maritime power and the consequent supremacy of the English navy.

The king always claimed that foreign affairs were too arcane for ordinary men to fully understand them. In England, at any rate, from Elizabeth through James II, this royal attitude seems to have had a good deal of validity. In the days of Charles I, and continuing on through the commonwealth and Protectorate, England was developing its commercial and naval power. The full emergence of England as a successful competitor in the scramble for trading outlets in North and South America and the Far East depended upon her ability to meet the Dutch maritime challenge on her own doorstep: in the English Channel and the North Sea. Before this challenge from the Dutch had been successfully mastered, three wars against the United Provinces were necessary. The first (1652–54) provided an issue around which Cromwell was able to rally a good deal of support for himself and the new regime. This war had followed the passage of the first Navigation Act (1651), and England's successes constituted the first step in the long climb to world commerical and naval supremacy. It whetted English appetites for more of the same. The first Dutch war also constituted the first break in the popular tradition that had developed since the Reformation that England must go to war only for the defense of the home island or for Protestantism.

But this old tradition was not completely dead, and was to be revived later on.

Charles II was to preside over two more wars against the Dutch (1664–67 and 1672–74). During the first the nation was more enthusiastic than the king. During the second the king was more enthusiastic than the nation. By the time the two wars were over, England was to find herself at a constitutional impasse and on the verge of civil war. Before examining these ultimate domestic repercussions of the Dutch wars, let us first look more closely at foreign policy itself. Whether or not anyone in England realized it, by the 1660s the role of France and its king, Louis XIV, was becoming decisive in Western Europe. The Anglo-Dutch maritime rivalry was in fact merely a part, and perhaps a minor part, of the growing struggle for the mastery of Europe. All three Dutch wars were merely but preludes to the new hundred years' war that England was to wage against France. The English triumph over the Dutch in America and on the seas was but the preliminary to the greater struggle to come. The importance of France was only slowly seen by the English nation. It was more quickly perceived by the king and by ministers such as Sir Thomas Osborne, Earl of Danby. And even among those who were early to recognize the immense importance of France, there were to be bitter disagreements as to what it meant for England and how it should be handled. On these crucial issues the king and Parliament were to disagree. The latter underestimated the importance of France at first, and the former, while recognizing its importance, sought to deal with the problem in a way that served his own and England's immediate interests, but in a way that drove a wedge down the middle of the English body politic.

Parliament had provided large sums for the second war, but the war generally went badly and the Commons rightly felt that the whole thing had been mismanaged, the nation not getting its money's worth. The mismanagement of the war was compounded by the twin disasters of plague and fire that swept London in 1665–66, during the middle of the war. All these disasters led not only to peace with Holland and the fall of the chancellor, Clarendon, but to the ruin of the old Tory concept of government by king and Privy Council. The Commons were to demand, and would secure, the right to appropriate money for specific, not general, purposes, and had the additional right through investigatory committees to oversee the expenditures.

Charles II was not yet ready to break with Parliament over foreign-policy differences, and therefore he actually added his support to the Commons' impeachment of the old chancellor. The king was happy enough, anyway, to be rid of the old man who had treated him like a schoolboy, and whose notion of the overriding importance of the Privy Council in government was repugnant to the king as well as to the Cavaliers in Parliament. The fact that this first use of the impeachment power by Commons since 1640 did not precipitate a greater political storm than it did was because the king, temporarily at least, was in no mood to pick up the challenge and defend his minister. But what it did do was to determine Charles never again to rely upon one dominant minister. From now on, the king would be surrounded by many advisers, but would in the last analysis make his own decisions, at least on those issues that were capable of arousing his interest in the first place.

Louis XIV came of age in 1661 and began his long career as the central pivot in Western European diplomacy. Not until near the end of the second Anglo-Dutch war did he begin to show the ultimately aggressive nature of his goals. During the Dutch war he switched from neutrality to an alliance with the Dutch, but took little part in the fighting. But at the back of Louis's diplomacy was the desire to keep England either neutral or in such political turmoil that she would be impotent to engage her arms against him.

Louis seemed to realize better than many Englishmen that England might have its maritime struggle with the Dutch, but that in a clear-cut struggle between France and the United Provinces, England would be impelled into a pro-Dutch posture for historical and strategic reasons. Therefore, it was not a military or naval alliance with England that Louis sought. Her neutrality would be sufficient for his purposes, and one way to secure this was to set the king and the Parliament at each other's throat. To achieve this he began the disbursement of vast sums of French money to various and sundry English politicians from the king on through the ranks of the aristocracy and the Commons.

The fall of Clarendon, in 1667, and his replacement by the Cabal (Clifford, Arlington, Buckingham, Ashley Cooper, and Lauderdale) set in train the many conflicting forces that were to set the crown at odds with the sentiments of most of the ruling class in Church and state by 1688. The seeds of the Glorious Revolution were there at the Restoration itself. These seeds began to sprout with the fall of Clarendon. Once Charles became more involved in the making of policy, the personal interests of the king were to be factors in politics. The impeachment of Clarendon, coming as it did in conjunction with parliamentary demands for its own supervision of military expenditures in the future, were to set the king and Parliament at loggerheads—not unlike the situation that faced the early Stuarts before 1640. But if Charles was to secure an adequate income, he either had to turn to Parliament or resort to extraordinary sources of revenue. One thing, at least, had been settled by the Puritan Revolution: there could be no forced loans, benevolences, grants of monopolies, the imposition by royal prerogative of additional customs duties, ship money, or distraint of knighthood. The restored monarchy had been assured a large but inadequate income. If the rest was not to come from Parliament, there was only one place left for the king to turn: Louis XIV. But in order to get more and more from Louis and on a regular basis, the king was more and more to become Louis's man. At least Louis had to be made to think that Charles was his man. In the process of convincing Louis, the king was unfortunately faced with the fact that many in England were also to become so convinced. Thus Charles II and England with him were to get caught up in a vicious circle. The more pro-French he was the more he got from Louis, but the more dependent he became the less Louis needed to buy his continued support. And the more he appeared to be in league with Louis the more Parliament came into open opposition and challenged him on those very matters of religion and foreign policy that mattered to Louis. But in this three-handed chess match—Louis XIV, Charles II, the English Parliament—Charles was quite capable of holding his own. Like his grandfather, James I, he managed to just get by and leave the dam to burst upon the head of his successor.

Now that the vital interests of the king and the nation as represented in Parliament began to come into open and serious conflict, the old constitutional conundrum was again to come to the fore. Where was the machinery to settle these conflicts of interest between the crown and the legislature? The failure to develop this machinery had led to civil war in 1642. Could it be developed in time to prevent another civil war? The issues at stake were to become so immense that civil war was to be a real possibility both in Charles's reign and in his brother James's. The issues in conflict were serious enough, but the real danger was that the constitution contained no machinery by which these conflicts could be reconciled peacefully. The necessary machinery cannot of course be thought of simply as a mere mechanical device. To prove workable in the midst of bitter conflicts between legislative and executive, any such machinery must in itself represent the conflicting parties and also in itself hold a position of respect in society. Politicians have to want to secure such machinery and they have to want it to work. Charles II gambled that the fear of civil war would be strong enough to guarantee his position, and he seems to have been right. In 1688 the fear of civil war was strong enough to weld the ruling political classes together in order to guarantee the position of Parliament. But since it was a near thing in 1688, the new machinery was to be the principal by-product of 1688.

Charles's growing reliance upon his French connections was not to be the sole cause of his estrangement from the Cavalier Parliament. For tied to the king's growing bond with Louis XIV was the matter of the king's own religious position and that of his heir, the Duke of York. The period of the Cabal was a difficult one for both contemporary and future historians to comprehend with any assurance. Of the five members, two were sympathetic to Roman Catholicism, two were sympathetic to Dissent, and only Ashley Cooper was an upholder of Anglicanism. Thus the Cabal, by the nature of its composition, was symptomatic of Charles's own spirit of religious toleration. The negotiations with France were officially secret, yet enough leaked out to create fears that Charles was closer in league with the French than in fact he was.

The Cabal's one strength was that the members were all able men and were capable of giving England a sound and efficient administration. And a buttress of this sound and efficient administration would be their ability to control the proceedings in Parliament. But as nearly ideal a form of government as this may have been in the eyes of the king, it was not the ideal as seen through the eyes of Parliament. The best efforts of the crown and of the Cabal did not succeed in breaking either House to their will. Religious toleration, reliance upon France, and *efficient central government* were policies considered to be anathema to the bulk of the landed classes. Throughout the seventeenth century the landed classes shied away from efficient government emanating from the crown. It was not efficient central government that they wanted but local self-government, whether it was efficient or not.

Thus the fall of Clarendon was to usher in a new era, an era in which the hopes and the pretense of unity between the restored monarchy and the country were to count for less. It was an era in which the king sought ever more resolutely to work his own will in determining policy, whether foreign, domestic, or religious. And thus it was also to be an era in which Anglicanism, localism, and parliamentarianism were to be united in a new country movement. Before 1640 the "country" party had been the combination of Puritanism, parliamentarianism, and localism. The new country was thus a rebirth of the old except that Anglicanism was to replace Puritanism as the religious component. The "court"-"country" conflict had led to civil war in the 1640s. Would it do the same again? How strong in fact was the religious element in the country party in these two eras? On one hand, since parliamentarianism and localism are the only two factors that remain constant before 1640 and before 1688, it might at first appear that they alone were really vital issues and that the religious issue was of only secondary importance. But this is not necessarily the case. Puritanism was to provide the catalyst that formed the first country party, and Anglicanism was to do the same in this new struggle. But being the catalyst still does not make it the first and overriding issue at stake. Religion provided the form of rhetoric and much of the ideological justification for these other points of conflict.

Just as the attempt to force the Anglican Book of Common Prayer upon the unwilling Scots precipitated the end of Charles I's experiment in personal rule, so a religious issue was to bring about the fall of the Cabal and the long, slow, but seemingly relentless slide to the revolution of 1688. As early as 1662 the king had issued his first declaration of indulgence, in which he offered to dispense with the Act of Uniformity as it related to Dissenters if Parliament would agree. But Parliament did not agree, and that was the end of the matter for ten years.

In 1672 Charles tried again. The new declaration technically waived the penal clauses of the Restoration settlement and provided for authorized places of worship for Dissenters. Roman Catholics were allowed to worship in their own homes. Even though the declaration called for the maintenance of the Church of England in all its authorized purity and rights, the effect of this declaration was twofold. On one hand it was seen by much of the public and by Parliament as toleration for Roman Catholics. On the other hand, a very real constitutional issue was being raised by the king's action. Ever since the Restoration, the king's dispensing power had been accepted when it had been used sparingly and in individual cases only, even where the individuals were Roman Catholics. Charles had used the dispensing power on behalf of Roman Catholics who had been of personal service to him during the Commonwealth and the Protectorate. Parliament and the courts had not protested, because this occasional and individual use of the dispensing power could be defended as a logical outgrowth of the royal power to grant pardons. But to suspend an act or whole portions of several acts of Parliament was quite another matter. In effect, the king was repealing statutes. When Parliament met again, in February 1673, it declared that the king had no power to suspend statutes, and it then countered by passing the Test Act, which Charles did sign into law. His signing of the Test Act and his subsequent enforcement of it succeeded, at least temporarily, in removing the constitutional issue from immediate discussion. Charles's withdrawal of his declaration restored harmony.

The Test Act required anyone holding an office of trust under the crown to (1) publicly partake of the sacraments of the Church, (2) take the oath of supremacy, (3) subscribe to the declaration against transubstantiation. This removed all devout Roman Catholics and Dissenters from public office, including that devout Catholic the Duke of York, the heir to the throne.

The secret treaty of Dover, binding Charles to Louis XIV, had been signed in the same year that Charles issued his declaration. Some already had quite accurate suspicions of the content of the treaty and knew that Charles had promised to work for the advancement of the Catholic interest in England and that he would himself eventually declare his own loyalty to that church. So 1673 saw the court officially and not so secretly working for the Roman Catholic-French interest, the country and Parliament openly in defense of the Anglican establishment and of the Anglican interest, and the Cabal being replaced by the Earl of Danby, who sought to control Parliament for the king while at the same time seeking to win the king away from Rome and France. The reign of Charles II was to close with the failure of both Danby and the parliamentary opposition.

CHAPTER 3

The Exclusion Crisis

Clarendon's hopes to govern England through the machinery of the Tudor and early Stuart Privy Council had failed. The efforts of the Cabal to govern England by a reliance upon the royal prerogative had also failed. It was now the turn of the Earl of Danby to try his hand at governing, but this time Parliament, which Clarendon and the Cabal had tried to ignore, was to be an integral part of the system.[1] But Danby looked upon Parliament not as a coequal of the king but as a body that with constant effort could be so managed as to provide a prop for the crown; because of Parliament's vague claims to represent the nation, opposition within the nation could be undercut. Parliament was to be managed, not consulted. But the successful management of Parliament was to require more than the twisting of arms, cajoling of friends and relatives, and the widespread use of bribes. Danby also realized that to manage Parliament and enhance the power and reputation of the crown required the crown to adopt policies that were in tune with the nation's interests. These interests were the Anglican establishment, an anti-French foreign policy, and efficient financial administration. If Charles II could be brought to give Danby a free hand in pursuing these goals, then

[1] See Clayton Roberts, *The Growth of Responsible Government in Stuart England*, Cambridge, 1966, pp. 197 ff.

he would be able to manage Parliament to the end that the king would be ultimately free from a financial dependence upon Parliament; and, other than the money necessary to provide for the military posture occasioned by an anti-French policy, the king would be secure on his throne and in his prerogative.

Thus Danby sought to save the royal prerogative by persuading the king himself to change those very policies he thought he had the prerogative right as king to pursue. Danby would save the king from himself and in spite of himself. What the king seems to have realized better than Danby is that saving the prerogative by repudiating his personal policies was a Pyrrhic victory at best. Parliament was to show that there was a very real limit as to how far it was willing to be managed, even if the management was in the interest of policies that it held most dear. Danby, in spite of his cleverness, forgot several important political truisms: Chief among these is that policies and interests are only part of what constitutes the political world. He ignored the lust for power, which he himself had in good measure. Danby's scheme secured power for himself and his policies, denied power to Parliament, and denied the king his policies. He also failed to anticipate the possibility that others besides himself could play at the game of parliamentary management or manipulation. And he forgot that if his scheme were to fail, he, not the king or Parliament, would prove to be expendable. One does not presume too much on the loyalty of kings (or parliaments).

Danby assumed that his policies were those of England itself, not of the king personally, and he therefore set out to manage Parliament not in the sense of winning a majority over to his policies, but to see that the majority that was already there would do its duty by king and nation and actually vote accordingly. Attendance was a very hit-and-miss affair for many members. This was especially the case among those who were already inclined to support the court. Danby's job was to see that those who were connected to him by personal loyalty and by the granting of pensions out of the secret-service funds would be constant in attendance and absolutely loyal in the division lobbies. On the whole, Danby had great success, but many of the Cavaliers soon came to feel that the jobs or pensions for themselves or their relatives were not theirs by grace, but by right. The failure of Charles II to restore the lost properties to the old Royalists was to come back to haunt Danby. For to many who had suffered losses during the Commonwealth and Protectorate, the new pensions were merely just compensation. And in any case, Danby was not to be the only one able and willing to secure votes in this way. Louis XIV did not allow himself to rely solely upon the king's good will. He subsidized many members of both Houses, in addition to the king.

If Danby succeeded in anything, it was in helping to sharpen the distinctions between the crown and the opposition and to hasten the day when the lines would actually be drawn tight. Regardless of how hard Danby might strive to forward his own "English" policies, the court was still seen as a reflection not of the policies of the minister, but of the king. The age-old truism that the king can do no wrong was dead in the sense that the opposition was quite ready to assume that if anything were amiss it surely could in all fairness be laid at the door of the king himself. Before the Puritan Revolution there had always been the need to feel that the king was personally righteous, only that he was the unfortunate tool of his evil advisers. The new spirit in the mid-seventies was more realistic. If the king had evil advisers it was because he himself had knowingly and deliberately chosen them. The revival of the impeachment process was to reflect this new spirit. The king must be denied his evil advisers and must choose advisers acceptable to Parliament. The new attitude differed from the old in that the opposition now thoroughly realized that the king might very well like and agree with his evil advisers and might not like or want those who would be acceptable to Parliament. The king's personal good will was no longer taken for granted. He must be made receptive to the views of Parliament whether he wished to be or not, even if this required occasional disruptions in the smooth functioning of the governmental machinery. The opposition was not averse to using obstructive and questionable tactics in order to accomplish its own ends. The old notion that Parliament consisted of the king's loyal lords spiritual and temporal and his loyal commons all working for a common goal with mutual trust and respect was dead. King and Parliament were locked in an increasingly fierce struggle for power, no less intense than that which had plagued Charles I. But this time the myths had been stripped away, and the true nature of the struggle for power was seen in the raw.

Even though Danby seemed to be successful in moving Charles toward an Anglo-Dutch alliance, the opposition could see only the not too well-hidden pro-French proclivities of the court. Even though Danby sought a truly Anglican ecclesiastical policy, the opposition could see only that the court was pro-Roman Catholic and that Danby's policy could well be nothing but a device to secure Commons seats for procourt Cavaliers. Thus the nominally Royalist majority in the Cavalier Parliament saw the coalescing of a real country opposition very much like that seen in 1640. But however delicate the situation might be, England need not have been plunged into a crisis as severe as anything seen before 1640 if it had not been for the work of one of the most unscrupulous men ever to stride across the stage of English history—Titus Oates.

Oates's "exposure" of the "Popish Plot" to overthrow the English government was one of the more fascinating and unsavory episodes in English history. But however much it is tempting to attribute the crisis caused by the attempt to exclude the Duke of York as heir to the throne to the work of Titus Oates, it must still be remembered that Oates did little more than create an opportunity for both the Earl of Shaftesbury and the king to flex their muscles and go to the brink of civil war in the hopes of achieving a lasting victory of either the crown or of Parliament. Oates lighted a match, but Shaftesbury and the king were both willing and able to fan the flames. In the end, the crisis of civil war was avoided and the crown achieved a nominal and temporary victory.

Ever since the fall of the Cabal, the Earl of Shaftesbury had waged a campaign both in and out of Parliament against the policies of the crown and the hegemony of Danby within the administration. He warned that if the present course was maintained, England would be subservient to France, the true Protestant religion would be subverted, the rights of property would be jeopardized, and the nation's ability to govern its own destiny through a free parliament would be lost. In fact, Shaftesbury and his friends in the opposition, or Whig party, recited over and over again the whole litany of anti-court epithets that had been the stock in trade of the country party since its emergence in the reign of James I in the 1620s. But Shaftesbury needed Oates and his exposés to bring things to a head. Oates in turn needed the Duke of York to make his charges plausible and politically significant. In the end it was not the Popish Plot but the person of James, Duke of York, that was the center of the storm.

That James was a trial for Charles cannot be denied. The relationship between a monarch and his heir is difficult enough in the best of times, but a brother can be even more a problem than a son. The two had very little in common beyond a determination to uphold and even enhance the powers of the crown, and a passion for women. But where Charles had a political astuteness, James was single-minded. Charles combined worldly wisdom with a dispassionate temperament and a becoming laziness. James, on the other hand, had neither a political sense nor an understanding of people or their motives. Both had the highest regard for the institution of monarchy, but James added to this a vast regard for his own personal prejudices. Charles was able to view his office and its problems with a certain philosophical and skeptical detachment, where James personalized everything. James could not understand any view or motive but his own, and expected blind loyalty to his every whim from all those who served him. Charles might be accused of being unscrupulous, lazy, or unprincipled, but James could be accused of immense obstinacy, narrow-mindedness, and political stupidity. Charles knew how to bend with the wind and also how and when to dig in and hold on. James merely dug in and commanded the winds to stop blowing. During the Exclusion Crisis James was saved by Charles, but when the winds blew again in the autumn of 1688 James just dug himself up by the roots and flew away. It was not out of love for his heir that Charles faced the storm over exclusion, nor was it to uphold the hereditary principle alone. On the contrary, Charles sought to protect his heir and to enhance the powers of the crown in the process. Charles was able to serve James much better than James ever knew or understood.

Charles II had developed a feeling of sympathy for the Roman Catholic Church and for French ways during his years of exile. How deeply his religious views went is certainly problematic, but there was an aura about the court at Versailles, Catholic and monarchical, that deeply impressed the young man in exile. It is certainly understandable that his experiences from 1640–60 would tend to the creation of a jaundiced view of England and its ways and a feeling that the French ordered things better. If subsidies from Louis XIV, which spared him from an overreliance on Parliament, required him to promise to openly convert to the Roman Church, so be it. At any rate, he would make his declaration in his own time and in his own interests.

James, on the other hand, had openly and warmly embraced the Roman faith in France. Ironically, however, James was to evince a much deeper spirit of English patriotism than his royal brother. Throughout the first years after the Restoration, the Duke of York's role was not particularly controversial. He had married Anne Hyde, the daughter of the Earl of Clarendon, and was thus tied to the strong upholder of the old Anglican tradition. His daughters, Mary and Anne, were both raised as Anglicans. The death of Anne Hyde, the fall of Clarendon, the diplomatic and religious indecisiveness of the years of the Cabal, and then his new marriage to Princess Mary of Modena, an Italian Catholic, weakened his position in the nation. The passage of the Test Act, in the same year as his marriage to Mary of Modena, compelled him to give up his office of Lord High Admiral of England. The mid-1670s thus found James more and more on the outside of affairs, not only in the nation at large but at court in particular. As much as possible, Charles tried to keep him out of the country, for James's good as well as his own. Whenever he was at court, James assumed the right of giving advice to his brother. Charles knew that the advice was usually worthless and that his mere presence tended to prejudice both James's and, even more important, Charles's political positions. Thus by the time of the Popish Plot the royal brothers were not on good terms personally. Charles knew that the throne and James's claims to it could be secured only if James stayed out of sight and out of mind and left the sole conduct of affairs to the king. James, however, had little confidence in Charles's political gamesmanship and on occasion even had sincere doubts as to whether or not Charles really did want to have him come to the throne. The presence of Charles's illegitimate son, the Duke of Monmouth, always hung like a sword over James's neck. Not only could the opposition advance his claims, but even more to the point was the very real possibility, at least for James, that the father might love the son more than the brother.

Shaftesbury and his country, or Whig, opposition were thus in a position to avoid a direct confrontation with the king and his policies by directing their shots at the heir to the throne instead. No one knew better than Charles how vulnerable he was on this flank. The eagerness with which the country took up the cry when the disreputable Oates first made his wild charges demonstrates the nearly paranoidal proportions that the fear of Catholicism had attained in England. Ironically, James's inherent patriotism was to count for nothing. Throughout the sorry history of seventeenth-century anti-Catholicism, it was the fear of the foreigner that usually provided the spark. In 1678 Charles, not James, was guilty of intriguing with the foreigner. Charles had his ties with France; James was the avowed Catholic. The symbol of James's religion was to seem more important than the substance of Charles's policy.

Titus Oates had been a failure at almost everything to which he tried his hand prior to the "exposure" of the "Plot." During his sordid career he had been ejected from school, from a naval chaplaincy, and from a French Jesuit college. In 1675 he had been charged with perjury, but had escaped from prison. He also claimed to have a doctor's degree from the University of Salamanca. At the time of the Plot he was officially an Anglican priest and a known liar. David Ogg has noted how much seventeenth-century life consisted of the hatching and searching for plots of all kinds in all places.[2] Oates was merely one of the most unscrupulous of these plot mongers. Both on the Continent and in England he had lived and worked with Catholics, and had many personal contacts with Jesuits. He was, therefore, not totally ignorant of the Jesuitical mind

[2] David Ogg, *England in the Reign of Charles II*, Oxford, 1934, vol. II, pp. 559–61.

and dreams. Being in dire financial straits in 1678 he teamed up with Ezerel Tonge, a much older man who had been trained in theology at Oxford and was an amateur scientist. The two men at first sought to find a real popish plot, and failing at that, they set about to invent one. Putting together the bits and pieces of Jesuitiana that they had each acquired over the years, they drew up a forty-three-point indictment of the "conspirators." The indictment charged that the pope had assigned to the Jesuits in England supreme control over the Catholic community so that they could in turn organize to overthrow both the king and kingdom. The Spanish Jesuits and Louis XIV's confessor were to provide the necessary funds. Two Jesuits had been assigned to shoot the king, four Irishmen were to stab him, and the queen's own physician was to poison him.[8] In addition, Protestants were to be massacred, the French would invade Ireland, James would be made king, and the Jesuits would serve as his advisers. Later emendations to the indictment specified the names of certain other proposed officeholders.

Presenting the indictment and the supposed evidence to support it proved at first to be a difficulty. Various members of the court including Danby, and even the king, were made aware of it but naturally tended to discount the alleged facts. Since neither Charles II nor Danby was either a fool or a man who little valued his own life, this is significant. The court, then, had no reasons to suspect any such plot. The country was to prove to be a different matter. Only one more spark was needed to start the fires of mass paranoia blazing. That spark was the death of Sir Edmund Berry Godfrey, a Westminster justice of the peace, before whom Oates had presented the indictment and who had held a preliminary hearing. Godfrey was a wealthy and respected figure in London, and when he was found lying on Primrose Hill, near Hampstead, with a sword run-

[8] Ibid., pp. 563–64.

ning clear through his body, the coroner's inquest returned a verdict of murder, and the whole nation immediately knew that this was just one more piece in the plot and that Oates was right. Parliament and the nation were thrown into hysterics, and the vacillation of the Danby administration, rather than damping the flames, merely served to implicate the Lord Treasurer himself.

From this point on, not Oates but the Earl of Shaftesbury took up the torch and sought to light his way back into power with it. Shaftesbury had had a long and unstable career. In the 1640s he had fought on the side of the Royalists against the parliamentary forces. During the Commonwealth and Protectorate he served on various commissions and strongly supported Cromwell against the Presbyterians. On Cromwell's death he worked for the restoration of the Stuarts and was one of the group that presented the formal invitation to the young king. He was rewarded with a seat on the Privy Council and served as a judge at the trial of the Regicides. He was created a baron in 1661, and from the Lords he opposed the Corporation Act and the Act of Uniformity. From his position as one of the opposition to Clarendon, he was able to ride back into power as a member of the Cabal upon the old chancellor's fall. The end of the Cabal saw him as Lord Chancellor and a supporter of the Test Act. After only one year on the woolsack he was dismissed with the connivance of the Duke of York and went into political exile as Danby took over the center of the political stage. The new Earl of Shaftesbury now saw the eclipse of his power as the responsibility not only of the Duke of York but of Danby as well. For the next five years he worked to organize his own "party" in Parliament by the use of methods very similar to those used by Danby himself. The personal rivalry of Danby and Shaftesbury thus worked unwittingly toward the creation of two parties in Parliament: Shaftesbury and his country opposition (the Whigs) and

Danby and his Anglican loyalists (the Tories). Just as the Cabal had been destroyed by the secret treaty of Dover, so the reign of Danby was to be destroyed by Shaftesbury's clever and ruthless use of the findings of Titus Oates and the murder of Sir Edmund Berry Godfrey.

Neither Charles II nor Danby really believed in the Plot's existence, but since they suspected, wrongly, that Shaftesbury and perhaps Buckingham were behind it, it was a serious political crisis and had to be treated accordingly. As for Shaftesbury's own role, he has been quoted as saying, "I will not say who started the Game, but I am sure I had the full hunting of it."[4] But it was not to be in the provinces and in London that Shaftesbury would make his pitch; he waited for the commencement of Parliament and then used all of his great parliamentary powers to weld together a country, or opposition, party that would be capable of at least driving Danby from power. Success here would inspire Shaftesbury on to greater and more dangerous quarry—the Duke of York.

Parliament quickly moved to establish two investigatory committees: one was called upon "to consider Ways and Means for providing Remedies for the better Preservation and Safety of His Majesty's Person," and the other was to investigate the death of Sir Edmund Berry Godfrey. These committees had very large memberships and all major factions were represented, but a quorum on most parliamentary committees was as low as three or five and with proper management the opposition could and did get control of both of them. In some cases meetings were scheduled in such a clandestine manner that court supporters either did not know about meetings or they could not find the meeting places even when they had been informed. These committees were soon to rival and then surpass the Privy Council itself in the zeal with which they

[4] Laurence Echard, *The History of England*, London, 1718, vol. III, p. 460.

operated and in the outside support they generated. Witnesses friendly to the idea of the existence of the Plot were obviously much more willing to appear before a sympathetic committee of the Commons than before the austere and skeptical Privy Council.[5] Since the Duke of York would be the obvious beneficiary of any plot to kill the king, it is self-evident that the moment Parliament began to concern itself with the Plot, the question of the succession was to arise as a spontaneous second thought. At first, however, it was not assumed that he was actually implicated. In October a bill was introduced in Commons that would have prevented Roman Catholics from sitting in either House of Parliament. This of course would exclude James as well as the others from any participation in searching through the tangled skein of the Plot and from any voice in the subsequent legislation.

James was soon to be thrust into the center of the stage. His duchess' secretary, Edward Coleman, had for years been in correspondence with the French court in order to secure James an independent pension from Louis XIV, comparable in scale to that which Charles had secured by the secret treaty of Dover. Coleman had done his best to persuade the French of James's virtues as a man, as a potential king, and as a firm supporter of the Catholic cause in England. The impression given was that the French could hope for much more from James as king than from Charles. Of course nothing was explicitly said that could prove that James's accession would occur prior to the natural demise of Charles II. But the loose wording of the letters, coupled with the atmosphere of hysterical anti-Catholicism and growing Francophobia, guaranteed that the discovery of the letters would reverberate like a bombshell throughout political England. Saving the king and kingdom now seemed to require the expulsion

[5] J. R. Jones, *The First Whigs: The Politics of the Exclusion Crisis, 1678–1683*, London, 1961, pp. 23–24.

and exclusion of the Duke of York, although no one in Parliament yet said so openly.

The publicizing of the Coleman correspondence certainly put the crown on the defensive, but Danby was willing to take a chance on holding on and even launching a counterattack. In the end, he failed, but Danby was undoubtedly correct in his belief that in spite of all the hysteria surrounding the story of the Plot, Shaftesbury might very well have reached too far too fast. Actually Danby was correct in his assessment of the political situation, but he himself was to be pulled down by the betrayal of his ambassador at Versailles, Ralph Montague. As Charles's chief minister, Danby had been obliged to carry on the official correspondence between London and Paris. As much as he abhorred the king's pro-French policy, he was obliged to conduct it nonetheless, and to work to change it from within. When Montague made public Danby's correspondence with Versailles, the result was to make Danby appear in the false light of an instigator of the hated pro-French policy rather than as the enemy of it, which in truth he was and had been.

In the last weeks of 1678 the king himself sought a way out of the whole crisis by offering concessions that would save his crown and his prerogative, and would also show him as a ruler who understood and sympathized with the hopes and fears of his subjects. Nothing came of the offer, but it did serve to put the king in a stronger position in the future, when he would choose to take a harder line. Charles spoke from the throne on November 9 and said that he would agree to any "reasonable" limits that might be imposed upon a Catholic successor so long as the line of succession itself was not tampered with.[6] William Sacheverel, in the Commons, commented that this concession on Charles's part was meaningless and that the only way to save England was to secure the succession in the

[6] *Journals of the House of Commons*, vol. IX, p. 536.

Protestant line.[7] Thus exclusion raised its head for the first time.

Perhaps one immediate by-product of the king's conciliatory attitude was Danby's success in securing by a majority of two votes a proviso excepting the Duke of York from the provisions of the new test bill, which called for the removal of all Papists from their seats in the House of Lords. As J. R. Jones wisely commented, the wave of anti-Catholic and anti-French hysteria alone was not a sufficient foundation upon which to mount a successful attack against the crown when the lines between the court and the opposition were not yet clearly drawn.[8] Too many of the opposition were fearful, or hesitant, for other reasons. Not until 1688 had the crown managed to provide further materials upon which the opposition could construct a successful revolution.

Early in 1679, with the crown conciliatory but on the defensive, the Cavalier Parliament was dissolved. During the eighteen years of its existence, it had proved itself to be Cavalier, or Royalist, in no sense that the king could understand. On the contrary, it had shown itself to be every bit as independent and even recalcitrant as the Long Parliament had during its first two years. The restored monarchy of Charles II had sincerely tried to heal the breech between the prerogative and Parliament that had led to civil war in the '40s, and, through a policy of toleration, he had tried to bind together the two religious nations over which he was to reign. On both these counts, these first eighteen years had ended in failure. The Royalists who had restored the king and had been returned to Parliament in 1661 had taken on all of the characteristics of the country party prior to 1640. The opposition was now Cavalier (or Tory, as they were soon to be called), but the name had ceased to disguise the fact

[7] Sacheverel's speech was interrupted by the secretary, Coventry, and by the Speaker.

[8] Jones, p. 27.

that it was a country opposition with both negative and positive policies of its own which it was determined to pursue. Of course the pursuit of these policies was not to be at any cost. The lessons of the Puritan Revolution were not that easily forgotten.

The king had sought a comprehensive church and had been rebuffed. Then he had sought religious toleration, and again he had failed. The so-called Clarendon Code had not only driven the old Puritan from the Church but from politics as well. The Test Act had removed Puritan and Catholic from all forms of service to the king and nation, with the sole exception of sitting in the Lords. The last act of the Cavalier Parliament had now removed even this. The king's efforts to provide himself with muscle by means of a standing militia had been rejected. The financial settlement of the Restoration had soon proved to be inadequate, but no steps were taken to guarantee the king an adequate income. In the field of foreign policy, the age-old royal prerogative was under constant and bitter attack. By 1679 Charles II still had his throne, but he can hardly be said to have had his policies. His almost clandestine relationship with Louis XIV was of course designed to preserve the royal prerogative and his throne, but the result by 1679 was to inflame the opposition yet again and to bring the nation close to the brink of civil war. The failure of his earlier hopes for a nation united in Church and state under the benevolent guidance of the crown determined Charles to change the nature of his rule and to trust to himself alone and his own interests as he saw them. But before he could reverse the trend of events and create a more truly royalist government based on the unfettered exercise of his prerogative, he had first to find a way through the perilous sands of the Exclusion Crisis. The dissolution of the Cavalier Parliament, it was hoped, would be the means to this end. As it turned out, the road to victory was to be a bit longer and more dangerous than he had hoped for. But victory was to be his in the end, nonetheless.

But what of the Cavaliers, who constituted a large majority of this Long Parliament? Does the name Cavalier have any meaning in light of the behavior exhibited by them in Parliament? Yes, for as estranged as they had become from the king, they were equally estranged from that group among them and in society who were soon to be called Whigs. There has long been a great controversy among historians as to whether or not the terms Whig and Tory have any meaning in the sense of modern parties either organizationally or ideologically. Were these names mere additions to the political vocabulary, useful only in distinguishing among the various and sundry groupings of this or that period on this or that issue? Or were there truly distinct groups of relatively fixed membership, organization, and ideology? The weight of evidence inclines one to the latter view. By 1679 the Cavaliers were already well on the way to becoming the Tory party of the 1680s and the subsequent two centuries.

Without anticipating the nature of the Tory party after the Exclusion Crisis, it is possible to piece together certain characteristics that justify our saying that by 1679 a distinct Tory point of view, if not ideology, was emerging. The Cavalier/Tory was a monarchist, and a hereditary monarchist at that, but he was no longer one who cared overly much for the free exercise of the royal prerogative—not by the king alone, at any rate. To some extent the monarchical idea was a mere counter to the supposed republicanism of the Whigs. Memories were not yet so short as to remind them that Charles I's loss of the crown was their loss too. The Cavalier/Tory also identified completely with the Anglican Church in the narrow sense of its establishment in 1661. The loss of the Church in the 1640s had also been his loss. The Cavalier/Tory was also well on the way to becoming a true supporter of the country interest against the court interest. The Tory peers and gentry sought throughout to hang onto their hegemony in their own bailiwicks. They were even willing to go further and showed signs of being willing to undo much of the centralizing of English government, which had been the growing tendency since the reign of Henry VIII. Yet their disillusionment with government at the center was not yet so complete that they were ready to retire from the field, as they would do after the Hanoverian succession. They still sought to influence, and even control, the central government, but for ends that would secure their roles in the country and preserve the old England in both Church and state.

None of the preceding should, however, lead us to picture the Tory as one who was concerned purely with his own parochial interests, nor as one who would concede to the central government merely the role of caretaker. The crown was in no guise thought of as the enemy. The king did have the right and the duty to protect the nation's interest in the world and to preserve the English people at home. But the England that they sought to preserve under the leadership of the king was an England that was religious in the Anglican sense, and an England in which the aristocracy and gentry held sway on local matters and provided the personnel and the policies for the national government. In negative terms, the Tory sought an England in which the Dissenter, the Catholic, the internationalist, and those who would meddle in the ways of traditional local arrangements would be powerless. Of all these competing and even contradictory policies, the goal was probably supremacy in local affairs, and the best means of securing this was probably the Church rather than the monarchy. In its liturgy the Church seemed to be an upholder of the monarchy and of the state. Yet it is highly likely that the monarchy in turn was looked to as the preserver of the Church. At least, that seems to be what it came to in 1688.

In order to understand the full course of the Exclusion Crisis and in order to see that crisis in the larger context of the Glorious Revolution, it is necessary to see toryism as a distinct ideology adhered to by men with interests of their own who, though sincerely loyal to monarchy and Anglicanism, were not so wedded to the one or the other that their own true ends should be lost in the struggle to protect either of those hallowed institutions. In sum, then, the Tory was a Royalist and an Anglican, but not in the same sense that either the king or perhaps even his bishops were. Any exact identity of interest between king and Cavalier, if it ever existed, had disappeared in the early days of the Convention Parliament in 1660. Charles II succeeded in surviving the Exclusion Crisis because he was able, temporarily, to revive that sense of oneness. Together they defeated the exclusionists, and king and Cavalier marched together beyond the death of Charles II and into the early days of James II.

The Cavalier Parliament had been dissolved in January 1679 to save the Duke of York and Danby. But the elections to the new Parliament did not turn out as either Danby or Charles had hoped. Charles had assumed that most of his troubles in the last days of the old Parliament had been caused by Shaftesbury's clever and ruthless faction building among the Londoners and other London-oriented members. He hoped that an infusion of new country blood would turn the tables against Shaftesbury. The election was the most bitter and energetic yet fought in England. New electioneering techniques were used, such as providing transportation to the polls for one's supporters, and the widespread use of the election pamphlet. Hitherto, English elections turned more on personalities and local issues. But this time the issues at the center were to dominate. The results were a victory for Shaftesbury. In every constituency where the race was a clear-cut struggle between Shaftesbury's allies and the supporters of the court, the former emerged the winners. Only about thirty men in the whole House of Commons could be called king's men. The king was even more completely thrown onto the defensive than he had been before. Danby was again impeached, even though he had resigned the lord treasurership. The king was now on his own, and the brink could not be far off. Charles, for all his reputed laziness and carelessness, was alone and had to become the master of his own fate. He brilliantly rose to the challenge, again by attempting to put the opposition on the defensive by taking the lead at reconciliation. Just before the opening of the new Parliament, James agreed to be banished in return for the king's statement declaring the illegitimacy of the Duke of Monmouth.

The king's efforts at conciliation were marred during the first month by his desire to protect Danby from the wrath of Parliament and by Danby's desire to exercise whatever influence he could muster to set the composition of the new administration. Danby had resigned the lord treasurership, but the king allowed him to nominate his successors as Lords Commissioners of the Treasury. On top of this, the king's speech to Parliament stated that Danby would receive a royal pardon from the impeachment charges. Danby defended himself by claiming that all his actions had been in response to the king's commands. This defense, coupled with a royal pardon, raised the grave constitutional issue of the ultimate responsibility of the ministers of the crown. Were they ultimately responsible to the king, or to Parliament? Clarification of this issue had to wait until the Act of Settlement of 1701. The disagreement of the Lords and Commons over the issue, however, contributed to the defense of Danby and of the royal prerogative. The Lords, however, were more concerned with defending their own position than they were with deciding on the great principle of ministerial responsibility which divided the king and the Commons. The court still had influence in the Lords, and their failure to be shocked by the king's pardon spurred the Commons on to challenge the Lords' arrangements

for the impeachment trial and also determined the
Commons to challenge the right of the bishops to
participate in the trial. The jurisdictional dispute between the two Houses prevented the impeachment
trial from ever proceeding, but the king was to keep
Danby in the Tower for the next five years anyway.
Danby's threats to "tell all" if he were turned over to
the Commons could not secure his release, but they
did at least keep him alive and free from trial. During
Danby's forced vacation from office the king more and
more took the reins of administration into his own
hands, relying for assistance upon the Earl of Sunderland.

The king's attempted conciliation, with the banishment of his brother, James, had thus been undone by
his declaration of a pardon for Danby. Even Parliament's granting money to disband the armed forces
was less a concession than an attempt to deprive the
king of troops that could be used to defend the king at
home as well as the kingdom abroad. Being unable to
vent their full wrath on the Earl of Danby, Commons
now turned directly upon the Duke of York and proceeded to debate exclusion. John Hampden's son Richard called for the introduction of the bill. At last the
issue was clearly in the open, and the next two years
found England living with the ever-present specter of
civil war.

As the argument over Danby's impeachment drew
to a close, and before the Commons introduced the Exclusion Bill, Charles made a further, and even grandi-
ose, attempt at conciliation. Following the advice of
Sir William Temple, sometime ambassador to the
Netherlands, a new Privy Council was installed. The
king promised that he would take advice from no other
sources and that he would defer to them. This was
Clarendon's old dream come to life again. In addition
to promising to rule with the advice of his Privy Council, the king would make this Council acceptable to
all factions by including in it the country leaders in

Parliament. The Earl of Shaftesbury himself was made Lord President of the Council. How sincere was Charles in these bold steps toward reconciliation, a reconciliation that in fact constituted a truly remarkable constitutional innovation? On the surface, it represented a remarkable victory for both the court and the country opposition. The new Council was composed of those men who were in control of both Houses of Parliament, and thus the king would be assured that all necessary legislation, including the granting of supply, could be passed with ease. On the other hand the Opposition, as leaders of Parliament, would have the only direct line to the king's ear and could largely determine the nature of the necessary legislation that it would be their duty to see through to passage. This was not yet the modern cabinet, but it was a large step in that direction. It was not the modern cabinet, because the king still made the decision as to whom to appoint and on what matters to consult them. And of course they were still in law responsible only to him. The Council was to control Parliament for the king; it was not yet assumed that Parliament would control the king through the Council. Regardless of the willingness of many of the opposition leaders to serve in the new Council, the ordinary member of Commons was not impressed. In fact he became downright suspicious. To the extent the opposition leaders now served the king, to that extent they lost their control over the country in Parliament. Sir William Temple's plan was but a dream, after all. But for the king it bought time and a propaganda victory.

The attitude of the opposition in Parliament to the new Council casts an interesting side light on the extent to which Parliament before 1688 sought power in the state and over the crown. Parliament did not want the king to become a Venetian doge. Parliament itself did not want to choose the ministers, since then it would itself be responsible for any failures on the part of those ministers. On the contrary, Parliament still wanted the king to freely choose ministers acceptable to them; thus the responsibility would be the king's, but Parliament could still hold the ministers to account. Therefore, the opposition was less than enthusiastic at having its own parliamentary leaders co-opted by the king for his new Privy Council. It all seemed like a clever plot to undermine Parliament's growing desire to have the king's ministers held responsible to the country as represented in Parliament. And of course Parliament was quite correct in its intuitive grasp of the situation, for this was exactly the king's purpose. Once the ministers were installed in the Privy Council, Charles immediately proceeded to ignore all but those whom he could trust on a personal basis.

The Whigs reacted quite solidly as a group in deploring the new Council. The Tories were torn between their old feelings of loyalty to the court and their newly acquired role as an opposition to the court. Those of the opposition who accepted appointment to office by Charles were now open to charges of being "careerists," and the memory of Sir Thomas Wentworth, Earl of Strafford, could come back to haunt them. After all, Wentworth had been one of the leaders of the opposition to Charles I and was bought off with the award of high office. Given his background over the past thirty years, Shaftesbury was especially vulnerable to such charges. Once he realized that the king was merely using him, he had to try even harder to maintain his leadership of the Whigs in Parliament. Fortified by the security that his new Council and ministers afforded him, the king proceeded to undermine the opposition's growing desire for exclusion by offering some really substantial concessions limiting the powers of a new and Catholic king.

On April 30, 1679, the Lord Chancellor, on behalf of the king, presented the royal concessions to the Lords: a Catholic king would have no powers to control either the judiciary or the Church authorities, and Parliament would either remain in session or reassemble upon James's accession. This latter concession was especially novel, because a Parliament was automatically dissolved upon the demise of the crown. The implication was, of course, that in return for these concessions exclusion was to be dropped. This was, however, not explicitly stated. That these concessions had the support of his new Whig ministers was to be one of the reasons why these concessions ultimately proved to be so helpful in the king's efforts to kill exclusion itself without actually granting concessions in the end. The opposition in Parliament was thrown off base and distrusted both the concessions and their erstwhile leaders. The Tories could not accept them because they were supported by the king's new Whig ministers, and the Duke of York himself considered them to be but the prelude to actual exclusion. The Prince of Orange, closely watching developments from the Netherlands, was not happy at the prospect of any limitations being imposed upon a hereditary monarch. It all smacked of republicanism and would constitute an unfortunate precedent. The effect, then, of Charles's concessions was to draw the lines more firmly around the main issue, and the opposition proceeded to introduce their Exclusion Bill. The Tories forthrightly opposed it. The bill passed the Commons, but Parliament was first prorogued and then dissolved before it could go to the Lords. The king had won the first round.

An election was held in August 1679, which returned a House of Commons as overwhelmingly Whig as its predecessor. Because of repeated prorogations the new Parliament did not actually get down to business until October 1680. The nearly sixteen months since the conclusion of the previous Parliament witnessed no abatement in the anti-Catholic hysteria, and found both Whigs and Tories debating among themselves and with each other about exclusion, limitations, and the rights of hereditary monarchy. The events of 1641 seemed to be repeating themselves. The king's illness during this period and the fear that his death would be followed by the Duke of York's accession again raised the specter of civil war. But this time few would or could seriously face the prospect of civil war. And yet the precipitate death of Charles II might well have resulted in this disaster.

Once the new Parliament finally did get down to business, exclusion was the only subject on its mind. This time the bill both passed the Commons and went to the Lords. But 1680 was not yet 1688, and the bill was defeated. The course of the debates and the stand taken by individual peers are highly illuminating, both in fact presaging the ultimate reversal in Tory sentiment in 1688 and 1689.

From the dissolution of the first exclusion Parliament, in June 1679, until the new Parliament finally met in October 1680, there had been a slight realignment of forces. Charles had finally dismissed Shaftesbury from the lord presidency of the Privy Council, and the erstwhile opposition leader, the Marquis of Halifax, was to remain loyal to the court. These two men came to represent the two opposing sides in the ensuing struggle. Once Shaftesbury had been dismissed by the king, he joined the opposition with a vengeance. He became the undisputed leader of the exclusionists, assigning to exclusion not just top priority but sole priority. For Shaftesbury the whole struggle between crown and Parliament, the cause of Protestantism versus Catholicism, of England versus France, of the people of England versus the imminent tyranny of the court, were all centered in this one great cause. No doubt he also realized that once he had drawn the lines so tightly, his own career and perhaps even his own life were no less at stake. It is little wonder that, now that the opposition Whigs were totally committed, Charles II was forced to become equally committed to the cause of preserving the hereditary succession and his own prerogatives. The untrammeled accession of James of York was now a necessity. No more concessions could be proposed except as a matter merely of temporary tactics. For Charles and for Shaftesbury it was a question of rule or ruin.

But the king was too clever to expose himself openly. His own strategy was one of "mastery and methodical" inaction.[9] He himself had openly offered his concessions a year and a half earlier. This time he would sit back and let others in the Lords try their hand at it. Men such as Halifax, still one of the king's councilors but seemingly allowed a free hand in the Lords, took the lead in trying to counter the intransigence of Shaftesbury by proposing limitations on a Catholic king. But these new concessions were not to be offered until after a momentous debate on the bill itself, a debate dominated by Shaftesbury and Halifax, with the latter emerging victorious. The bill was defeated on first reading by a vote of 63–30, a decisive majority for the court. Both contemporaries and most historians since have awarded the laurels of victory to the eloquence of Halifax, but it is more likely that the king should be given the bulk of the credit. Charles attended the debates in person and let it be known openly that he both opposed the bill and would offer no more concessions on his own. In the face of this new-found royal intransigence, the waverers really had no choice but to avert the possibility of civil war or revolution by joining the court faction. With the Exclusion Bill defeated, the attempt to introduce a new bill in the Lords calling for limitations upon James's prerogatives was doomed to defeat. The Whigs in both houses had staked all on exclusion and could not contemplate limitations. It was still all or nothing. The subsequent dissolution of Parliament killed the matter for the time being.

In what remained of the parliamentary session, until January 1681, the opposition in both houses gave vent to their wrath over the defeat of exclusion by proposing

[9] Sir Keith Feiling, A History of the Tory Party, 1640–1714, Oxford, 1924, p. 183.

several bills and resolutions that anticipated parts of the settlement following the revolution of 1688–89. Even Halifax and the waverers in the Lords associated themselves with some of these. One proposal called for denying James the power of veto when he became king. Another would have assigned him the status of a minor, thus necessitating a regency. It was proposed that his marriage to Mary of Modena should be dissolved and that he should be made to marry a Protestant. A Protestant association of bishops, judges, royal officials, and members of Parliament was suggested. The members of the association were to take up arms in the defense of the kingdom and of the Protestant Establishment and would stay under arms until a new Parliament could meet. This proposal closely resembled the association created by the opponents of Mary Queen of Scots in the reign of Elizabeth I, and Charles II certainly was no happier with it than Elizabeth I had been. After all, this was vigilantism on a huge scale and suggested the creation of a state within a state. A resolution in the Lords backed by Halifax actually provided that no armed forces could be raised without the consent of Parliament, the Duke of York was to be denied his seat in the Lords, and the veto and appointment powers of a Catholic king would have to be circumscribed. This resolution, however, was killed by the eventual dissolution of Parliament.

The House of Commons had its own proposals, which were far more extreme: Parliament would meet frequently, tenure of judges would be based on good behavior rather than the king's pleasure, taxation without the consent of Parliament would be a treasonable offense, the Lords' jurisdiction over trial of peers would be circumscribed, impeachments begun in one session of Parliament would carry over into the following session even if the previous session had been ended by prorogation or dissolution, and no member of the Commons could accept any office or place of profit under the crown without the consent of the Commons.

All these proposals, except the one dealing with impeachments, were to be enacted into law after 1688; thus there was a prophetic quality about them, even if at the time there was no chance that a monarch aroused to the defense of his prerogatives would consent to their passage.

These proposals for a shift in the balance of power were not, however, all that Commons sought to secure. Exclusion was still the primary goal, and the power of the purse was to be brought to bear on it. In January of 1681 the Commons resolved that no money would be supplied to the king until the Exclusion Bill was passed. All those who had or would advise the king to prorogue or dissolve Parliament to prevent passage of the bill were declared to be defenders of the French interest. The depths of their passion can be seen in the resolution declaring that the Great Fire of London in 1666 had been the work of Papists. With all the bills to give effect to these resolutions still pending, Charles dissolved Parliament.

Elections were soon held for a new Parliament to meet in Oxford, that ancient redoubt of the Royalist cause. Not only were the lines still drawn sharply, but it was now absolutely clear to all participants that they were drawn. All the bills and resolutions in both Houses calling for limitations on a future Catholic king and on the royal prerogative itself had been killed by the dissolution. Would a new Parliament start all over again or would they go to the heart of the matter and vote directly for exclusion? Halifax and his friends who supported limitations in the Lords had fallen out with Charles over the dissolution of Parliament in January and were removed from the Council. Sunderland, who had actually voted for exclusion, had also been removed. These two men each represented a part of the Tory tradition and the Tory party. Halifax was the "trimmer," who opposed exclusion and permanent infringements on the prerogative but also sincerely sought limitations on a Catholic king. Halifax's new proposals

were said to have the support of the king, but once
again it is likely that this support was for tactical purposes only. The proposals called for James's accession
to the throne but also for his banishment from the
kingdom for life. His daughter, Princess Mary of
Orange, would be regent unless or until a Protestant
son of James had reached maturity. The regent would
appoint members of the Privy Council with the approval of Parliament; all would be done in the name of
James, but it would be a capital crime to bear arms on
behalf of James's person. That these proposals could
have had the king's support is really incredible. In any
case, only one member of the Commons supported
them. If there had really been royal support for these
limitations, certainly the court could have found some
Tories in the Commons who would have adhered to
them. David Ogg states that the issue was exclusion or
limitations.[10] The issue was in fact much simpler: exclusion or the unfettered accession of the Duke of York,
Catholic or not.

Even if the king might have actually toyed with the
possibility of accepting Halifax's scheme at the beginning of the new Parliament, within a few days he had
no need to. Lawrence Hyde, Earl of Rochester, son of
Lord Clarendon and brother-in-law of James, had
just managed to cement a new arrangement between
Charles and Louis XIV, securing a new subsidy for
Charles at almost no cost to the king. The secret treaty
of Dover was reborn, this time the king being required
to promise almost nothing of substance in return for
the political, diplomatic, moral, and financial support
of France. Now the king did not need Parliament at
all. The only serious question was, how could the king
rid himself of this and all subsequent Parliaments without driving the Whig opposition to arms? If Parliament
had met in London as usual, not only would there have
been the mob, which Shaftesbury could have rallied

[10] Ogg, II, p. 615.

on his behalf, but there were many halls available for an illegal meeting of a rump Parliament if worst came to worst. In anticipation of this possibility, Hyde himself had suggested holding the new Parliament in Oxford, which was good royalist ground and a place where neither a mob nor an alternative meeting hall would be available to the opposition.

There was no doubt that the setting was favorable for Charles. Lord Oxford had soldiers friendly to the king stationed along the roads, the university students had been sent home, and all the university facilities were at the disposal of the two Houses, so long as the king wished it that way. As the king himself arrived, crowds in the streets chanted, "Let the King live and the Devil hang the Roundheads." If this was to be a repeat of 1641, at least this time the king was not fleeing from Parliament to a friendly Oxford, but was dragging his Lords and Commons with him. With Halifax's futile plea for limitations out of the way, and with his new arrangements with Louis XIV completed, the king could sit back and enjoy the ensuing spectacle. It would be just a matter of time before Shaftesbury would crawl too far out on the limb. When that point came, the king knew what to do.

February and March 1681 had found the king strengthening his own position, but even though the elections themselves had been lost, Shaftesbury, whose forces had won the elections to the new Parliament, was indeed farther out on a limb than theretofore. The election of February 1681 had seen the consolidation of the Whig party organization and the involvement of the electors in the grand political issues on a scale never before seen in an English election. Many of the victorious Whigs were returned to Parliament with specific instructions from their constituents calling for exclusion and for the cleansing of the realm of all Papist influences. For Shaftesbury to have fought and won an election in such circumstances was to make it impossible for him to openly accept a compromise from whatever source it derived. To accept concessions from Halifax, who had done so much to kill the Exclusion Bill the previous autumn, would have been political suicide for Shaftesbury. His only chance was to press for exclusion. Both during and after the election a pamphlet war was in full sway, a war not unlike that of the 1640s and 1650s. One of the fruits of the Whig organization was the ability to flood the court and its adherents with petitions demanding exclusion. The Petitioners were naturally going to be opposed by the "Abhorrers," those who abhorred the contents of the petitions as well as the pressure that was being brought to bear.

In the previous Parliament Shaftesbury and the Whigs had proposed reforms of the monarchy that could appear to be extreme, but their proposal for an association was also particularly frightening, not only to the king but to many of the ordinary gentry and the middle group of citizenry in general. The most alarming and dangerous element of all for his cause was the flirtation with Charles's illigitimate son, the Duke of Monmouth. This flirtation had quite openly begun in the summer of 1679, with Monmouth offering to assist Shaftesbury in regaining his position at court. Naturally James had a dreadful fear of his nephew, who was not only the king's natural son but a convinced Protestant as well. Monmouth was to become the darling of the Whigs to the same degree that he became anathema to the court and the Tories. The king was indeed fond of him, but at the same time was able to realize the impossibility of preserving the monarchy by supporting his candidature as against that of James. Naturally his religion was a tremendous asset, but his illegitimacy was a liability of truly dangerous proportions. Restoration society may well have been freer and looser in its moral tone than the preceding, Puritan era, but there remained, nonetheless, a strong current of traditional morality running deeply through the ordinary members of both the landed and the urban societies. For the court to openly indulge in sexual promiscuity was one thing; for the fruits of this promiscuity to be raised to the throne was to prove to be quite another. The Church certainly could not bring itself to ignore this indelible stain on Monmouth's character. His accession would have been a violation of both the moral law of the Church and of the common law of the realm. (The common law of England was traditionally stricter on this matter than the canon law, Roman or Anglican, of the Church.) For Shaftesbury, however, Monmouth's birth and religion were both seen as assets. As a Protestant, Monmouth could be expected to preserve the Protestant establishment. As an illegitimate child his non-claim to the throne would substantially weaken the royal prerogative in his hands, thus tilting the balance of power from the crown to Parliament and a Council subservient to it. Shaftesbury and his like-minded followers hoped to gain the summit of power by using Monmouth.

A backlash was going to develop, however. If the anti-papal and parliamentary causes had to stoop to such depths to secure a victory, then for many—perhaps most—Englishmen the cause itself was tainted. It was only for the king to read the lines of development carefully for him to protect the prerogative and the succession by exposing this alliance between Shaftesbury and his son Monmouth. The Prince of Orange, who had a good deal of support in his own right as Charles's successor, as well as in his wife Mary's name, and who was the only adult, male, Protestant heir to the throne, could not possibly support exclusion if Monmouth was to be the beneficiary. And the loss of Orange's support was a serious matter, because the opposition had always assumed the possibility of relying upon him militarily if need be to secure the enforcement of exclusion. Shaftesbury's one hope was that the personal popularity of the young Duke would be sufficient to overcome all obstacles and secure victory and power for the exclusionists.

Shaftesbury thought that Monmouth was the stick with which he could beat James and Charles. In fact it was the limb, far out on which he had now crawled. Shaftesbury himself handed Charles the ax with which to cut off the limb on March 26, on the floor of the Lords' chamber. The king was present, and the Marquis of Worcester passed a note from Shaftesbury to the king. The note proposed that Charles should guarantee the Protestant cause by immediately and openly declaring Monmouth to be his successor. Charles and Shaftesbury then engaged in conversation, with Monmouth listening in. When the king declared that the proposal was both illegal and unjust, the earl replied, "If you are restrained only by law and justice, rely on us and leave us to act. We will make laws which will give legality to a measure so necessary for the quiet of the nation."[11] The king in turn replied to Shaftesbury, "Let there be no delusion, I will not yield, nor will I be bullied. Men usually become more timid as they become older; it is the opposite with me, and for what may remain of my life I am determined that nothing will tarnish my reputation. I have law and reason and all right-thinking men on my side; I have the Church [pointing to the bishops] and nothing will ever separate us."[12] It was now clear beyond a doubt that the struggle had reached a climax. The king had shown that he was willing to go to the brink, and over the brink if need be. There was nothing for Shaftesbury to do now but throw in the towel or go over the brink himself and attempt a *coup d'état* or even a revolution. Civil war, of course, would undoubtedly have been the result in either case. With the king armed with the open support of the Church and the Tory conscience, as well as a sizable segment of the national conscience, the use of force would have been dangerous, if not foolhardy in the extreme. Both the protagonists seemed to under-

11 Ibid., p. 618.
12 Ibid., pp. 618–19

stand this very well. Shaftesbury was beaten. And he must have known this too.

Two days later the announcement was made dissolving Parliament. David Ogg has brilliantly summed up the conclusion of this momentous but aborted Parliament: "It was while Magna Carta was being cited in support of their impeachment of Fitzharris [an Irishman who helped the crown by exposing some of the fabrications in the Popish Plot] that the Commons were startled to hear the knocking of Black Rod on the door; this time they were not prorogued, but dissolved. 'It is His Majesty's royal pleasure and will that this Parliament be dissolved; and this Parliament is dissolved'; such was the formula in which the chancellor announced the sequence of cause and effect. Round them were tennis courts and college gardens on which the Commons might have reunited themselves by an oath more solemn than any which they had yet sworn; but they dispersed: some to London, others to the country, and many to the horse races at Burford." [13]

The Exclusion Crisis was over. Is it possible to say whether or not anyone won or lost? If so, who and why? Was this crisis a distinct event in its own right, or was it merely the first act in the larger crisis that culminated in the Glorious Revolution? If the Exclusion Crisis is looked at only in relation to the remaining years of Charles II, it was without question a great victory for the king and the prerogative. The country was seen to have come close to civil war, and it was the Whigs and Shaftesbury, not the king or his brother James, who were blamed by the country. There followed a reaction distinctly favorable to the crown, and Charles was willing and able to take full advantage of it. The reaction will be discussed in more detail later. But suffice it to say at this point that the crown sought and was able to effect a decided revenge upon its enemies and was also able to achieve a sufficient change in the political,

[13] Ibid., p. 619.

administrative, and judicial institutions of the country to enable Charles to finish out his reign with enhanced power, prestige, and financial security. Parliament never met again in this reign. The reaction in favor of the crown and the institutional reforms carried over into James's reign, but James quickly spent the political capital he had inherited and soon proceeded to dig his own grave. It is, of course, impossible to say how successful Charles would have been if he had lived for another five or ten years. Yet perhaps we can hazard the guess that he might in fact have succeeded quite well.

There are certain parallels between the transition of Charles II to James II and the earlier one of James I to Charles I. In each case the problems started in the earlier reign but the explosion came in the succeeding reign. A possible explanation may be that the personalities and the characters of the kings involved were the deciding factors. James I, for all his foolishness and posturing about his rights, still had enough common sense to glimpse the trend of events and make the minimum adjustments they required. He was more a verbal tyrant than an actual one. His son, Charles I, was a man of rigid principle and at the same time a man whose word was not his bond. Either he would not give at all, or he would make promises that he then would not honor. Some of the blame for the outbreak of civil war in 1641 can safely be laid at the feet of Charles I himself.

A similar juxtaposition can be seen in the reigns of Charles I's sons. Charles II was, beneath all the exterior of the lazy playboy, a shrewd and calculating politician who knew how to time his actions and his non-actions and knew the difference between form and substance and the difference between winning a battle and winning the war. His brother, James II, was rigid like Charles I, politically stupid, and lacking in all common sense. The blame for the disastrous conclusion to his reign can be largely laid at his feet. None of this

can, however, constitute a denial that the form that
Charles II's revenge took from 1681–85 created a situation of the utmost danger for the crown in the long
run. A Charles II might have better succeeded in tem-
pering his own revenge later on. James II did not know
the meaning of the word "temporize." He was to devote
his reign to the institutionalizing of the Caroline
revenge.

The more difficult question to answer is why the king
was able to come out of the Exclusion Crisis trium-
phant. The answer to this question will help us to understand the basis for the successful revolution of 1688
–89. The best way to get at the answer is to look again
at the forces arrayed on the two sides during the years
of the Exclusion Crisis. First of all, the exclusionists:
Shaftesbury and the Whigs had on their side the hysterical and paranoidal fear of French- and Jesuit-
supported Roman Catholicism that was sweeping the
nation. This whirlwind was in turn given political substance by the triumph of the Whigs in the two elections
of 1679 and the election of 1681. The Commons in
turn controlled the power of the purse and could bring
forth impeachments of the king's servants. These two
powers were formidable indeed. The former, after all,
had led to the undoing of Charles I. As long as Parliament met in Westminster, the London mob was always
available and could be recruited into action to bring
additional pressure on the House of Lords and the court.
Since the House of Lords itself was divided between
court and country, Shaftesbury and his supporters in
the Lords had at least an even chance of getting control
of that House as well. Even many Tory peers were affected by the anti-papal crusade and were also willing
to oppose the court because of the king's failure to include them in his administration. Danby had antago-
nized their lordships, and this legacy lived on even
though Danby was out of office and in the Tower early
in 1679. Even a supposed high Tory such as the Earl
of Sunderland had come out for exclusion. In addition

to all these potential strengths there was the legacy of the Puritan Revolution. That revolution had supposedly taught both the king and the country that in a show-down the will of the nation as expressed in the House of Commons could not be thwarted with impunity. A king had been beheaded, and there was no reason why it couldn't happen again. The highly efficient electoral organization and the equally efficient organization of public opinion and exclusionist propaganda would certainly suggest that the Whigs could have organized a military force if it actually came down to that. But all these potential advantages enjoyed by the opposition were to prove worthless in the end precisely because the will to resort to the ultimate weapon of war was just not there. And the king knew it was not there.

Arrayed on the side of the king and court, if not precisely on the side of the Duke of York, was of course the Church and all of the ecclesiastical, moral, political, and religious pressures that it could command. While the full force of this power could not show any appreciable effect on the election results in 1679 and 1681—the Whigs, Dissenters, and Low-Churchmen carrying all before them—the king certainly knew that he could rely upon the bishops in the Lords to hold the line against exclusion. The position of the Establishment was certainly made clear in 1681, following the dissolution of the Oxford Parliament, when the Archbishop of Canterbury suggested to the Privy Council that the king's declaration be read out in all the churches. The declaration stressed how unhappy the king was with the late Parliament and how determined he was to adhere to and protect the Protestant religion.[14] As long as the king took no overt action to undermine the Protestant cause in general and the Church of England in particular, the full weight of the bishops and clergy behind the cause of hereditary mon-

[14] Bishop Gilbert Burnet, A *Supplement to Burnet's History of My Own Time*, edited by H. C. Foxcroft, Oxford, 1902, pp. 106–7.

archy and obedience to its authority can be assumed. The power of Dissenters and Low-Churchmen in the elections is a bit misleading. Skilled organization, the passions inflamed by the Popish Plot, and the pro-French proclivities of the king all had redounded to the great Whig electoral triumphs.

But there was however, another and more important reality behind the reality of elections. Both the crown and the Church had been inextricably tied together since the signing of the Solemn League and Covenant, in 1643. None of Charles II's actions had yet endangered this fundamental alliance for their common protection. This alliance in turn made possible the perpetuation of the Clarendon Code as a political system by which the governance of local and provincial England was guaranteed to remain in the hands of the Anglican and Cavalier interests. As long as the Cavalier interest of 1660 still required the maintenance of the Anglican establishment in order to perpetuate their own local authority, and as long as the Establishment continued to preach the twin doctrines of hereditary monarchy and passive obedience to the crown, so long would the "ruling class" stand beside and behind both Church and king and oppose exclusion. Nothing that Shaftesbury and the Whigs could do could shake this alliance. And in any case, by 1681 enough of the truth concerning the Popish Plot had been exposed for there to be a growing skepticism about the whole Plot and its political ramifications. In the reign of James II a different pattern of events would emerge and of course with a different outcome. Once the king and the Church split, the Church, not the king, would win. Charles II may have been a Roman Catholic in his soul but he was not so foolish or so unconcerned about his throne as to say so openly. He might have become a pensioner of France and a supporter of toleration, but he never allowed himself to be seen in the guise of an enemy to Protestantism in general or to the Church of England in particular. Charles's original offer of concessions and his later willingness to let others suggest limitations upon a Catholic successor were designed to keep the Church in league with him as much as they were designed to keep the opposition off balance. In both respects they proved to be of great value to the king.

Another factor helping the king's cause was the possibility that exclusion might in fact fail. Those who had careers to make or to protect had to be careful. Most of these careerists were in the Lords, and too much wavering could be a dangerous game. Once it came to the real issue, most of the waverers came down against exclusion, the Earl of Sunderland being the principle exception. The breakdown of Sir William Temple's scheme for Privy Council reform and the dismissal from office in the summer and fall of 1679 of those who had not totally supported his cause would certainly have impressed anyone with hope of future office of the importance of not opposing the king in what might prove to be a losing cause.

But the greatest weapon in the king's arsenal, the thing that really deterred the opposition from going all out for exclusion by any means necessary, was the fear of civil war. The new alliance with France and the subsidies flowing therefrom meant that Charles could now afford to rule without Parliament, but the Whigs in turn had to be made to realize that they could not live without the king. The legacy of the Puritan Revolution was indeed to be double-edged. The nation could get rid of a king if it wanted to, but at what a price! The king understood very well what the price of civil war would be for the Church, the aristocracy, the gentry, and even the urban bourgeoisie. These in turn also understood what civil war might hold in store for them. It was a price that no one wanted to pay in return for the exclusion of James. Prior to the dissolution of the Oxford Parliament, Shaftesbury was reported to have considered keeping both Houses in session regardless of whether the king dissolved them or not. This would

of course have constituted revolution. No such plans
seem to have been made, and certainly no such thing
was done. Shaftesbury and the king had gone to the
brink, each thinking that the other would be forced
to give way rather than face the prospect of civil war
and revolution. Shaftesbury gambled on the hope that
Charles would sell out his brother to keep his throne.
The king gambled on the hope that the nation would
prefer a middle-aged Catholic king with Protestant
heirs to civil war. The king won the gamble, and exclusion was dead. It was now left for the king and his
friends to reap the rewards of battle and to consolidate
the victory. The reaction that set in was to be much
more favorable to the crown than the Restoration of
1660 itself. It was also to show that the Exclusion Crisis
had neither been the prelude to the Glorious Revolution of 1688 nor was it to provide the solutions to those
grave constitutional problems that had caused the
Puritan Revolution and had not been solved in 1660.
The political and constitutional issues that had bedeviled the entire seventeenth century were not only
not yet solved, but were in fact to take on an even
greater urgency after 1681.

The revenge that Charles II now sought and
achieved was not to diminish his popularity, nor that
of his brother James upon his own succession to the
throne in 1685. But nonetheless it was to sow the seeds
of destruction for James II. The crucial essence of this
reaction was not that it saw Parliament disappear from
the scene for the remainder of Charles's reign—even
though the Triennial Act called for a new parliament
in 1684. The real significance of the reaction was that
it struck out at the vested rights of local authorities and
attempted to destroy the careers of several men of great
substance. The attempt to restructure local government
from the center and for the benefit of the center was
to prove a highly dangerous thing in the end. Not until
after the Reform Bill of 1832 would it be possible for
the national government to effect a wholesale restruc-

turing of the local authorities, and then it was done by a Parliament that had some claim to being representative of those who controlled the local authorities. The reactions of Charles II and of James II were enacted solely on the authority of the royal prerogative and with the support of the judiciary, which in turn served at the pleasure of the king. But the king did not blindly strike out at all entrenched local privileges. His principal targets were the enfranchized boroughs. He simply sought to diminish the electoral weight of the boroughs and thus of the Whigs, to the advantage of the gentry and thus of the Tories. The king was clever enough to realize that if he was to make powerful enemies he must also make powerful friends.

With public opinion now in a decidedly pro-court mood, the crown swiftly proceeded to write finis to the remains of the Popish Plot and its chief ringleaders. Many, including Titus Oates and the Earl of Shaftesbury themselves, were brought to trial on charges ranging from treason to perjury to seditious libel. All were found guilty of one or another of the charges. Shaftesbury was arrested on a charge of high treason and sent to the Tower, even being denied the right for several months to make use of the new writ of *habeas corpus*, which the first Exclusion Parliament had passed in 1679 as one of its few successful acts. But the earl had been arrested under the royal prerogative, not common law, and therefore he had no claim to common-law rights until the Court of King's Bench met several months later. Eventually a grand jury returned a verdict of "ignoramus" (no grounds for prosecution), and with bonfires blazing in his honor Shaftesbury left the Tower to go into exile and soon after to die. Even though he could not be tried, he was effectively destroyed. Many other peers or sons of peers who had co-operated in stringing out the Plot or who had joined in planning the attempt at exclusion were either arrested and tried and found guilty, or were at least removed from whatever offices or influence they still retained.

But the punishing and eliminating of those persons who had associated themselves with either the Plot or exclusion were not as important as the royal attempt to restructure English local government. One of the all-pervading struggles of the seventeenth century had been the struggle between the centralizing tendencies of the court and the countereffors of the gentry and the merchant classes to restrict this tendency and even to reverse it by acquiring even more autonomy for local authorities. At stake was the power to make the vital decisions required in governing England in those day-to-day, mundane matters that affected the lives of the masses of ordinary people. Until the early days of the reign of Charles II, the principal battleground had been the administration of the Elizabethan poor law of 1601. The local justices of the peace sought autonomy from the Privy Council in its enforcement, and the Council in turn sought to bind the justices ever more firmly to its centralizing will. The Act of Settlement of 1662, passed in the early days of the Cavalier Parliament, had represented a major victory for the J.P.s, reversing the earlier victory that the court had achieved in 1631 with the issuance of Charles I's Book of Orders. The victory of the court on this issue in the early days of the personal rule of Charles I was one of the major factors in generating the country opposition to the crown in the Long Parliament. The Cavaliers in 1662 had thus gotten their revenge, and for all practical purposes the J.P.s were quite free of Privy Council control in the following years.

Influence over the local authorities was not solely important for its own sake or merely in order to better regulate the application of the poor law, however. Two other matters, of far greater concern to the king, were involved: elections to the House of Commons and control and use of the country militias and trained bands. If Charles II was going to make his own personal rule a success, he had to strengthen his grip on those who controlled the local militias and upon those who controlled the parliamentary elections. For if the day should come when he did need a Parliament, he certainly did not want those loyal to his own cause to be at such an electoral disadvantage as they had been in the three elections from 1679 to 1681.

To reverse the trend of his reign in the rural areas by bringing the J.P.s back under the direct supervision of the crown would be difficult, if not impossible, because they numbered in the hundreds. But to regain control over the militias and the trained bands by means of reconstituting the ranks of the lords lieutenants and deputy lieutenants would not, perhaps, prove to be so difficult. Throughout his reign, Charles II had sought to strengthen his authority in these areas by dismissing large numbers of J.P.s and appointing new ones, while at the same time strengthening the hands of the lords lieutenants at the expense of the justices. The effect had been to create a series of semifeudal fiefdoms in the hands of a few great noble landholders. These "over-mighty" subjects had in turn proved to be of little use to him when the crisis came over exclusion. Many had sided with the exclusionists in Parliament. Only their common fear and abhorrence of civil war had provided one of the foundations upon which Charles could base his clever handling of the crisis. But Charles wanted more than a network of local officials who would support him when it was manifestly in their own interests to do so. He wanted a network that would more readily serve his own interests, whether or not it was in theirs. Charles II therefore resorted to the unprecedented act of removing several of his lords lieutenants and deputy lieutenants and replacing them with new men who would be more likely to remember the source from which their new authority sprang. In his hour of victory Charles was thus attempting to reverse the trends that had been impelling local England for nearly a century. James II would carry on this practice until he reaped the whirlwind.

Of less importance for its short-run political impact since no parliamentary elections were contemplated in the foreseeable future, but of far greater significance in the long run, was the institution of quo warranto proceedings to revoke, or threaten to revoke, borough and corporation charters. Here, more than patronage was involved; rights enshrined by both law and custom were at stake. Were the "rights of Englishmen" again to come under attack? This was a serious matter indeed. The quo warranto proceedings—a judicial inquiry as to the validity of the borough's charter of incorporation—began with London in 1682. There had in fact been a few such hearings throughout the reign of Charles II, but from 1682 the practice was stepped up and was without question a part of the court reaction. Even court sympathizers admitted as much. London was indeed the only corporation to fight for its rights through a whole gamut of appeals before finally losing. But by striking out at London first, the court won a psychological victory, many other corporations voluntarily surrendering their charters before proceedings were even begun. The new charters that were granted usually rewarded these boroughs by granting them extra economic advantages, such as the rights to hold new or additional markets. However, the political impact was severe. Not only did the new charters tighten the controls on how the boroughs would be governed and by whom, but the new charters actually specified the names of pro-court individuals who would be placed in the new positions of authority within them. The Whigs were not going to embarrass the court again by winning decisive electoral victories, as they had done twice in 1679 and once in 1681. This was proved by the election that James II called in 1685, when the Tories won a great victory for the new king. But the revenge against the Whigs and their merchant followers did not stop with the granting of new charters to boroughs. A great number of trading corporations were also affected, both those with overseas interests and those with strictly domestic trading outlets. For what proved to be the last four years of his reign Charles II intended to be the sole decision-making power.[15]

The last years of Charles's reign found much that was changed and much that was left unchanged. In foreign affairs, the king ended his days as a pensioner of France and with a neutral but pro-French foreign policy. This was essentially the same policy that Charles had pursued throughout his reign. The fact that Louis XIV had extended his aggressions into the border areas of the Low Countries, Luxemburg in particular, may have made this traditional policy of Charles more dangerous in the sense of England's European and world position, but at home it was to meet with even less opposition than a similar policy had met with in the days before the Exclusion Crisis. The real change was that the royal prerogative now seemed to be more secure than at any time in the seventeenth century. Neither Henry VIII nor Elizabeth I, nor James I, nor even Charles I during his personal rule seemed to have been as secure politically and financially as Charles II now was. He didn't even depend solely upon any one or any group of advisers or administrators. If Sunderland and Godolphin seemed to be entrenched in power it was because they were willing to serve Charles and administer his bidding with both loyalty and expertise. Without a Parliament in being, there was no way for the nation, short of riots or rebellions, either to challenge the king or even to effectively make known its discontent. If Charles relied upon anyone besides himself it was the Duchess of Portsmouth. As J. P. Kenyon has wisely said, late-Caroline England was adopting the methods and the

---

[15] See Jennifer Levin, *The Charter Controversy in the City of London, 1660–1688, and Its Consequences*, London, 1969.

style of the court of Louis XIV.[16] England was now to be administered by the prerogative power, not governed by the classic mixture of king, Lords, and Commons. The impulse toward this kind of prerogative rule was of course a part of the English heritage since the reign of the first Tudor. What made it now possible was that the Whigs had succeeded in destroying the creditability of the country, so that the court was left supreme on the field. Of particular significance was that the supposed court party—the Tories—were also left out in the cold. Throughout Charles II's reign the Cavalier/Tory interest had pursued its own form of opposition to the crown. By excluding the Tory interest from a role at court, Charles was, however, creating a potentially dangerous situation. From 1681 to 1685 the opposition of the country may have been moribund, but once the opposition was effectively reconstituted in James's reign, it was to be an opposition that combined Whig and Tory together. Again, what Charles II sowed, James II was to reap.

Perhaps it will be best to conclude the reign of Charles II with a word about the position of the Prince of Orange in Europe in 1685. Spain was still in a state of suspended animation waiting for its aging, incompetent, and childless king to die. Austria and its Holy Roman Empire was moribund, the pressure from the Turks beginning to occupy most attention. Sweden was still more concerned with its struggle with the Emperor over German affairs than it was with the threat from France. With England leaning toward the French, William was isolated. Even in the Netherlands he did not have a united country behind him either as regards the French menace or in terms of his own political authority. Many Dutchmen thought of William as being as great if not a greater menace to their personal and provincial liberties as Louis XIV himself. One thing was still in his favor, however. His father-

16 J. P. Kenyon, *Robert Spencer, Earl of Sunderland, 1641–1702*, London, 1958, pp. 90–91.

in-law was still the unfettered heir to the English throne, and his wife, Mary, was still the heir of James. Even though James appeared to be friendlier to France than even Charles II, the future would not necessarily be all bad. In addition, William had a trump up his sleeve in that during the exclusion years many of the Whig opposition had looked to him as their savior and he still had some following in England right through the reign of Charles. Even if a pro-French and Catholic James came to the throne there was some, if limited, political pressure that William could exert upon him. Even more important was the fact that Charles's illegitimate son Monmouth was now in exile in Holland and William was looking out for him. It surprised many how well William looked out for him. Certainly William could not support Monmouth's claim to the throne as against that of James (and his wife's and his own), but the possibility that he might, would always be enough to keep James on his toes. And in any case, by watching out for Monmouth, William did manage to please Charles. A pro-French but still neutral Charles was still better than an England actually allied to France. The death of Charles and the rebellion of Monmouth which soon followed was to change all this.

PART II

---

*The Bloodless
Revolution*

CHAPTER 4

James II and the Descent into Tyranny

Charles II fell ill on February 1, 1685, and died five days later, after receiving the last rites of the Roman Catholic Church. James, at last, was king. The years of worry and waiting in the wilderness of a Scottish exile were over. He was immediately proclaimed king amidst a mixture of regret for the death of Charles and rejoicing at the lawful and peaceful accession of the brother. During his last four years Charles II had punished the Whigs and ignored the traditional Tories, ruling by virtue of his royal prerogative through the instruments of his two able timeservers Sunderland and Godolphin. James II immediately sought to reconstitute the ministry and bring back into the center of affairs those traditional Tory and Anglican leaders who would give the new government an appearance of traditionalism as well as a firm political and ecclesiastical base. Lawrence Hyde, Earl of Rochester, the king's brother-in-law and younger son of old Clarendon, was made Lord Treasurer and titular head of the ministry. His older brother, Edward Hyde, Earl of Clarendon, was made Lord Privy Seal. Nothing could have done more to reassure the Tories, the Church, and the nation that all would be well in the new reign.

This high-Tory appearance of the new ministry, however, was not much more than a gloss on the old ministry of Charles II. Sunderland and Godolphin both
stayed on; though they had both been exclusionists, at
the same time both were more than willing to serve a
king who was determined to rule by a policy of
"Thorough," reminiscent of the days of Charles I, Strafford, and Laud, and who needed the diplomatic expertise of the one and the financial expertise of the
other. The Marquis of Halifax, advocate of limitations,
stayed on as Lord President of the Council. James thus
began his reign by concocting a ministry that represented all three Tory factions: the high-Anglican and
anti-exclusionist Hydes, the exclusionist but "Thorough"
administrators such as Sunderland and Godolphin, and
the advocate of limitations on a Catholic king, Halifax.
But whatever the appearance, the new reign soon
proved that James was king and worked best and most
often through the instrumentality of Sunderland.

James did not, however, limit his reassurance of the
Tories to his new appointments alone. Within fifteen
minutes of his brother's death he went before the accession council and said:

I have been reported to be a man for arbitrary power, but that
is not the only story that has been made of me; I shall make
it my endeavour to preserve this government both in Church
and State as it is now by law established. I know the principles
of the Church of England are for Monarchy, and the members
of it have showed themselves good and loyal subjects; therefore I shall always take care to defend and support it.[1]

This statement was later published as a royal proclamation signed by James himself. The whole nation
was now reassured that, whatever his personal religious
beliefs may have been, he would reign and rule as a
firm upholder of the law in both Church and state.
Anglican, Dissenter, and Catholic alike had no recourse

[1] Rev. J. S. Clarke, *Life of James II*, London, 1816, vol.
II, p. 4.

but to accept this at face value, for if James had any reputation at all, it was as a man of his word. Throughout the Exclusion Crisis and during his exiles in Scotland he had never wavered in public or in private from his position. Where Charles II had given many the impression of a king who was irresolute and devious at the same time, the Duke of York had given the impression of a man of firm and unwavering principle, whatever one may have thought of those principles. It is the contrast between his reputation as Duke of York and his actions as king that have made it so hard for both his contemporaries and later historians to comprehend the real man. Later, when he claimed to be seeking nothing more than religious toleration for non-Anglicans, Catholics and Dissenters alike, almost all thought that he was being as devious as his brother before him and was in fact working merely for the return of England to the Roman fold. The events of the next four years shed further light on the problem, but suffice it now to observe that the words and actions of a man out of office and power should not be compared to what he says and does when in power. What the man and the reign would have been like if there had been no Monmouth's Rebellion during the first year is of course an unanswerable question. But that rebellion did give James both the opportunity and the need to indulge in a policy of repression. Did the repression bring out the true James or was it just that he did, after all, have to change in order to survive? At any rate, at the beginning of the reign he was thought to be a man of honor and a welcome change after Charles.

After issuing his proclamation and reconstituting his ministry, James arranged for the holding of elections for a new Parliament. This was thought by Sunderland to be a tricky and dangerous business, both because Louis XIV might not approve and because recent royal experience with Parliaments was not conducive to creating much optimism among men like Sunderland or the Hydes that anything but chaos might come of it.

Why rock the boat when all was proceeding smoothly and the financial situation was well in hand, with the king continuing to collect the customs and excise duties recently farmed out by Charles and with a prospect of a handsome subsidy from Louis? James, however, quite shrewdly hoped to capitalize on the present euphoria that surrounded his accession and to secure his image as a law-abiding monarch by quickly calling a Parliament which would then be asked to provide him with an adequate income for life. By calling a loyal Parliament now, he might have no need of any Parliament later on. James also seems to have realized more accurately than his ministers that, the wholesale restructuring of the boroughs would return a loyal majority. And this indeed proved to be the case.

The composition of the new Parliament was enough to have made any Tudor or earlier Stuart king weep with envy. The new House of Commons contained 513 members, four hundred of whom had never sat in a Parliament before and all but forty of whom were well disposed to support the court. Charles II had certainly done his work well during his years of revenge. The Whigs were apparently destroyed and the Tories now seemed to be reconciled to the court with an enthusiasm not seen since the first few weeks following the Restoration. The House of Lords, with its continuity of membership, might be expected to show a sense of its own dignity and respect for its own authority as a continuing part of the trinity of king, Lords, and Commons which had been expected to govern the nation since the Restoration. But a House of Commons in which nearly 80 per cent of the members were new lacked any such sense of tradition, and the few months during which the House was actually in session would hardly be enough to create any such feelings. The Commons that opposed Charles I had contained many men of outstanding ability who had also had many years of consecutive service and had become imbued with a deep respect for the traditions and the authority

of the House. The Cavalier Parliament of Charles II
had likewise had eighteen years in which to recapture
this old feeling. But James's Parliament had no such
feelings at its inception and was not to be given time for
any such feelings to take root, although by the time of
its prorogation in late November there were signs that
a small nucleus of opposition sentiment might be ready
to take hold and expand.

Even before the new Parliament could be elected,
James was personally in touch with Barillon, the French
ambassador, explaining his reasons for calling a Parliament so quickly and without the prior approval of
Louis XIV. He also expressed his keen desire to receive
a subsidy from Louis and intimated that Louis would
find him even more co-operative and committed to the
Catholic cause than his brother, Charles, had been.
Louis had gotten little from Charles but neutrality and
a vague commitment to declare for the Roman faith;
Charles had in fact, back in 1680, during the Exclusion
Crisis, signed a treaty with Spain and Holland and had
waited until death approached before making his Catholicism known. James was anxious to give the impression that he would let the treaty remain in limbo and,
as an already avowed Catholic, would work with Louis
for the common religious cause. Just what that cause
was and how far he would implement it remains one of
the great unsolved problems of James's reign.

M. Barillon seems to have been the only person, besides Admiral Penn, whom the king took into his confidence. Certainly there is little evidence that anyone
in his own ministry was ever close to him on a personal
basis. Sunderland, of course, had enough ability to divine quite accurately the king's aims and to act accordingly in accomplishing them. But it is largely through
the continuous flow of dispatches from Barillon to his
master in Paris that we get any real feeling for what
James was thinking and striving for. The danger of
relying overmuch on these dispatches is, however, that
James may have merely used his confidential relation-

ship with the ambassador to further his own ends, which he still kept to himself alone. With this caveat in mind, it is useful to read excerpts from the following dispatch, for it does give us a clue to James's thoughts at the commencement of his reign:

I [James] have resolved to call a parliament immediately, and to assemble it in the month of May. I shall publish at the same time a declaration that I am to maintain myself in the enjoyment of the same revenues the King my brother had. Without this proclamation for a parliament, I should hazard too much by taking possession directly of the revenue which was established during the lifetime of my deceased brother. It is a decisive stroke for me to enter into possession and enjoyment. For hereafter it will be much more easy for me either to put off the assembling of parliament, or to maintain myself by other means which may appear more convenient for me. Many people will say that I determine too hastily in calling a parliament; but if I waited longer I should lose the merit of it. I know the English; you must not show them any fear in the beginning; the malecontents [sic] would have formed cabals to demand a parliament, and thereby have gained the favor of the nation, which they would afterwards have abused.

To this the King of England added all kinds of protestations of gratitude and attachment to your Majesty; he told me, that without your support and protection, he could undertake nothing of what he designed in favor of the Catholics; that he knew well enough he should never be in safety, till a liberty of conscience was established firmly in their favor in England: that it was to this he was wholly to apply himself as soon as he saw a possibility; that I had seen with what facility he had been acknowledged and proclaimed King; and that the rest would come about in the same manner, by his conducting himself with firmness and wisdom.[2]

Even before Louis received this dispatch, he had sent Barillon five hundred thousand livres, to be doled out to James as Barillon saw fit. The news of this vast

[2] Sir John Dalrymple, *Memoirs of Great Britain and Ireland*, London and Edinburgh, 1771–73, "Barillon to Louis XIV, February 19, 1685," Appendix, pp. 103–6.

sum, granted by Louis before James even had time to request it, made the deepest possible impression upon James. Both the king and his chief ministers, Rochester, Sunderland, and Godolphin, were thunderstruck with joy, and professed eternal gratitude to Louis. It was clear that James and his closest servants intended to rule as far as possible without recourse to future Parliaments and that they knew that this was possible only with the financial support of the French king. That this financial support also entailed a pro-French policy is apparent from the statements made about the lack of need to uphold the Spanish treaty and the obvious coolness in James's opening correspondence with the Prince of Orange and his first emissary to England, Overkirk. There was, then, much less secrecy in James's reign about the nature of his reliance upon Louis. Charles II had always been much more anxious to have the full extent of his French connection kept not only from public view, but even from the eyes of most of his ministers. On the other hand, James's ministers do not seem to have been apprised of the king's hopes of achieving toleration for his Roman Catholic subjects. It was on this point that James shared his thoughts only with Barillon. And now, secure in the fact of full support from Louis and already having proclaimed his right to collect the customs and the excises, the new king met his new Parliament.

In his speech from the throne the king repeated the usual formula of expressing his determination to uphold the laws in both Church and state, and then he went on to ask for sufficient permanent revenues so that he would not have to call frequent Parliaments. The "feeding me from time to time by such proportions as they shall think convenient" was not to be thought convenient either for him or for the nation. James's announcement that Archibald Campbell, Earl of Argyll, had landed in Scotland had the desired effect, and all the revenues of Charles II were voted for life to James. Argyll was the son of the great Presbyterian and pro-

Cromwellian landholder whose opposition to the Stuart rule in Scotland had been carried on by the son. He had been condemned to death for treason in 1681 and managed to escape to Holland, from whence he now returned to his native land. The news a month later that the Duke of Monmouth had also landed in the West of England gave James an opportunity to go before Parliament again to ask for even more money. The effect of the two grants was to guarantee James a lifetime income of nearly two million pounds, or twice what his brother, Charles II, had been guaranteed on his return in 1660. This one and only Parliament of James II has often been called the most sycophantic Parliament in English history. But it is also of some significance to notice the nature and the composition of the minuscule opposition that did emerge. On the first vote on supply, granting James the revenues of Charles II, there was only one dissentient, but that lone negative voice belonged to Sir Edward Seymour. During the last session of this Parliament, in November, after the two rebellions of Argyll and Monmouth had been crushed, a few others would join him in opposition.

Sir Edward Seymour was a descendant of the protector Somerset in the reign of Edward VI, and he was the acknowledged "King of the West country." Seymour was a very wealthy, powerful, arrogant, and ambitious upholder of the Cavalier/Tory tradition who had served as Speaker of the House of Commons in the 1660s and was a leader in the cabal that brought down Clarendon. His role in the movement to destroy Clarendon, who was supposedly a fellow Cavalier and Tory, is merely the first episode in the career of a man whose subsequent role in and out of Parliament or ministerial office sheds a good deal of light on the true nature of the Cavalier/Tory/Anglican viewpoint and faction that was so largely responsible for the failure of exclusion, the destruction of James II, and the success of the Glorious Revolution.

It has been pointed out before that each segment of the Cavalier/Tory/Anglican trinity must be looked at in isolation in order to gain an understanding of each, the relationships among them, and the ultimate nature of the Tory party itself. Clarendon was a Tory/Anglican, but he was not in any true sense of the term a Cavalier, even though he was a stanch Royalist after the commencement of civil war in 1642. Clarendonian Toryism was stanchly monarchical but was not equally enamored of the royal prerogative as such, at least not in the sense that this prerogative would be exercised by the king personally. It was monarchical in the sense that they understood the much older Tudor tradition. The crown was supreme in the nation, comprehending both Church and state, and both national and local government, but this power was to be exercised by the king through the instrumentality of his Privy Council. The Privy Council in turn would represent the traditional landed interests of the nation and would collectively supervise the workings of the king's servants nationally and locally and would tender all necessary advice to him, not as individual ministers but as a group. There was also a definite role in this Tory structure for a Parliament that would represent the landed as well as the commercial and local interests, and that would supply funds for the crown and the supreme legislator. Thus Clarendon saw the crown in a role not unlike that advocated by Sir Robert Filmer in his work *Patriarcha*. The difference between Clarendon and Filmer, however, was that Filmer would assign to the king the role of father and protector of his people, where Clarendon would hedge the king about with a powerful Privy Council and a Parliament. The two versions of monarchical government shared the view of the monarchy as the natural leader of the entire nation in all its aspects: Church, state, national, local, land, and commerce.

It was the desire for comprehension in Church and state that separated Clarendonian Toryism from the interests of the Cavaliers, as well as the emphasis upon the crown, either through Council or directly by personal prerogative, as being the leader of all, nationally and locally. Clarendon had opposed the Clarendon Code, which had driven Dissenters and Catholics alike outside the national Church and he had also advised the king to take his old Royalist friends "for granted" while "rewarding" his and his father's old enemies. The Cavaliers were a people and even a party in their own right from the earliest days of the Cavalier Parliament. Men such as Sir Edward Seymour had opposed religious comprehension and had enacted the Clarendon Code. They resented deeply the policy that Clarendon evidently shared with Charles II that the old Puritans and Parliamentarians should be accommodated in the newly restored England. But perhaps even more important than these differences was the insistence on the part of the Cavaliers that the king must have a truly *English* foreign policy and that the supreme duty of the monarchy was to preserve the safety and unity of England in both Church and state while guaranteeing that local magnates would be left alone and supreme in their own bailiwicks. Perhaps the key, then, to an understanding of the Cavalier mentality is the word "patriotism"—loyalty to England and its interests rather than subservience to any foreign power, and loyalty to one's own county, town, or village, rather than to a remote government in London. On each of these counts of patriotism, the monarchy of Charles II and of James II was to be found wanting. In foreign policy these kings were inclined to the French interest, openly or covertly, and in domestic affairs there was still the old Tudor and early Stuart tendency to subordinate local to national interests. Danby had been successful in his early years in managing Parliament, because he at least tried to have an "English" foreign policy, and Seymour had supported Danby. But when those similar in view to Seymour were not in ministerial office, it was Parliament itself that these men had to turn to and use to accomplish their goals. Seymour had in fact become a "Parliament man" by the time James II acceded to the throne.

Seymour also was typical of the new sort of politician who emerged in such strong numbers after the Restoration, and was to remain a vital and ever-present part of the English political scene, in fact any democratic political scene, ever since. He was highly ambitious, always desirous of ministerial office, power, and perquisites, and tending to adjust his political views when and how necessary in order to advance himself, or at least maintain himself, in power. Modern responsible and constitutional government really seems to be dependent upon a combination of four interacting but complementary and necessary elements: general elections at fairly frequent intervals; the presence of parties or factions, or at least, temporary electoral groupings; leadership provided by a few highly ambitious and somewhat unscrupulous office seekers; and a sufficient cohesion among the groups and leaders so that the winners would not seek to exterminate the losers, nor would the losers seek to eliminate the winners by a resort to arms or foreign intrigue or both. It is in the post-Restoration era that we can begin to see the first real signs that these various and vital factors are beginning to come into play. The Exclusion Crisis itself served to provide a catalyst, or at least the point in time in which they can be clearly seen in more than mere embryo. The dissolution of the Cavalier Parliament, in 1679, brought to an end the last Parliament for a long time that would last as long as ten years. And those future Parliaments that were to enjoy a ten-year life span were the fruits of World Wars I and II. The election of 1685 was caused by the death of Charles II, and the election of 1689 by the Glorious Revolution. But following the revolution, elections were never more than seven years apart, and Parliaments were in annual session, as a result of the Revolution itself. The Exclusion Crisis, then, had marked the end of the old tradition of either exceedingly long and/or infrequent Parliaments. The crisis also marked the undoubted appearance of the political party with candidates and a program. While it may be true that only the Whigs really met both these criteria of a party, nonetheless they did, and the Tories were thereby forced to defend themselves by learning to do likewise.

Highly ambitious and somewhat unscrupulous office seekers have always existed in the political sphere, but before the Restoration the office seeker or officeholder, whether thought of as a careerist, a timeserver, or a statesman, was not generally identifiable by program or electoral faction. In the past a faction had been a network based on family or patronage on a more individualistic patron/client relationship. The monarch chose his servants both to please himself and to reward or punish groups at court or in the nation, but there was little if any connection between this and the holding of elections or even the managing of Parliament when it was in session. The Grand Remonstrance and the Nineteen Propositions, of the early 1640s, had brought together the rival "parties" of Royalists and Parliamentarians, and England was to be plagued or blessed with them and their successors ever since. The old tradition of serving one's king regardless of differences of policy or program fell with Clarendon. Danby tried to be a link between the old and the new, in that he loyally served Charles II in advancing causes in which he did not believe, but at the same time he sought to bend Charles to his will and to use his control of Parliament both to serve the king and to assist himself in bringing the king around to Danby's will.

The failure of the exclusionists was a close thing, and in that failure can be seen the extent to which the ingredients for a stable constitutional monarchy were present, as well as the elements still missing. The crisis certainly was marked by frequent elections—three elections within two years. There is no doubt of the existence of party, at least as far as the Whigs are concerned.

And there was also no lack of ambitious men who sought office and power for themselves and their program. What was still lacking, and this proved to be crucial, was the true spirit of cohesion or compromise, whereby whichever side won, the other would accept defeat. That there was no resort to arms was not because of the presence of such a spirit, but because of the fear of what a resort to arms could mean for all the participants in the political drama, as well as for the classes and interests they represented and the realm as a whole. There was, then, a fear of civil war, not a positive desire or willingness to achieve an agreed solution that all could live with. And perhaps the basic reason why this positive element was missing was that where the Whigs were already a distinct party, with leaders, a program, and an electoral and propaganda organization, the Tories were still torn between being a distinct party in this Whig sense and being the traditional Cavaliers, who instinctively looked to the king for both leadership and policy. Where the Whig exclusionists were quite clearly united under Shaftesbury and were agreed on exclusion—even though they were admittedly divided on to whom the crown should go— the Tories were divided into three factions: exclusionists, supporters of limitations, and anti-exclusionists. The Tories really had no policy and no leader. The king was, then, free to enter the vacuum and provide both. His willingness, once personally engaged, to go to the brink, provided a solution to the crisis, and a solution that all had to live with, but it was a solution that was achieved in a fashion and with results that were soon to be seen as inimicable to the interests of both Tories and Whigs alike. But this was a lesson that both groups quickly took to heart. When the next crisis occurred they would have to meet on common ground as equals or the crown could once again move into the vacuum and serve its own—not necessarily the national —interest, as before.

The failure of the new, party system to solve the

Exclusion Crisis was succeeded by Charles II's adopting an almost Continental style of royal administration, under which England would be centrally administered rather than being governed in the grand political sense. A system in which all decisions, high and low, are made on the basis of *raisons d'état*, rather than on the basis of accommodating and compromising personal, party, class, and provincial interests, is not a system that any society that had already reached England's high degree of political sophistication would tolerate except in case of real danger from an external enemy or the fear of civil war at home. Once the Exclusion Crisis showed that no one in England wanted or would even contemplate civil war, that specter disappeared as a sufficient excuse for tolerating government by administrators rather than by politicians. Charles II managed to work this kind of administrative system for the remaining four years of his life. His brother, James, failed after four years. With these thoughts in mind it is possible to see the vast significance in Sir Edward Seymour's lone opposition to the bill to grant to James the lifetime revenues of Charles II. For Seymour represented the Tory who was capable of understanding, intuitively, that England needed to be governed by politicians and not by remote, non-responsible royal administrators. The years from 1681–88, with the exception of 1685, came to resemble the years of the personal rule of Charles I, except that this time the king himself could be held directly responsible in the public mind, not just the king's evil advisers. And just as the personal rule of Charles I succeeded in uniting all factions except the court itself into the country opposition, so the "personal" rule of James II would have the same effect. As we shall see, the main difference between 1642 and 1688 was that in the former the opposition was to split and create a "king's party." In the latter year the opposition was to remain united, at least until after the revolution had been irreversibly accomplished.

Both the composition of his Parliament and the cir-

cumstances of the Argyll and Monmouth rebellions
served to assist James in acquiring the financial support
he wanted, but in the matter of religious toleration it
was to be a different story. The king's request that the
Test Act be repealed was ignored. At least during this
first year on the throne James was shrewd enough not
to push the matter of toleration too far or too fast.
There were, however, signs enough for those who
wanted to see them that James was not going to lose
interest in his co-religionists, even though the statement
of intent he had transmitted to Louis XIV via Barillon
had not been made public. Following the dissolution
of the Oxford Parliament, in March 1681, Charles II
had, as part of his revenge and as part of his determination to appear to be a good Anglican, resumed the
vigorous execution of the penal laws against all trans-
gressors, Dissenter or Catholic. For the next two years
the receivers of recusancy fines were averaging £5000
per year. The return of James from his Scottish exile
brought a drastic reduction in the amount collected,
and during the king's last year the receivers were dismissed from office. This seems to have been at the
urging of James himself.[3] Shortly after his accession to
the throne he created a truly unofficial and private
"privy council" of his own, in which he was advised by
known and admitted Catholics such as Lord Wardour
(Henry Arundel), Lord Belasyse, the Earl of Tyrconnel
(Richard Talbot), and Lord Dover (Henry Jermyn).
While the existence of this cabal might not have been
widely known, surely those in the official ministry and
in the royal household must have been aware of its
existence.[4] The king's taking of advice from those not
formally a part of his Privy Council had been a serious
political issue ever since the days of James I's close relationship with Count Gondomar. It would be very sur-

[3] J. P. Kenyon, *The Stuart Constitution: Documents and
Commentary*, Cambridge, 1966, p. 453.
[4] David Ogg, *England in the Reigns of James II and William III*, Oxford, 1955, p. 143.

prising indeed if suspicions and resentment were not to be aroused by the existence of such a group.

Even though neither the public at large nor the members of Parliament were aware of the existence of this Catholic cabal, or of the hope of achieving toleration that had been communicated to the French king, there was, nonetheless, a feeling of uneasiness in the early days of Parliament. Sir Edward Seymour, in his speech against granting the king a life revenue, devoted most of his effort to denouncing the court's interference in the parliamentary elections in the West country, which he and his family traditionally had considered the preserve of the Seymour interest; he did, however, range a bit farther afield and raised the issue of whether or not it would be possible to safeguard the Anglican interest if parliamentary elections were not free and unfettered. To this scion of the old school of Cavalier and aristocratic politics, a freely elected Parliament was the nation's principal bulwark against an interference with its liberties. He also indicated that there were rumors that the Test Act and the Habeas Corpus Act would be repealed. While Seymour was hissed into silence by his fellow members and could not even get a seconder to his opposition motion, his warnings evidently did not go completely unheard or unheeded, for the Speaker accompanied the presentation of the revenue bill with the comment, "We bring not with it any bill for the preservation or security of our Religion, which is dearer to us than our lives, in that we acquiesce, entirely rely, and rest wholly satisfied, in your Majesty's gracious and sacred word, repeated declaration, and assurance."[5] There were doubts and perhaps even fears, then, but James was the king, and as both the king and the man he was thought to be honorable and would keep his word.

Three weeks after the opening of Parliament the

[5] William Cobbett, *Parliamentary History of England*, London, 1806–20, vol. IV, p. 1359.

reign was to begin anew. The Duke of Monmouth landed at Lyme Regis, in Dorset, on the Channel, about 130 miles west of London. He came from his exile in Holland on one ship loaded with ammunition and a few followers. It was hoped that by the time he had landed in the Southwest that the king's forces would be out of the way, fighting the Argyll invasion in Scotland. But the immediate failure of the Argyll expedition made any large-scale dispatch of English troops to Scotland unnecessary.

More than timing, however, was at fault with the Monmouth scheme: The few assets that Monmouth had personally and that he could command were far outweighed by the liabilities. He was perhaps the only member of the Stuart dynasty throughout the seventeenth century who had any real personal popularity and a rapport with a sizable segment of the public. He was dashing, a Protestant, and the son, albeit illegitimate, of Charles II. He had been credited with a military victory over the Scottish Covenanters at the Battle of Bothwell Brig, in 1679, gaining favor with Englishmen in general and Anglicans in particular. But his real support in England came from the poor farmers of the old Puritan Southwest and the depressed artisan class of the old Puritan villages. There was a nostalgic ring of the old Roundhead-Covenanter tradition about the supporters of Monmouth, and England was certainly not ready to go this far in challenging James's throne. Both the rural gentry and the urban middle classes lay low at first to see how the wind would blow, but this in itself was sufficient to deny Monmouth the quick and massive support that would have been necessary to achieve victory. The old Puritan nature of Monmouth's support also served merely to bring James and the Anglicans closer together, for Monmouth himself had been involved in the Rye House Plot, in 1683. That plot had been the concoction of the remnants of the New Model army, of Civil War days, and had hoped to achieve a final, if belated, victory for "the good old cause" of yesteryear. At one point in the campaign, Monmouth's soldiers were forced to seek refuge in Wells Cathedral, whose chapter book for July 1 contains a passage that helps to point out the Puritan nature of the rebellion: "The civil war still grows. This cathedral church has suffered very grievously from the rebel fanatics, who have this very morning laid hands upon the furniture thereof, have almost utterly destroyed the organ, and turned the sacred building into a stable for horses."[6] Monmouth's cause was thus too thoroughly tainted with the aura of Puritan dissent, republicanism, and social upheaval to have any chance of securing the support of men of substance or of Anglicanism. The king moved his own forces massively and decisively, and the rebellion was quickly crushed.

William of Orange had quickly dispatched three contingents of Scottish troops and three of English troops that had been stationed in the Netherlands, and this act should have dispelled any of James's doubts as to William's essential loyalty. The rebellion had provided a trying moment for William as well as for James. But the issue was at least more clear-cut for the latter. William, whose relations with the Stuarts were touchy at best, had never been on good terms with his father-in-law. James was always suspicious, and rightly so, of the ultimate aims of the prince and was always more willing to judge his actions than his words, both of which were often cryptic enough indeed. Obviously William was loath to sit back quietly and watch James become ever more dependent upon Louis XIV. On the other hand, the usurpation of the throne by Monmouth would dash any hopes that William had that either he himself or his wife would succeed to the throne. The only possibility that Monmouth's rebellion held out for William was that it might succeed in removing James, but not succeed in placing Monmouth on the throne as his

[6] William Holden Hutton, *The English Church from the Accession of Charles I to the Death of Anne (1625–1714)*, London, 1903, pp. 218–19.

successor. William could then move in to fill the vacuum. The dispatch of the English and Scottish troops at James's request showed that William would do nothing overt to upset James or to help Monmouth. Whether he would have or could have volunteered more to help James was the question. Outwardly, at least, William had been perfectly loyal. But to James, who always suspected those not totally subservient to his interest, the doubts were to remain.

Even though, in retrospect, Monmouth was easily and quickly defeated, James was sincerely frightened by the experience. No more than three thousand rebels had united beneath Monmouth's standard, and at the decisive Battle of Sedgemoor the loyalists numbered about seven thousand. But James was shaken, and perhaps rightly so, by the fact that many of the local aristocrats and gentry either did not act or did so half-heartedly. It was the regular forces from London that provided the backbone to the loyalist army. Once the rebellion was crushed, James knew that he could not rely in the future upon the traditional ruling class of England. He must secure armed forces dependent solely upon himself—a standing army. James was also aware that the support of Louis XIV was more verbal than actual. Very little of the money in Barillon's hands had as yet been turned over, and once James had crushed Monmouth, Louis seemed even more reluctant than before to dispense the cash. Safe on his throne, but wary of the future and of his friends, allies, and relatives, James sought revenge at home and a more openly pro-Catholic policy. In foreign affairs he felt that there might have been some merit, after all, in his brother's habit of getting more out of Louis not by fawning over him, but by moving away and toward the Dutch side. Louis was to be even less amused with James than he had been with Charles. It can at least be said for James that he was not now and never had been anybody's man but his own. The key to an understanding of the man is found by examining James himself, not the machinations of a Louis XIV or a Pope Innocent XI.

The government's success in crushing Monmouth's rebellion had two immediate effects. There was the judicial repression of the rebels conducted in the West country by Judge Jeffreys, and the king's attempt to retain and enlarge the number of Catholic officers in the army in violation of the Test Act. Of these two products of rebellion, the Bloody Assizes of Judge Jeffreys has gone down in history as the event that made Englishmen fear for their liberties, as it presaged the inauguration of a reign of terror. The effort to pack the army with Catholics has been viewed, with far more sympathy by recent historians, as an example of the extension of full civil and political rights to his Catholic subjects. What is really important, however, is not how we in the twentieth century judge these two phenomena, but how contemporaries judged them. For the men of the 1680s the Bloody Assizes did no more than give rebels the justice they deserved, while the commissioning of Catholic army officers was viewed indeed as a most serious violation of English laws and liberties. Sir Edward Seymour, the king of the West country, told the House of Commons that "this last rebellion has contributed to our future peace, and those engaged in it have sung their penitential psalms and their punishment rejoiced at by all good men."[7] Those who would oppose James in 1688, the gentry, the aristocracy, and the Church, were pleased with his victory in 1685 and were by no means shocked at either the numbers of those punished nor the severity with which the sentences were carried out. The most that was said against Jeffreys was that he was a bit too zealous in his methods, resembling more the prosecutor than the judge. Seventeenth-century Englishmen admired the conqueror who showed mercy, but they were by no means either shocked or horrified at the lack of mercy.

[7] Cobbett, IV, p. 1374.

Consciences were not quite so tender as they would become in the nineteenth and twentieth centuries. But to the extent that there was criticism of the revenge, both James and Jeffreys tried to put the blame on the other. James was to tell William that he was ignorant of much of what Jeffreys was doing, and Jeffreys claimed that James knew all about it and gave encouragement. Historically, the Bloody Assizes were for James II what the murders of the princes in the Tower had been for Richard III. There had been little if any discussion of the death of the princes until after Henry VII had defeated Richard at Bosworth and turned the full force of Tudor propaganda to work, destroying whatever reputation Richard had left. So with James II. His defeat, in 1688, required those who succeeded him to take great pains to destroy his reputation and to make the Bloody Assizes strike horror in the hearts of post-Revolution Englishmen.[8]

Catholic army officers were quite a different matter, however. The county militias in the West had proved unreliable during the rebellion, and the king had had to rely upon the regular troops in London to defend his throne. Since these regulars were directly under royal control, unlike the militias, it was easy for the king to make hasty appointments of untried and untrained Catholic officers. Since it had now been twelve years since any Catholic had held a commission, it was surely not for their skills but for their presumed loyalty that they were chosen. When Parliament reassembled in the autumn, James told the Houses of the appointments and asked that they be retroactively condoned. It was, however, one thing to ask for approval of these emergency appointments and quite another thing for him to ask that a regular army be maintained at Hounslow Heath and that Catholics be eligible for service in the future. The import of the king's wishes was thoroughly understood even by this most obsequious of Parliaments. Barillon informed Louis XIV on June 25, 1685, and portrayed James's motives in exactly the form that the House of Commons understood them: "It seems to me that the King of England is very glad to have a pretence for raising troops, and he believes that the Duke of Monmouth's enterprize will serve only to make him still more master of his country." And on July 30, Barillon reported, "The King of England's scheme is to abolish the militia entirely, the uselessness and danger of which he found on this last occasion, and if possible to make the Parliament apply the fund intended for the militia, to maintain the regular troops. All this entirely changes the state of this country, and puts the English in a different condition from what they have been in till now. They know it, and perceive very well that a King of a different religion from that of the country, and who is armed, will not easily renounce those advantages which the defeat of the rebels, and the troops he has on foot, give him."[9]

Naturally the king did not use the same blunt language in his speech to Parliament at the beginning of the new session that he had evidently used in his discussions with Barillon. In the process of surveying the recent rebellion, James pointed out the need to maintain a standing army and the great trust he had in the Catholic officers. While admitting that some malcontents might try to use this as an excuse to drive a wedge between the king and his loyal Parliament, James concluded his arguments by saying, "When you consider what advantages have arisen to us in a few months, by the good understanding we have hitherto had; what wonderful effects it hath already produced in the change of the whole scene of affairs abroad, so much more to the honour of the nation, and the figure it ought to make in the world; and that nothing can hinder a farther progress in this way, to all our satisfactions, but Fears and Jealousies amongst ourselves; I will not

[9] Dalrymple, Appendix, pp. 169–70.

apprehend that such a misfortune can befall us, as a division, or but a coldness, between me and you."[10]

James sensed that he was treading on dangerous ground in asking for both a standing army and for the condoning of the violation of the Test Act. Therefore, on the one hand he had to appeal to the patriotism of the members of Parliament and on the other he was giving them a veiled threat that he would achieve his objects anyway and they had better co-operate for their own good as well as his. But November was not May, and the desire to satisfy all the king's wishes was no longer the only unanimous impulse at work among the members of the two Houses. This time a genuine debate would take place, and Sir Edward Seymour would find several worthy allies.

Parliament was unquestionably pleased that Monmouth and his band had been defeated. Members of Parliament were also aware that it was the royal troops from London, and not the local militias, that had borne the brunt of the fighting, culminating in the royal victory at Sedgemoor. Why, then, was there this mounting apprehension in the Commons? James had some very real justification in claiming that his victory had also been theirs and England's. Dissent had been crushed, the rising of the southwestern artisans had been crushed, and James's relations with the Dutch were becoming outwardly more friendly while those with Louis XIV were outwardly more strained.

There would appear to be two sets of reasons for the developing sense of unease in Parliament. On the one hand, the country had come to fear the presence of a standing army since the days of Charles I and Oliver Cromwell; and there was also the memory of the early Stuarts ruling without regard for the law of the land as enacted by Parliament. If there was any legacy from the Puritan Revolution, it was the fear of a standing army and an unbridled prerogative. But, for this

Parliament in particular, there had to be more substantive reasons for distrust than these throwbacks to an earlier era. These two issues were merely the symptoms of the real disease: religion. In spite of the king's declarations at the beginning of the reign testifying to his support of the Church of England, there had been a continuing pattern of behavior on James's part that created embarrassment for some and doubts for others. James had been ostentatiously attending Mass since his accession. Since he made his attendance a state occasion, he expected to be accompanied by his ministers, some of whom did attend, but others opted out. The Earl of Rochester, the leader of the Anglican Tories, would spend his weekends in the country. The Earl of Ormonde would not go beyond the antechamber to the royal chapel. But making Mass attendance into a state occasion could still be thought of as just a peculiar royal whim, had it not been accompanied by more substantive actions. Within a month of his accession, the king had ordered William Sancroft, the Archbishop of Canterbury, and Henry Compton, the Bishop of London, to put a stop to all anti-Catholic preaching in their jurisdictions. And Barillon had reported to Louis XIV at the beginning of March that James was already reinterpreting his announced support of the Church, implying, at least, that his support of the Church depended upon the Church's support of him and his policies.

James began his reign in Scotland with an already existing program he had enacted during the days of the Exclusion Crisis, while serving as his brother's viceroy during his enforced exile to the northern kingdom. He had had enacted a test act that was far more severe than that enacted in England, and aimed at the Dissenters. However, since Lowland dissent was still intimately bound up with the marauding bandits that continuously terrorized the region, it is not unfair to say that lawlessness rather than religion was the real object of the Scottish test. But after his accession,

James's forces pursued with zeal and cruelty the rampaging Covenanters of the Lowlands and attempted to force them to take an oath of loyalty to the Scottish Episcopal Church. Macaulay has said that his actions and policies in Scotland are proof that James was no real friend either of dissent or of religious toleration, which he later claimed to be in England. But by 1685 his stance in Scotland really proves no more than that he expected his royal authority to be respected and that he was upholding the Episcopal cause. The methods used were harsh in the extreme, however, and the justice meted out was extreme even by Scottish/Roman standards. Even if Englishmen had as yet no valid grounds to question James's loyalty to the religious establishment, they did have grounds to fear his wrath if he were opposed while in possession of an adequate military force.

The arrival in London in September 1685 of Dr. John Leyburn, an English Dominican, as bishop *in partibus infidelium* was followed in November by that of Ferdinando D'Adda as papal nuncio, an event unprecedented since the death of Mary I, in 1558. If this was merely a step in the direction of religious toleration, it is nonetheless not surprising that doubts were raised and fears were planted. The revocation by Louis XIV of the Edict of Nantes also was to have its repercussions in England. The month of November saw the reassembling of Parliament, the arrival of D'Adda, and the wave of French Huguenot refugees streaming into London. The edict had been revoked in October, the same month that Lord Halifax, the one minister who opposed a pro-French policy, was dismissed from the presidency of the Council. It was now possible to suspect that the upholding of the Test Act was not only a guarantee of Anglican exclusiveness but a bulwark of English liberty. Within the ministry and the royal household, changes were taking place also. Rochester, weak but a strong Anglican, was being pushed more and more into the background, and Sunderland was moving to the fore. Sunderland was now obviously pro-French and was already showing an ambivalence concerning religion that was merely the presaging of his ultimate conversion to the Roman Church. Edward Petre, a Jesuit, was clerk of the closet to the king, and another Jesuit, John Warner, was the king's confessor. For the first two and one half years of the reign Petre held no other official post, and there is, therefore, some difficulty in determining exactly what his personal relationship and influence with the king were. He does, however, seem to have been very close to Sunderland, the one minister that James seems to have trusted. It is known that representations were made to the Papacy to have Petre appointed to the archbishopric of York. The archdiocese was kept vacant for two years in hopes that the Pope would agree to the appointment of a Jesuit to the second most prestigious Anglican post. Neither the archbishopric nor the latter request for a cardinal's hat was compatible with the Pope's "conscience." For whatever reason, James and Sunderland were anxious to reward Petre, and to place him well in the hierarchy of the Anglican Church. The question is whether the Pope opposed their plans because of his low regard for the Jesuits in general, or because he thought James was going too far too fast.[11] Contemporaries were well aware that a Roman Catholic and a Jesuit were distinguishable, although it was rarely in the Protestant interest to make the distinction.

It was not in and of itself illegal to be a Roman Catholic, but it was a crime to be a priest or a Jesuit. This legal distinction was a reflection of the fundamental difference in outlook and program of the lay Catholic and the clergy, and the Jesuits in particular. A large proportion of the lay Catholics were noble or gentry families of great antiquity, who had proved their loyalty to the crown and the kingdom in Elizabethan times and to the monarchy in the days of the Puritan

[11] *Dictionary of National Biography*, vol. XV, p. 977.

Revolution. In the post-Restoration era they sought little more than to be left alone to believe as they would and to practice their religion in the privacy of their own country houses, perhaps with a priest who was kept in hiding, perhaps without a priest. The clergy are harder to categorize, since many were content to remain secreted away in country houses and to perform the sacraments for their protectors and await better times, if and when they might come. Other clergy were willing to assist in advancing the arrival of those better times. The Jesuits were a different story altogether. Nominally at least they were the shock troops of the Papacy and the advance guard in the movement to extirpate heresy from the lands of its adoption. It had been the Jesuits who had taken the lead in the attempts to overthrow Elizabeth, and throughout the seventeenth century it was they who acted as a fifth column on behalf of French and papal interests. To say the least, the Jesuits had a "forward" policy. By 1685 the Jesuits throughout Western Europe were inextricably bound up in the great struggle for religious and secular power, both domestically and on the international stage. In effect, their great ally was Louis XIV and their enemy was Spain. Pope Innocent XI himself was caught up in the contest for the mastery of Europe, and to preserve his own freedom of action he generally had to side with the Spanish and Imperial forces against the might of France. Thus by the time James II came to the English throne, the Jesuits were more the shock troops of the king of France than they were of the Pope himself. That James should admit Jesuits to his private household and listen to and perhaps take their advice was a shocking thing indeed—shocking not only to English Protestant, but even to English Catholic, laymen and the Pope himself. How far James was in fact influenced by them was not, and possibly is not, as important as the image their presence conjured up. It did, at the least, create an extra burden for those otherwise predisposed to place their trust in James's

protestations of seeking nothing more than the attain-
ment of equal treatment for Catholics before the law.
It also made it hard to trust his conduct of foreign
policy and to really believe his protestations of English
patriotism and his denials that he was but a tool of the
French king. If James were in fact seeking nothing but
toleration for Catholics and the advancement of England's national interest, it would have been much wiser
to keep the Jesuits at arm's length.

Upon the conclusion of the speech from the throne,
the king left and the Lords proceeded to debate
whether or not they should give a vote of thanks to the
king for his "gracious" speech. There was some opposition, but the opposition was undone by the Marquis of
Halifax, whose satirical comments were turned against
him and the opposition by the supporters of the court.
Halifax said that "they had now more reason than ever
to give Thanks to his Majesty, since he had dealt so
plainly with them, and discovered what he would be
at."[12] Of course, Halifax undoubtedly meant that the
king was now admitting his intentions to play the role
of tyrant. But the satire failed, and the king was now
armed with the support of the Lords. The burden of
resisting the king now fell solely upon the House of
Commons, and resistance was not found wanting. Sir
Winston Churchill, a Tory and the father of John
Churchill the future Duke of Marlborough, took the
lead in advancing the royal cause. He unwittingly
helped the opposition when in the course of the debate
he opposed the suggestion of a supply of £200,000 as
being too little and said, "Soldiers move not without pay. No Penny, No Paternoster."[13] But as with
Halifax, so here too, the unwitting satire was not understood, and the Commons sitting as a committee agreed
to bring in a bill offering the king £700,000 for the
army, a compromise between the opposition's sugges-

12 Cobbett, IV, p. 1371.
13 Ibid., p. 1380.

tion of £200,000 and the court's hope for £1,200,000. But the debate was not really over money at all. Everyone was happy that the rebellion had been crushed and knew that money was needed to discharge the cost of crushing it and to provide for the future defense of the king and kingdom. The real issue was, what kind of defense? An army, which meant royal control; a militia, which meant local control; or a navy, which meant that the only danger was from overseas? The court wanted a royal army, controlled by the king, taking to heart the lesson learned from Monmouth's Rebellion. The opposition thought otherwise.

It is interesting to see how this debate brought together several disparate elements of the House and presaged that coming together of many diverse groups in 1688–89. Sir Edward Seymour was again found among the opposition and he was joined by Sir Thomas Meres and Sir Thomas Clarges. Meres was an old Parliament hand who had been a part of the old Country party, and therefore inclined to be a Whig. Clarges was a brother-in-law of old General George Monck, who had commanded the Cromwellian army in Scotland and had provided the military backing for the Restoration. Clarges was also associated with the Presbyterians. By diverting the debate away from the matter of mere money, they were in the end successfully to deny James both the money and an army.

There does seem to be little question that James II knew not at all how to handle a Parliament. It was not merely that as a king he thought it politic to take a firm hand with them in order to get as much as possible out of them. James was not thought of in terms of tactics. He was a man of principle, and his principle concerning Parliament was basically that of his father and grandfather before him. Parliaments existed to supply the king with the funds and the statutes deemed necessary by him to further his own objects, which in turn, of course, were assumed to be identical with the interest of the kingdom. James was always convinced that his brother, Charles II, had been much too weak and vacillating in his handling of Parliaments. He felt, also, that his father had come to disaster because he was not firm enough with Parliament and that the Exclusion Crisis need never have arisen if Charles II had taken a firmer hand. James may well have been an English patriot, but he had a view of the monarchical role steeped in the myths of his grandfather's theories as outlined in *The True Law of Free Monarchy*. Where for James I this had been a well-worked-out essay in political theory, for James II it was just an extension of his own personality. James had a very poor understanding of other men and no appreciation whatsoever of the complexity of motives and issues. One was either for him or against him. The slightest hesitation in total compliance to his wishes was sufficient to convince him that you were in fact his enemy and must be dealt with accordingly.

The debates in Parliament in November 1685 show clearly that even though the fear of a standing army and of Catholic officers was very great and was increasing, it is also clear that James could have gotten his £700,000 and that his previous employment of Catholics would have been condoned. But the willingness to debate these matters and, to express doubts about the future course of events infuriated James and he prorogued Parliament after only eleven days, without seeing any money formally voted at all. Further prorogations followed, and Parliament was finally dissolved on July 2, 1687. James now seemed set on a policy of personal rule like that of Charles I, financed by the French, like that of Charles II. James's new policy can only be described as "forward," if not "thorough," or as David Ogg has said, a policy of "infiltration."

James felt secure to proceed with his "forward" policy, since he was well aware that the Church had never weakened in its adherence to the doctrine of passive obedience and non-resistance, even during the thick of the Exclusion Crisis. He was convinced that he could go to any length in integrating Catholics into the political, military, and religious life of the nation without having anything at all to fear from the clergy; through their use of the pulpit the ordinary subjects would be kept in check. In addition, the aristocracy and gentry would be immobilized because there would be no Parliament through which to organize any opposition to him. After all, when Charles II precipitately dissolved the Oxford Parliament, in 1681, Shaftesbury and his Whigs just slunk away and caused no more trouble. The English never resorted to the calling of illegal Parliaments, and without a Parliament there could be no effective opposition. Whether James did in fact seek to restore England to the Roman fold or whether he merely sought full equality for his fellow Catholics has become a subject of intense debate in recent years. Some writers, notably Maurice Ashley, have gone so far as to credit James with a devotion to true religious toleration that was far ahead of his time. It is well known what the traditional view has been. Suffice it to say at this point that whatever James's ultimate goal may have been, no one, with the lone exception of William Penn, believed that he merely sought toleration; and in any case, even if that were his goal, the way he went about achieving it made the Church and even the nation fear for their liberties. Since religious toleration was indeed one of the fruits of the Glorious Revolution, it seems plausible to say that those who opposed James were not merely opposing toleration, or seeking to perpetuate privilege, but were also moved by the fear that a new era of royal tyranny was at hand. Even if his goals were admirable, which is debatable, the means used to achieve them were certainly less than politic and were in fact less than legal.

In appointing Catholic officers to his army, James was exercising an ancient right of the crown to dispense with the rigors of statutes when their enforcement worked to the injury of either the king or a particular subject. This exercise of his prerogative powers was far more inflammatory than a similar use of the prerogative in James I's "forced loans" or Charles I's "ship money." Whether the wide use of the ancient prerogative or the use of it to staff the army with Catholics was the greater crime in the eyes of the public is a difficult, but crucial, question. At the time, it would appear that the use of it on behalf of Catholics was the more inflammatory. But after the Revolution, events were to move toward the granting of religious toleration and the restriction of the prerogative.

Two distinct but quite separate prerogative rights were at stake, prerogative rights that have often been incorrectly handled by many later historians—the dispensing power and the suspending power. An attribute of sovereign power in the ancient Roman Empire and in the medieval monarchies was the right to set aside a law in a particular case (dispensing power) or to set aside a law in all cases (suspending power) in which the enforcement of the law in general or in particular was deemed by the sovereign authority to be detrimental to the upholding of the sovereign's interest or where the enforcement would in itself lead to an injury not contemplated by the law itself. The dispensing power has often, but incorrectly, been likened to the royal right to grant pardons. Superficially there is a similarity, but in substance the two powers are quite distinct. When the king grants a pardon, the recipient is still considered to be guilty of the crime. He is merely excused from paying the penalty for the crime. When the law is dispensed with in a particular case, the defendant is neither punished nor considered guilty. The law just did not apply to him in that particular case. Dispensing is equivalent to repealing the law in that one instance. Of course a widespread, across-the-board use of the dispensing power is the equivalent of the use of the suspending power. In other words, the law has for all practical purposes been repealed. That is, then, the crux of the issue, for the power to repeal laws is just as fully a part of the law-making, or legislative, process as the power to make law. From the reign of Henry VIII on, it was established that new law could be made only by the king and the three estates of the realm—the king-in-Parliament. The dispensing power was used on occasion in the Tudor and early-Stuart eras in the situations previously referred to. The suspending power was rarely used and was rarely an issue in the sixteenth and early-seventeenth centuries, since the Tudor sovereigns were sufficiently in tune with the two Houses to be able to get the legislation they desired or could live with. The broad use of either of these powers is a symptom that the necessary unity between king and Parliament does not exist and that a struggle for political power is imminent, which in turn means that a constitutional struggle for sovereignty is at hand. James II, by his frequent use of the dispensing power and his use of the suspending power in respect to the Test Act, was, whether he knew it or not, creating a grave constitutional crisis and a new "struggle for sovereignty." The issues were in fact far more serious than whether or not Catholics should be brought into the mainstream of English life. James II may have hoped to avoid the mistakes of his father, but in fact he seemed bound and determined to repeat them.

There was another aspect of the legality of the dispensing power at issue as well. The medieval and Tudor view of the dispensing power was premised on the distinction between *malum prohibitum* (a prohibited evil) and *malum per se* (an evil in itself). The distinction was essentially medieval, and the foundation was divine law and/or natural law. Restrictions considered man-made (*malum prohibitum*) could be dispensed with. Restrictions that were thought to have been authored by God or Nature (*malum per se*) were not to be dispensed with. These distinctions permeated both the secular and the ecclesiastical structures of the medieval world. The Tudor era, especially after the English Reformation, saw the gradual secularization of political and legal thought and the gradual erosion of

the distinction, because the whole conception of divine
and natural law was one of the victims of the new age
of science and its concomitant *mechanical* laws of nature, which were coming to the fore in the seventeenth
century. One result of the pre-1640 struggle for sovereignty and the constitutional struggle of the Puritan
Revolution itself had been the triumph of the principle
that sovereign power was identical with the lawmaking,
or legislative, power. Neither the Long Parliament nor
the government of the Protectorate felt any divine or
natural limitations upon their ultimate freedom to exercise total legislative authority. The lesson of the Restoration had been that the supreme or sovereign
legislative authority did exist in the English state, and
that it existed in the triple-headed institution of the
king-in-Parliament. The problem was very complex. Because if the king-in-Parliament can make or unmake any
and all laws, then there is no longer any practical distinction between *malum prohibitum* and *malum per
se*. All laws are merely *malum prohibitum*. The state
is supreme, not God or Nature. The result is that the
king could now feel free, at least in theory, to dispense
with any law, while those who might oppose his particular use of this power, as in the case of James II's appointment of Catholic officers, would be thrown back
upon the old medieval distinction between the human
and the divine.[14] English constitutional development
was to be unique in seventeenth-century Europe in that
these same intellectual tendencies on the Continent
were indeed leading to just this justification for royal
absolutism, while in England the struggle for power
between the king and Parliament would continue un-
abated. If the old theories were not workable in modern
circumstances, then new theories would have to be
developed. One way or the other, the royal prerogative
had to be restricted. Where Hobbes and Filmer, each

[14] See Sir William Holdsworth, *A History of English Law*,
London, 1937, vol. VI, pp. 217–25.

in his own way, tried to accommodate the old with the new to the advantage of the crown, John Locke in theory and the Whigs in practice were developing new devices to fit the new circumstances. The tragedy of James II was that he forced the Tories and the Church to go a good deal of the way down the new paths Locke and the Whigs were blazing. They were convinced, regardless of the old theories, that the suspending power and the widespread use of the dispensing power were in practice nothing more than a royal usurpation of the power to repeal legislation. This was intolerable, as it was thus an affront to the principle of the sovereignty of the king-in-Parliament, which had been struggling to the fore since the reign of Henry VIII and had supposedly triumphed with the Restoration.

Within a few months of the prorogation of his one and only Parliament, James tested his dispensing power in *Godden* v. *Hales*, a case that ranks with that of the *Five Knights* in James I's reign or the *Ship Money Case* of Charles I's reign. Sir Edward Hales was a Roman Catholic gentleman whom James had commissioned to a colonelcy at the time of Monmouth's Rebellion. With the co-operation of the crown, his servant Godden, acting as public informer, brought suit against Hales for holding a commission without having taken the required test. James undoubtedly felt certain that the judges in the Court of King's Bench would rule in his favor. Ever since Monmouth's Rebellion the king and his new lord chancellor, Jeffreys, had worked to cow the judges by periodically removing those who gave the appearance of valuing their judicial independence. As was predictable, the judges did indeed rule for the king and his dispensing power. Sir Edward Herbert, the Chief Justice, ruled for the defendant, Hales, and for the king's prerogative in the following terms: "1. That the kings of England are sovereign princes. 2. That the laws of England are the king's laws. 3. That therefore 'tis an inseparable prerogative of the kings of England, to dispense with penal laws in particular cases, and upon particular necessary reasons. 4. That of those reasons and those necessities, the king himself is sole judge: and then, which is consequent upon all, 5. *That this is not a trust invested in, or granted to the king by the people, but the ancient remains of the sovereign power and prerogative of the kings of England; which never yet was taken from them, nor can be.* [Italics mine.] And therefore such a dispensation appearing upon record to come time enough to save him from the forfeiture, judgment ought to be given for the defendant."[15] The only aspect of the dispensing prerogative that the judges seem to have doubted was the timing of the dispensation. Since the king had in fact dispensed with the penal clauses of the Test Act prior to the appointment of Hales, the judges considered all to be well. If Hales's appointment had preceded the dispensation, then they at least hint at the possibility that the dispensation would not have been valid. In that case a pardon would have been necessary, but the act would still be in force and Hales could not have continued to serve his king in a military capacity. But except for the matter of timing, this decision was a victory of profound theoretical and practical significance for the king, and consequently a profound defeat for the notion that the sovereign power rested with the king-in-Parliament.

Charles I had come to rule by the consent of his courts and in the process drove all good men into the arms of the country opposition. The same result was to ensue with the rendering of this decision in the case of *Godden* v. *Hales*. But if James had not pushed on with renewed zeal, no great harm would have been done. The interaction between the legal and the political situation must always be kept in mind, however. The decision of the judges in upholding the royal prerogative of dispensation would not have had nearly the

[15] *State Trials*, edited by T. B. Howell, London, 1816, vol. XI, p. 1199.

same political impact if the statute involved had been other than the Test Act. In *Glanvil's Case*, in 1628, it was stated that the royal prerogative of dispensation and suspension did not apply when the "liberties" of the subject were at stake. There could not be any dispensation or suspension from Magna Carta, for instance. The Test Act was held in exactly the same esteem by Englishmen in the 1670s and the 1680s. It was not thought of as a denial of freedom but, on the contrary, as a sure defense of the freedom of England and of its citizens. It must be constantly borne in mind that the great mass of Englishmen sincerely believed that the free expression of Roman Catholicism and the integration of the Roman Catholics into all aspects of public life was in fact a threat to the freedom and independence of the nation. It must also be borne in mind that this was not solely a religious matter, but a political and military one as well. As long as international Catholicism was led by a powerful and expanding French monarchy, it was, with a good deal of justification, thought of in a fashion similar to that in which the Nazi Bundists were regarded in the 1930s or the Communists were regarded in the 1940s and 1950s. When this "international conspiracy" was looked upon sympathetically by the English court, as in the days of Charles II, and when the king himself was an avowed Catholic, as was James II, it is little wonder that anti-Catholicism was the touchstone of freedom and patriotism. The accession of William of Orange was to change the situation in the direction of toleration and "benign neglect," because William was the acknowledged leader of the anti-French alliance. With an avowed Protestant and anti-French king on the throne, anti-Catholicism was to lose its sense of urgency, although it would linger on in the form of a "folk wisdom" for almost 150 years. Charles II at least had enough political sense to grasp the real basis of English anti-Catholicism and, therefore, make the necessary political adjustments to the facts. James II had no such political sense, and merely drove on to his ruin.

Emboldened with his triumph in *Godden* v. *Hales,* James took the final and perhaps fatal step of suspending the Test Act altogether by issuing his Declaration of Indulgence. This followed hard on the heels of his re-establishing the Court of High Commission, entitled the Court of Ecclesiastical Commission. The Tudor Court of High Commission had been a court of first instance, exercising all aspects of the Act of Uniformity, without the right of appeal; and by use of the oath *ex officio,* the defendant was denied all common-law rights, such as the right not to have to testify against himself. It was a court wholly dependent upon the monarch's status as the supreme governor of the Church, and in contrast to the common-law tradition, it combined the two elements of being both an administrative tribunal and a court of justice. In this respect, it was often the judge in cases involving its own administrative decisions, and was thus wholly at odds with the common-law tradition that no one could be a judge in a case in which he was one of the parties. In all these respects, the High Commission was at one with all the other "prerogative" courts, and met the common fate in the early days of the Long Parliament. (The Court of Chancery was the only prerogative court to survive, and that was because it did so much important work and nothing could be found to replace it.)[16] By using the prerogative to revive this court, after it had been abolished by statute, James hoped to be able to deal firmly and thoroughly with any clergy who might attempt to frustrate his efforts to introduce Catholics into the Anglican establishment itself. The new Lord Chancellor, Jeffreys, was made president of the court, and his presence was always needed to make a quorum.[17] William Sancroft, the Archbishop of

[16] See S. E. Prall, *The Agitation for Law Reform During the Puritan Revolution, 1640–1660,* The Hague, 1966.

[17] *State Trials,* XI, p. 1143.

Canterbury, was also appointed to the commission, but he declined to serve. James could well have taken this refusal as a hint of things to come, although Sancroft's stated reasons for his refusal may have seemed to be based on technicalities, more than on substance; he refused to serve on an ecclesiastical court presided over by a layman. But James did manage to get Lord Crewe, the Bishop of Durham, and Sprat, the Bishop of Rochester, to serve. Both were considered friendly to James's policy. The use to which the High Commission was put is enlightening. James and his defenders have said that he sought nothing more than religious toleration, both for his fellow Catholics and for Dissenters as well, but Jeffreys immediately used his new authority to harry the Dissenters, or their supporters within the Church. This harassment was short-lived, but the savage treatment meted out to the aged and great Puritan divine Richard Baxter is symptomatic not only of Jeffreys' ruthlessness, but also of why all James's later efforts to woo the Dissenters were to fall on deaf ears, except for those of William Penn.

Remembering that whatever James said to Barillon may well have been only what he wanted Louis XIV to believe, what James did say to Barillon on the occasion of re-establishing the Court of High Commission is significant in understanding James's intentions; his views, if known in England, would have given support to those who feared the worst:

God had permitted that all the laws which have been passed for the establishment of the protestant, and to destroy the catholic religion, should now serve as a basis for what he wished to do for the re-establishment of the true religion and should give him the right to exercise a power still greater than Catholic kings in other countries exercise over ecclesiastical affairs.[18]

In even stronger language is Barillon's report to Louis of a conversation he had had with Lord Sunderland,

[18] Turner, p. 317.

the Secretary of State and the one minister who does seem to have understood James, although there is always the possibility that Sunderland's tendency to be a sycophant and timeserver may have led him to presume too much as regards the king's hopes for Catholicism. On the other hand it must be borne in mind that Sunderland was the one minister whom James seems to have trusted throughout his entire reign. On July 16, 1685, Barillon wrote Louis:

Lord Sunderland has entered very far with me, and appears to be informed to the bottom of what has passed between the King of England and myself upon the subject of the catholic religion. This minister said to me, I do not know if they see things in France as they are here, but I defy those who see them near, not to know that the King, my master, has nothing so much at heart, as to establish the catholic religion; that he cannot, even according to good sense and right reason, have any other end; that without it he will never be in safety, and always exposed to the indiscreet zeal of those who will heat the people against the catholic religion as long as it is not fully established.[19]

Statements such as these have traditionally been quoted as proof that James II did indeed seek to convert England officially to the Roman Catholic Church. But some modern historians, especially Lucile Pinkham and Maurice Ashley, have contended that even remarks such as those quoted above indicate no more than that James sought to "establish" the Roman Church on a basis of equality with the Anglican and that full toleration was all that was intended. This view just cannot be reconciled with the sequence of events during the remainder of the reign. The use of the Court of High Commission and the subsequent issuing of the Declaration of Indulgence were not accompanied by the "establishment" of a separate but equal Catholic Church but by the mass infiltration of avowed Catholics into office within the Anglican establishment itself. That

[19] Dalrymple, Appendix, p. 175.

this was done merely to achieve a body of established clerics who could then use their new positions of power in order to bring the Church around to a position of tolerance is an equally incredible notion. But even if it does not sound incredible to some modern scholars, it certainly sounded incredible to James's Anglican, and dissenting, contemporaries.

The re-establishment of the Court of High Commission and the royal victory in the case of *Godden* v. *Hales* emboldened James to raise his sights and to accelerate his pace. The rector of Putney, Edward Sclater, openly announced his Catholicism and duly received a dispensation to remain in his post. This was followed by the appointment of other Catholics to livings within the Church. The decision in *Godden* v. *Hales* had been based on the king's prerogative right to defend himself and the kingdom by using the advice and services of those whom he deemed useful to himself and the kingdom—in a military capacity. That case had not specifically stated the king's right to do likewise within the ecclesiastical establishment. In very practical terms, there might well be a case for the king to staff his army from all ranks of his subjects, but it does seem to be stretching things a bit to say that the Church established by law was to be defended by appointing non-members—even enemies—to positions of rank and authority within it. And there is no question of James's making these appointments so as to bring the Church around to a position of comprehension, as was once discussed in the days following the Restoration. It is hard to believe that contemporaries could see these appointments and dispensations as anything other than a power play. It is equally difficult to understand how present-day scholars can see it in any other light. The events at Oxford the following year should be sufficient confirmation of this.

Not content to infiltrate his own men into the Church, James also sought to bend to his will or break the backs of those already in the Church who dared to speak out against his policies. The degradation, pillorying, and whipping of Samuel Johnson, a former chaplain to Lord Russell, can be understood, because he called upon soldiers to refuse obedience to Catholic officers. Since the Catholics now held their commissions with judicial approval, and since Johnson was actually exhorting mutiny, the harsh treatment of Johnson may well have been deserved; but the treatment of Henry Compton, Bishop of London, and Dr. Sharp, a London priest, was something else again. Sharp had preached against popery, which in law was surely a proper thing for an Anglican priest to do, but Compton was ordered to make him stop. When Compton attempted to defend Sharp by stressing his true loyalty to the king, the bishop himself was brought before the High Commission, found guilty of disobedience to a royal order, and suspended from his office. That a king sought to exercise a firm control over his clergy was, of course, not a unique event in the history of the Church. But that he should do it in order to assist the enemies of that Church and by means of a court that had been expressly abolished by statute nearly half a century earlier, could not help but revive memories of the reign of Mary I, over a century before. The folk knowledge of that reign was that Roman Catholicism and tyranny went hand in hand. Not since Mary had burned Thomas Cranmer at the stake had it been possible for the English people to think of the Anglican hierarchy as defenders and even martyrs for the cause of freedom and the rights of Englishmen. James was striving hard to re-create that image of the Church in his own reign. Within two more years he would succeed in doing so, and pronounce sentence upon himself and his own reign in the process.

Other efforts were also made to both humiliate and dominate the traditionally Royalist and Anglican establishment at Oxford University. John Massey, a layman and fellow of Merton College, was appointed by the king to the deanery of Christ Church. This was the

first time since the Reformation that a layman had
held a deanery. On top of this, Massey was dispensed
from all religious obligations. In the Middle Ages, laymen were frequently granted high ecclesiastical office,
but it was always assumed that the purpose was political, not religious. Whenever it was done, it was to serve
the king, not God. This was, indeed, an insult to the
Church and to the university.

The culmination of James's policy was the issuing
of the Declaration of Indulgence, in April 1687. It is
really not possible to truly divine James's ultimate
aims and motives. All that can be done effectively is
to examine the declaration itself, the situation in which
it was issued, the various reactions to it, and James's
own response to those reactions. It has been repeated
many times that however innocent or even farsighted
the royal policy may have been, it was to strike nearly
all as a blow for Catholicism and its "establishment,"
whatever the term might have meant. In the seventeenth century the word "establishment" in the religious sense carried two distinct meanings: On one hand
it meant an "established" church in the sense of a
state church—the Church of England. But it could
also mean the "establishment" of a non-state church
on a basis of equality or toleration alongside the state
church, as in the post-Revolutionary era. Both meanings
can be found in the king's own statements, depending
upon the occasion and the audience to which the
words were directed. Whenever Barillon was told that
the king hoped to emulate the policies of Louis XIV
in the days after the revocation of the Edict of Nantes,
it would appear to be clear that James hoped to establish Catholicism as the one and only officially recognized religion in England. In other words, England
would officially return to the Roman fold, as it had
in the reign of Mary I. James's writings to the Prince
of Orange and to non-Catholics in England seem to
mean that he sought nothing more than equality and
mutual toleration for all while still maintaining the

Church of England as the official religious institution. But as has been said before, whatever ultimate goal the king sought, the important thing is to see how contemporaries at the time looked at it and how they responded to it. Given the proposition that James II was indeed far more enlightened and tolerant than most Englishmen of his era, and that the scourge of mindless anti-Catholicism still plagued the great body of the nation, still it is true that James sought to achieve his noble aims by a policy and by means that were, and were largely considered to be, anathema to the maintenance of mixed monarchy and of the autonomy of local authorities, both of which had supposedly been accomplished by the Puritan Revolution and confirmed by the Restoration.

That James was willing and able to continue his advancement of the pro-Catholic policy, and that this policy was indeed anti-Anglican as well, was made clear to all in January 1687, when he removed from office the symbol and personal embodiment of high-Tory Anglicanism—the Earl of Rochester, Lawrence Hyde. The Lord Treasurer had refused to serve on the new Court of High Commission, and had opposed its treatment of Bishop Compton. But Rochester was the personal symbol of the maintenance of the Anglican establishment, which had been created in his father's name in the early years of Charles II. He had gained the personal enmity of James's queen, Mary of Modena, and to Sunderland and the papal nuncio, D'Adda, his retention as the formal head of the administration was utterly incompatible with any move to repeal the Test Act. His refusal to convert to Catholicism at the king's request was the last straw. Of course if he had been willing to acquiesce in the repeal, keeping him in office would have been a great propaganda victory for the king. Rochester, however, did not limit his opposition to making his views known in private. He would neither acquiesce in the repeal nor refrain from doing all in his power to stop the repeal. His fall was a great shock to the political and diplomatic world. Barillon considered it a sign that the "Catholic cabal" had triumphed. If James hoped that Rochester's removal would break the spirits of lesser officials, the move was not entirely successful. Several others were going to have to follow Rochester into oblivion. For the next two months James met with various known Anglicans in the administration, and the Tory/Anglican ranks seemed to hold. This solidarity was met with Rochester himself being removed from the keepership of the wardrobe, his brother Clarendon being deprived of the Privy Seal, and both the treasurer and the comptroller of the household being removed. A similar rash of removals fell upon the armed forces—even the great popular favorite Arthur Herbert, the Vice-Admiral of England, was to fall. The deprivations did not stop on the highest level, either, but extended far down into the ranks, even to minor officials in the customs office. Up and down the country, justices of the peace sounded out members of the oft-prorogued Parliament, and other men of substance, to see how they stood on the question. The results showed sufficient Tory and Anglican solidarity to determine the king not to attempt another session of Parliament, at least not yet. (The day was, in fact, never to come.)

Rochester held firm in his refusal to convert, and James's daughter, the Princess Anne, likewise refused to abandon her religion at her father's behest. (Even the Pope, who generally opposed James's forward policies, had urged the king to seek his daughter's conversion.) Only the Earl of Sunderland succumbed to the realities at court and implied his own conversion. The Prince of Orange expressed his absolute refusal to condone a repeal of the Test Act and the penal laws against Dissenters and recusants. The king was bent on isolating himself from his family, and his court from the country. Even hints that the line of succession would be changed to eliminate James's daughter Mary, the Princess of Orange, did not sway William. It merely

stiffened his own resolve and tended to move the
Anglicans into looking at William not only as a potential ally, but perhaps even as a potential savior.[20]

Now that James seemed determined to effect the
repeal of both the Test Act and the penal laws by use
of the prerogative powers which had just been so greatly
strengthened by the *Godden* v. *Hales* decision, the
failure of the king to allow Parliament to meet shows
how difficult, if not impossible, it would be for the
opposition to challenge him. A Parliament in session
could threaten to cut off the king's funds, it could
initiate impeachments against those who acquiesced in
the hated policy, and it could serve as a forum from
which the opposition could rally the nation to prove
to the king the error and folly of his ways. The absence
of Parliament was proof both that when in session a
Parliament is a mighty thing indeed, and that the
king's right to determine if and when it would meet
was a mighty weapon in the royal arsenal. Parliament
might not be able to secure legislation that the king
opposed, but it was able to deny the king what he himself wanted. And the seventeenth-century revival of
the old medieval device of impeachment had, by the
end of Charles II's reign, gone a long way into forcing
ministers of the crown to walk warily in advising the
king on matters deemed repugnant in the eyes of a
concerted parliamentary opposition. The absence of a
Parliament left only one other institution that could
serve as a check to the royal policies—the judiciary.
James II, even more than his brother, Charles II, was
to understand and make use of the courts so as to deny
the opposition even this last remaining defensive
weapon.

One thing at least that had been accomplished in
the early-seventeenth century, in the days of Sir Edward Coke, was that the law was supreme and that the
law was what the judges said it was. And unlike Parlia-

[20] Stephen Baxter, *William III*, London, 1966, pp. 218–21.

ment, the courts met in regular sessions each year and every year. The judiciary was a permanent institution whose sessions were not subject to the whims of the monarch. But the crown did have the ultimate authority here, too—the judges' tenure of office was subject to the royal pleasure or whim. The law may be what the judges said it was, but the king alone could decide who those judges would be and could make or break them at will. The ancient royal prerogative to appoint and dismiss judges was used sparingly until the seventeenth century. When the country opposition to James I and Charles I had found themselves impotent to block the king and his "evil" advisers in Parliament, they had turned to the bench for relief. The crown had immediately counterattacked by pressuring the judges into subservience to the royal will. Charles I had managed to rule for eleven years, not by the grace of Parliament but by the grace of his judiciary. James II was to do the same. The decision in *Godden* v. *Hales* became a symbol for all to see that any new effort by the opposition to rely on the courts in the absence of Parliament would prove to be as fruitless in the 1680s as it had been in the 1630s. But James was not content to rely solely upon that one decision as a sufficient weapon. Nor was he content merely to warn the judges that they would co-operate or else. He resorted to wholesale dismissals in advance in order to guarantee that if and when the need should arise the judges would be his men and would be thoroughly reliable. Sir William Holdsworth had said that James could not have found twelve lawyers who would have supported his claim to have the power to repeal the Test Act and the penal laws by means of the suspending and the dispensing powers, or of his governing of the army by means of martial law in peacetime. Yet even though he could not find twelve such lawyers, he could and did find twelve such judges. Judge Jeffreys, the Lord Chancellor, expressed the king's view in unmistakable fashion in a speech he gave upon the oc-

casion of the appointment of Sir Edward Herbert to
the chief justiceship of the Court of King's Bench: "Be
sure to execute the law to the utmost of its vengeance
upon those that are now knowne, and we have reason
to remember them, by the name of Whigs; and you
likewise to remember the snivelling trimmers [the
Earl of Halifax, who had written in defense of a free
and learned judiciary]; for you know that our Saviour
Jesus Christ says in the Gospell, that 'they that are not
for us are against us.' "[21] James's treatment of his
judges showed that they, too, were considered as either
for him or against him, and if the latter they received
short shrift.

Not all cases were to be decided by the judges alone,
however. In the criminal sphere, there was still trial
by jury. Juries could be packed, warned, and bribed,
but twelve honest men might still be a more difficult
nut to crack than twelve timeserving or careerist judges.
Of course in the realm of criminal law the initiative
lay with the crown to bring actions against defendants,
and the king could fail to enforce those criminal
statutes that he did not like, without resorting to the
suspending or dispensing power. The penal laws against
recusants and Dissenters, however, allowed ordinary citizens to make the complaints, thus forcing the king
to resort to the dispensing power.

Where the criminal law could be used by the crown
to coerce and punish its enemies, the rights of the
defendants were a thorn in the king's side. The right
to a trial by jury was one such thorn. The writ of
habeas corpus was another. Customarily in use since
the Middle Ages, the writ had been enshrined as a
right of Englishmen in the famous Habeas Corpus Act
of 1679, the only positive thing accomplished by Parliament during the Exclusion Crisis. If those whom James
sought to coerce by means of the criminal law had the
statutory right to a writ of habeas corpus and were

[21] Holdsworth, VI, p. 509.

thus guaranteed a fair and speedy trial following their arrest, on specific criminal charges, and then the right to have the case heard before a jury in their own district, then the king was unable to freely use the criminal law for his own purposes. James opposed the requirement that specific warrants were necessary to effect an arrest; he favored the use of general warrants. He also opposed the habeas corpus. Since the subject, not the crown, had the initiative of calling the writ into play, the suspending and dispensing powers of the king were of no use here. So James let it be known that he wanted the repeal of the Habeas Corpus Act. But such a repeal would necessitate the calling of a Parliament. Even his most subservient of Parliaments, oft prorogued, could not be trusted to strip from the subject this one last shield by which he could defend himself from the clutches of a "tyrannical" king. This was the last legal weapon in the opposition's defensive arsenal, and it could not lightly be cast away. While it was true that James needed a Parliament in order to secure the repeal of the Habeas Corpus Act, it must also be admitted that he wanted the suspension of the penal laws and of the Test Act to be confirmed by act of Parliament as well. The king was neither so bent on establishing absolutism nor so dense as to be unaware of the great benefit that parliamentary approval would render to his hopes of toleration for Catholics. He spent the next year trying to see if a Parliament could be put together that would give him this approbation, but it proved to be a hopeless task.

On April 4, 1687, the king issued his momentous Declaration of Indulgence. The penal laws were suspended by virtue of his prerogative, and it was announced that the Test Act would be effectively repealed by his assertion that "from time to time" he would, by letters patent, issue dispensations so that he would be free to employ in his service men of his own choosing, regardless of religion. In any case, the tests and oaths called for by the Test Act would no longer be administered. The decision to issue the declaration was not really the triumph of royal policy that it might appear to be. It is more realistic to see it as a dangerous gamble on the king's part to achieve by force what he had up to now been unable to achieve by pressuring and cajoling. His efforts to break the Anglican monopoly of service in both Church and state had failed to win them over. On the contrary it had merely strengthened resistance to him.

If the Catholic cause could not be advanced with the approval of the Anglicans, then it would have to be done without them. The approval of a Parliament would be the best of all, but that still was not possible. Realizing that some public demonstration of support for his policies was needed, and knowing that even the Catholic laity were unwilling to openly grant him support, James really had no place to turn except to the Dissenters. Mention has earlier been made of James's policies toward the Dissenters. In spite of his occasional statements that he favored freedom of conscience on religious matters, he did in fact have a decided record of fierce opposition to Dissent. This was especially true in Scotland. If nothing else, a son of Charles I could hardly help looking upon the heirs of the Puritans as rebels, regicides, and republicans. Up to the issuance of the declaration, at any rate, it is completely understandable that Dissenters would look with great suspicion upon James's protestations of toleration as founded upon little more than sheer political opportunism. Indeed, there will always be the nagging suspicion that his zeal was purely political and that he was to persist in it for the rest of his life in order to justify himself and make those who effected the Revolution appear to be mean and narrow-minded bigots. It bears repeating that it does seem incredible that a man whom almost all historians admit was stupid, narrow-minded, and obstinate, could really be so far in advance of his age on this one issue of religious toleration. In any case, very few of his contemporaries could bring themselves

to believe it. But even if James's support of toleration
was tactical, there was still a chance that it might succeed, because the Dissenters themselves would not
necessarily have to believe in the king's purity of conscience in order to seek to advance their own cause.
They could adopt the same tactics and effect a temporary alliance for their own advantage. Prior to the
issuance of the declaration, at any rate, there was still
no hard evidence that there was any mass support of
the Anglican monopoly among the Dissenters. Before
James's policy of toleration would fail irrevocably, there
first had to be forged a firm alliance between Anglicanism and Dissent. This alliance could not be formed
by the Dissenters and the Anglicans acting either alone
or in concert. The gulf that separated them was obviously too deep and too wide. What was necessary was
that there be a common danger working from the outside. Only the king was in the position to provide that
common danger, and a royal policy of toleration was
not alone sufficient to do that.

The suspension of the Bishop of London and his
treatment before the High Commission had temporarily served as the necessary catalyst, but it was hardly
more than an isolated incident. James still had a chance
to achieve at least a tacit alliance with the Dissenting
leaders. In the summer of 1686 the king used Sir John
Baber, a courtier on good terms with the Dissenters,
to sound out Roger Morrice, the Presbyterian, and
other leaders as to the possibilities for a court/Dissenter
alliance. James knew that the success of his plans to
issue the declaration depended upon the Dissenters'
publicly praising the declaration rather than merely
accepting it passively. The contents of the declaration
were still negotiable. Baber offered toleration supported
by parliamentary statute. Would the Dissenters respond
openly and favorably? These were to prove to be the
crucial issues: a statute and the open declaration of
support from the Dissenters. Could James deliver the
one, and would the Dissenters deliver the other if the

king could not get a statute? Could an alliance be formed on the basis of James's intentions, or would he first have to prove that he could deliver? Put this way, the king's task does appear to be almost hopeless, unless some erosion were to first take place within the Anglican ranks. This was not necessarily impossible if the Anglicans were forced to join the competition for Dissenter support.

Morrice felt that the Dissenters had three options: They could join with the Anglicans in order to stop the court. However, this would expose them to the wrath of the king, and the Church would undoubtedly leave them to bear the full brunt of that wrath alone. A second possibility was to be patient and let God's will work in its own good time. A third course was to go ahead and support the king in his endeavors. This course, however, meant that a Parliament was to be held. This last was the course that Morrice favored, and by it he hoped that they would succeed in establishing "such a liberty by a law as should give them unalterable liberty, the court dissolving this Parliament and the court and Dissenters joining in choosing another Parliament. . . ."[22] To achieve a sympathetic Parliament, however, would be most difficult, considering that the borough franchise had recently been altered to the benefit of the Tory/Anglican establishment. Perhaps this would entail a restoration of the old charters or another wholesale surrendering of charters so that a new and more favorable electorate could be created. Neither course would be easy or safe. The next few months were rife with rumors that James did indeed contemplate a wholesale reorganization of local government, and the sitting justices of the peace began to step up their pressures on the non-conformists.

Attempt by James to secure a promise of support from the Dissenters for his proposed declaration was

[22] Douglas R. Lacey, *Dissent and Parliamentary Politics in England, 1661–1689*, New Brunswick, N.J., 1969, pp. 177–78.

fraught with many difficulties. Some of these were James's own doing and others were the result of the basic disunity within the Dissenting camp itself. The pre-Civil War Puritans were really a united and homogeneous group in comparison with the post-Restoration Dissenters. They were first of all divided into four main groups, or denominations: Presbyterians, Congregationalists, Baptists, and Quakers. Within each group there were those who were more fundamentally inclined as well as those who were willing to make certain necessary compromises with the law and with the Anglican establishment. Some were already on the road to being the "occasional conformists" of a future age. The only things the Dissenters really were apt to be united on was their hatred of Roman Catholicism (which would hardly tend to incline them to look kindly upon a Catholic monarch), and also the old Puritan political tradition, which had its anti-monarchical, even republican, tendencies. Neither of these potential areas of Dissenter unity could provide much hope for James. But at least the king did understand them well enough to know that toleration granted by virtue of the prerogative alone would cause more harm than good. It would be necessary to secure parliamentary sanction for toleration, or at least every effort would have to be made to seek it.

The moment word got out that James was contemplating his edict of toleration, the various Dissenting groups began discussions among themselves and with each other. In general the Baptists and the Quakers, under the powerful leadership of the king's dear friend William Penn, were more inclined to go along with the king, assuming of course that a Parliament would be called. The larger and more powerful Presbyterians and Congregationalists, however, were inclined to oppose any step that might "tend to bring in popery." The months of advance warning of what the king intended to do gave Anglicans as well as Dissenters a chance to think through the implications of toleration and to rally their own forces. They would have to see that every step would be taken to make sure that any new Parliament would not bear witness to a revival of Dissenting political power, for this would mean not only toleration but the end of the so recently won Anglican monopoly of the franchise and of local government both urban and rural. What James utterly failed to see was that Anglican opposition to the edict of toleration was not based solely on religious bigotry, nor was it based on the use of the prerogative for its achievement. In fact, the use of the prerogative was less frightening than the use of Parliament as a means of achieving toleration: a mere proclamation under the prerogative would not necessarily lead to a shift in the balance of local political power, but a co-operative Parliament would mean that such a shift had already taken place or might soon be accomplished. Far more than religion itself was at stake. This is what Presbyterians and Congregationalists seemed to understand more thoroughly than did the Baptists and the Quakers.

On the other hand, the Quakers had felt the full weight of the penal laws far more systematically than had any of the other Dissenters. The most intriguing aspect of the Quaker reaction was the special relationship between William Penn and the king. The relationship did indeed appear to be so intimate that David Ogg has compared it to that between a guardian and his ward.[23] The close relationship had begun in the days of Penn's father, the admiral. That William Penn himself was thoroughly dedicated to the principles of religious toleration cannot be questioned. To what extent James shared these views is and has been the crucial question. Did they see eye to eye? Did Penn actually have a significant influence on James? Or was it that James would listen politely and nod in approval whenever Penn engaged in one of his discourses on the matter? Ogg has again summed up the traditional

---

[23] Ogg, *James II and William III*, p. 180.

view when he says that Penn was either overly opti-
mistic or just plain dense in his appraisal of James
and his motives. On the other hand, Miss Pinkham,
Dr. Ashley, and Dr. Buranelli seem inclined to take
James, and Penn's estimation of James, at face value.
But it must be said again that if they are correct,
James's conversion to toleration was a new-found thing.
Too many of his past acts and words, both in England
and especially in Scotland, tend to belie any but a
most recent and sudden conversion. Because of Penn
and because of the particular grievances of the hard-
pressed Quakers, James turned to them with special
hopes of forging the first link in a Catholic/Dissenter
alliance in order to achieve the desired "establishment"
of Roman Catholicism. Charles II had tried it in 1672
and had been beaten. James was determined not to
be beaten.

In anticipation of issuing his Declaration of Indulgence and as a tactic to build up support for it, James
encouraged Dissenters to petition him for special dispensations or licenses at a cost of fifty shillings. These
licenses would entitle a family to immunity from the
penal laws for non-conformity. Where the Quakers and
the Baptists did make use of this new device to evade
the full rigor of the law, the Presbyterians and the
Congregationalists were most reluctant. The latter denominations were composed to a greater extent than
the Baptists or the Quakers of men of some substance
in rural and urban society. They and their fathers had
been caught up in the throes of the Civil War to a far
greater extent than had either Quakers or Baptists.
They were and had been part of the political element
in English society. While obviously in favor of toleration for themselves, they were too experienced politically to fail to see that the winning of this toleration
by illegal means could only hurt them and the nation
in the long run. The Quakers and the Baptists, however, were men of lesser substance and of little or no
political experience. The Quakers, in particular, had

almost completely avoided active involvement in the struggles of the Civil War and the Commonwealth and Protectorate. They were not political and did not think of the political or the constitutional implications of their actions. As the leaders of the old Puritan movement, the Presbyterians and the Congregationalists were in the forefront of the anti-Catholic hysteria. They were, in fact, the very ones who had aroused anti-Catholicism as a weapon against the encroachments of the royal prerogative upon English national and local life since the days of Elizabeth. To expect them to all of a sudden put aside a century of anti-Catholic and anti-prerogative tradition in order to form an alliance with a Catholic king bent on achieving his goals by means of the prerogative was something that few could contemplate. Thus, while James had set out to create a political/religious alliance by which he could achieve his aim of establishing Catholicism, the Presbyterians and the Congregationalists seem to have begun to comtemplate a political/religious alliance of their own.

As Charles II had quickly discovered in the early 1670s, a Catholic/Dissenter alliance really could not work. The two put together did not come close to constituting a majority of the English nation and could find no foreign ally to make up for the lack of numbers within England itself. As long as the Anglicans were the majority, and a massive majority among the men of substance, the best that could be expected realistically was either a temporary victory or even a Pyrrhic victory. The politically astute Presbyterians and Congregationalists seem to have realized early in James's reign that the one best hope for the toleration of Dissenters was an Anglican/Dissenter alliance. Ironically for James, only he could create such an improbable alliance. And tragically for him, he seemed hellbent to do it. James II was to be even more unlucky or more stupid than his father, Charles I. At least Charles I had been able to have John Pym create a

1   "Odds fish, then I'm an ugly fellow."—Charles II.

2   James II.

3   William of Orange, later King William III.

4 Sir Thomas Osborne, Earl of Danby (later Duke of Leeds).

5 Mary of Modena, consort of James II.

6 Queen Mary II.

7 Princess Anne of Denmark (later Queen Anne) with Duke of Gloucester.

8 Duke of Monmouth, bastard of Charles II.

9 Titus Oates.

10 Laurence Hyde, 1st Earl of Rochester.

11 Sir Anthony Ashley Cooper, 1st Earl of Shaftesbury.

12 John Churchill, 1st Earl of Marlborough
    (later Duke of Marlborough).

George Savile . Marq⁹ of Halifax.

13 George Savile, 1st Marquis of Halifax.

royalist party for him in the Long Parliament. The son played his hand far less astutely and paved the way for toleration for Dissenters—but not his beloved fellow Catholics—by letting the Anglicans and the Dissenters begin to forge an alliance against him. Such an alliance, however, required that contradictory forces must be at work within Anglicanism and Dissent. It meant that unity within Dissent must break down and that unity among Anglicans must be increasing. While Presbyterians and Congregationalists must be dividing from the Baptists and Quakers within the Dissenting ranks, High- and Low-Church Anglicans, or Tories and Whigs, must be reuniting within the Anglican fold. James's actions tended to accomplish both these ends.

When one looks at the various religious and political elements that made up English society in the 1680s, one cannot help but feel a certain sympathy for James's plight. Unfortunately for him and for his fellow Catholics, there does not seem to have been any combination of forces that would have won toleration for Catholics except an alliance with the Anglicans. Whether such an alliance could have been put together is not known. We do know that James had in fact tried it and had failed. Whether his failure was due to his tactic of forcing the alliance down the throat of the Church, or whether it was because the Anglicans remembered the disasters that had befallen them forty-five years earlier, when they had both supported Charles I, or whether it was because of the later Stuarts' willingness to secretly ally themselves with France in violation of what appeared to be England's national interest, is the unanswerable question. But if such an alliance was theoretically possible, James II certainly did not know how to go about creating it, and the Anglicans were unwilling to give him any help.

And so James II, the Roman Catholics, and the Dissenters all had to confront the dilemma faced by minorities in all pluralistic societies in modern times. How can toleration and equality be achieved against the will of the majority without recourse to illegal, or even tyrannical, methods? It is seemingly impossible in anything but the long term. James's actions were judged to be tyrannical by the Anglican majority, and the Dissenters' decision to put the law and the constitution above their own goal of toleration, at least in the short run, proved to be a very shrewd political tactic. One result of the fall of James II was in fact the granting of toleration for the Dissenters. But the Catholic cause was postponed—and may have been set back—by James's hasty and illegal actions.

On April 4, 1687, the Declaration of Indulgence was issued, and in effect war had been declared on the Church of England. In spite of the lukewarm response from the Dissenters, James went ahead with his efforts to keep his promise to them that he would seek to have the penal laws and the Test Act formally repealed by a Parliament. Sunderland was assigned the task of sounding out the members of the oft-prorogued Parliament as to their willingness to co-operate when and if Parliament were reassembled. But two highly significant acts were to destroy any chances Sunderland may have had to come up with favorable replies: the refusal of William to co-operate, and James's attack upon Magdalen College, Oxford. First, James approached the Prince of Orange to secure his open support of the repeal of the obnoxious acts. James and William had allowed their relations to deteriorate during 1686, and hints coming out of England that James might attempt to alter the succession, depriving Mary (and William) of their rights, convinced William of the need to patch things up with James. Any such accomodation would not, however, go so far as to bring William to support the "establishment" of Catholicism. The Whig and Dissenting interests had looked to William as a potential savior ever since the Exclusion Crisis. His firmness in rejecting James's demand that he support repeal of the penal laws and the Test, helped to clarify the issue. William's decision meant that the enemy was the Catholic cause in England, united with the aggressive imperialism of Louis XIV. The Dissenters were encouraged not to co-operate with James now, since he might well be dead soon anyway; then, with Mary on the English throne, a Protestant William could secure toleration for Dissent.

If William had been willing to give James the co-operation he sought, the Catholic/Dissenter alliance might well have been effected. But even in this episode, the blame for his failure must largely be assigned to James himself. He made no efforts to win William over. On the contrary, he tried to force William into accommodation by his rude refusal to see William's emissary Dyckfeld, and by his implied threats to alter the succession. It seems to have been an unchangeable trait in James's character to refuse to understand any interests but his own, and to bully his opponents rather than cajole them. As a political tactician he was a total failure. To expect that William would submit to threats was to completely misunderstand William's character and best interests. William certainly would have had nothing to gain in the long run if he won the temporary favor of James II at the expense of his standing among the Anglicans. The Anglicans constituted the big battalions, and there was really no point in anticipating Mary's accession to the throne by alienating the Church of England and the vastly powerful political forces behind it.

With William's opposition to the declaration and to any parliamentary legislation known to all, the Protestant forces were to stand firm. The attack on Magdalen College, Oxford, was to be the decisive factor in destroying James's dream. William would keep the Dissenters in line, and the attack on Magdalen would destroy any hope of co-operation from the Anglicans. Once again it was Sunderland who was assigned the task. He was reluctant to take on the chore, but having cut his last ties with the Anglicans by his own conversion to the Roman Church, he either had to go down

the line with James or be destroyed. Sunderland's father
and his own son were Magdalen men, as were his own
tutor and his personal chaplain. He knew the resistance
that would result, but he had long since learned that
kings are to be obeyed and that this was especially
true of James II. If James was willing to take revenge
on his brothers-in-law the Hydes and his own daughter
Mary, Sunderland, a mere courtier, had no choice but
to give his all for the king's cause.

On April 5, 1687, the day after the issuance of the
Declaration of Indulgence, a warrant was issued to the
vice-president and Fellows of Magdalen College ordering them to elect Anthony Farmer to the presidency
of the College. Farmer was, in the words of J. P. Kenyon, "a worthless Catholic sympathizer."[24] A doctor
Younger, a Fellow of Magdalen and Chaplain to Princess Anne, had earlier signified his willingness to be
nominated to the post, but he was told "that the King
expected that the person he recommended should be
favourable to his religion."[25] It was now obvious that
the king meant to use this vacancy as a means of in-
filtrating the Anglican Church, not just to put pressure
on them to become more co-operative, but to take
over for the Catholic cause a piece of the Established
Church. This is an important distinction. If Anglicans
viewed this merely as one more pressure tactic, some
at least might have been willing to bow to the pressure;
but viewing it as an outright "take-over" bid could
only result in the Church's standing even firmer in
defense of its own. Anthony Farmer's nomination infuriated the Fellows, Oxford itself, and the Church,
because Farmer was not only a court sympathizer, but
a person of scandalous character; nor was he even a
past or present fellow of either Magdalen or New College, which the governing statutes of the college required the president to be. The nomination was thus
illegal as well as unseemly.

[24] Kenyon, *Sunderland*, p. 154.
[25] J. R. Bloxam, *Magdalen College and King James II,
1686–1688*, Oxford, 1886, p. xi.

The college immediately drew up a statement of their objections to Farmer and a petition calling upon the king to nominate someone who would bring credit upon both the college and the king. Four days after depositing the documents with Sunderland, there came the answer that "the King must be obeyed."[26] It is possible that the king himself never even saw the documents. If so, it shows that Sunderland felt certain of the king's mind and so acted on his own. According to the college statutes, April 15 was the deadline for the election of a new president. The Fellows duly met, and a few suggested that the election should be delayed in order to have time to petition the king again. This suggestion failed of adoption, so in the midst of much scurrying about, they proceeded to the election of Dr. John Hough, who was qualified under the statutes. The necessary documents certifying his election were drawn up and he took the required oaths of office. The taking of these oaths had been specifically barred by the king in his nomination of Anthony Farmer—they were now unnecessary, having been suspended by the Declaration of Indulgence. Up to this point, then, Magdalen College had defied the king on three counts: they had refused to elect the royal nominee, they had proceeded to elect their own candidate without royal permission, and they had ignored the Declaration of Indulgence by administering the traditional oaths to their new president. Could the king take this insubordination lying down? No.

Formal word of the election of Hough had been duly sent to the College Visitor, the Bishop of Winchester, who immediately agreed to its statutory validity and so informed Lord Sunderland. The bishop was warned to stop the proceedings, and the vice-president and the Fellows were summoned to appear before the High Commission to explain their disloyalty. The proceedings before the High Commission lasted six months, and the end result was a total victory for the king and

26 Ibid., p. xii.

the virtual destruction of the college. The only attempt the king made at reaching a compromise solution was that he followed his veto of Hough's election with a demand that the bishop of Oxford, Samuel Parker, be elected instead of either Hough or the king's first choice, Anthony Farmer. Since the Fellows were determined to defend their satutory rights to elect, as well as the maintenance of an Anglican tradition at Magdalen, Parker, an all but professed Catholic, was just as unacceptable as Farmer had been. Throughout the commission hearings, the vice-president and the Fellows of Magdalen rested their case solely on their statutes of incorporation, denying that the Declaration of Indulgence had or could release them from any legal or moral obligation to defend them. But "the statutes of colleges," they were told, "had been always considered as things that depended entirely on the King's good pleasure; so that no oaths to observe them could bind them, when they were in opposition to the king's command," and so they were dismissed.[27]

William Penn tried to mediate the dispute, urging the college to make concessions while at the same time stressing to the king the depth of feeling within the college that it was their bounden duty to remain steadfast in their obedience to their statutes. A good deal of controversy has been generated over Penn's role in this affair. Macaulay, of course, attacked Penn as being a tool of the king. Vincent Buranelli argues that Penn and the king were in agreement that the overriding issue was religious toleration—that it was intolerable that Dissenters and Catholics could not freely attend and participate fully in the life of the ancient universities.[28] Even Sunderland has been quoted as saying that it was insufferable that the richest college in Europe should be the private preserve of one religious institution.

[27] Bishop Gilbert Burnet, *History of His Own Times*, Oxford, 1833, III, 155.
[28] See Vincent Buranelli, *The King and the Quaker*, Philadelphia, 1962.

Granted that the affair and the motives of the participants were complex, there are certain clues that can help find a solution. The petition that the Fellows first sent to the king does not seem to have gotten by Sunderland. He himself either knew or anticipated the king's mind and rejected the petition in the king's name on his own. But since it is known that Sunderland was very reluctant to take on the struggle against Magdalen in the first place, it is possible that he did indeed inform the king, but in his Catholic council, not the Privy Council. In any case, Sunderland does seem to have worked closely with Father Petre, who in turn was certainly on close terms with the king. It again seems incredible that James's sole motives were religious toleration; certainly Petre's motives were not so lofty. The king must also be viewed as a man who may have believed in toleration but who had an equally ardent belief in his prerogatives; the Magdalen College episode gave him the rich opportunity to link the two together and to advance both causes simultaneously. Even Dr. Buranelli, a devoted believer in the purity of James's motives, has to admit that the attack on Magdalen was unwise and was in the end a setback for the good cause. To blame Sunderland alone for the setback is surely to go too far in exculpating James and Petre.

Regardless of where the initiative lay within the court, the king was determined to have his way and in the end the election of Hough was disallowed. Parker was sent to the college and took physical possession of his presidential office. The Fellows were ordered to receive him as their leader. All but two newly installed Catholic Fellows refused and were dismissed. The king had his chosen president, but the college was in a shambles—two Fellows and a president, all Catholic, and all the appointments made in violation of the college statutes.

The victory was a hollow one indeed. Even the High Commission began to see fissures in its ranks. Even Lord Chancellor Jeffreys showed signs of regret. Un-

doubtedly James would not again attempt such a struggle against an Oxford college. After all, the Fellows of
Magdalen had managed to defy the king and his High
Commission for seven whole months, with no other
weapons than their loyalty to their statutes and their
oaths. They had remained true to their own consciences
and showed that it was not only those who believed
in toleration who had consciences and were willing
and able to remain true to them. And not only the
Anglicans were impressed by the resistance of the Fellows. The king's utter disregard for the law had at
least mildly shocked members of his own entourage.
Even Penn was willing to plead on the Fellows' behalf
that they were legally in the right and that it was a
matter of conscience as well as law for them.

The Magdalen College affair brought into the open
the same fundamental issues that had been so widely
aired in the decades preceding the civil war of the
1640s. Is the law of England supreme, or are there occasions when a higher law takes precedence? For William Penn religious toleration was a natural law. To
deny full toleration to the king's subjects because of
particular human laws was unjust. If it was necessary
to use the royal prerogative to trample down these unjust laws, so be it. The Jesuits, of course, would be in
complete agreement, at least in so far as justifying a
disregard of the common and statute laws that worked
against the interests of God's one true church. Penn
believed in toleration and would go to almost any
length to get it. The Jesuits believed in the establishment of a universal Catholic world and, in league with
Louis XIV, would go to almost any length to achieve
their goal. James II is a bit more difficult to categorize,
but at least it can be said that whether or not he believed in toleration or a divinely ordained natural law
(and as a Catholic he must have), he certainly did
believe in the existence of a nearly all-powerful and
overriding prerogative power which was in his sole
discretion to use for what he considered to be his and

the nation's interest. The greatest of the Dissenters, the greatest of the Catholics, and the king did have two common areas of agreement: they were determined to destroy the monopoly of the Church of England, and they were willing to go around, above, and below the law of England to achieve their goals. Given the structure of late-seventeenth-century English society, it is not surprising that the mass of Englishmen—Anglican, Dissenter, and Catholic—distrusted Penn, hated Petre and his Jesuits, and feared the king. The rush of enthusiasm for concepts of "fundamental law" in the reigns of James I and Charles I had its culmination in Cromwell's military dictatorship, during which there were times when it seemed that there was in fact no law at all beyond the will of the army. It is not surprising that a generation later similar appeals to a higher law—whether prerogative or natural—would increasingly be distrusted. The events following the exile of James II show that it was not that toleration per se was opposed, but that resort to any and all means to achieve it was the enemy.

David Ogg has written that the Dissenters did not distrust the gift of toleration but the giver of that gift.[29] That the attack on Magdalen College followed so quickly on the heels of the declaration itself was enough to arouse the suspicions even of the most naïve. It seemed that the Marquis of Halifax had prophesied correctly in his *Letter to a Dissenter*, which had been published anonymously during the summer of 1687 but whose true authorship was quickly and surely made known. In this "letter," which has been called the most successful political pamphlet ever published,[30] Halifax warned the Dissenters of the true motives behind the king's declaration. He reminded them that he had first tried an alliance with the Anglicans and had turned to

[29] Ogg, *James II and William III*, p. 181.
[30] The pamphlet went through three editions and 20,000 copies within a year. H. C. Foxcroft, *A Character of a Trimmer*, Cambridge, 1946, p. 237.

the Dissenters only after this effort had failed. Thus James was in principle no particular friend of Dissent as such; this new-found friendship was just a political ploy. He then said, "This alliance, between liberty and infallibility, is bringing together the two most contrary things that are in the world. The Church of Rome doth not only dislike the allowing liberty, but by its principle it cannot do it. Wine is not more expressly forbidden to the Mahometans, than giving heretics liberty is to Papists. . . ."[81] He warned the Quakers in particular that the Roman Church had often denied that they could even be called Christians (a Protestant might be called a heretic, but at least he was admitted to be a Christian). Halifax went on to counsel patience. After all, James would not live forever, and in the reign of his daughter Mary, surely a new day would dawn for the dissenting Protestant. Why sell their souls to the Devil now, when in a few years they would peacefully and legally achieve their hearts' desire, and probably with Anglican approval to boot. (A very good prophecy, indeed.) The great and aging Puritan divine Richard Baxter admitted the force of Halifax's "letter" and knew that it would have a great impact upon the Dissenting conscience.

James II was not the shrewd political tactician his brother, Charles, was, nor was he even as good as his father, Charles I. His handling of the situation during the year 1687 was really disastrous. Since he truly believed that his father had been lacking in firmness, as he thought his brother had, James was determined to press on. He never understood the necessity to let time do his work for him. After issuing the declaration and seeking the open approval of the Dissenters, he should have tried hard to present an image of wise and benevolent toleration. If he was determined to make appointments in Church and state outside the purview of the Test Act, he could at least have appointed

[81] Cobbett IV, p. cxc.

a few Dissenters along with the host of Catholics. But no, it was clear that James was willing to suspend the penal laws for both Catholics and Protestants, but the dispensations under the Test Act were primarily for the benefit of Catholics. Given the rate at which James began to place Catholics into positions of authority, it was clear that the day would come sooner than anyone but James wanted when the administration of the Church and the state would be in Catholic hands. The English people may not have been led en masse to Rome, but the Church and the administration were inexorably speeding down that very road. The publication of Halifax's "letter" did not occur in a vacuum. It became more and more clear as the year wore on what was at stake. The Dissenters were not unimpressed. The attack on Magdalen was itself hardly an example of a benign and tolerant monarch bent on bringing his people together.

Since the declaration and the attack on Magdalen aroused more suspicion than enthusiasm among the Dissenters, James was forced to do everything in his power to carry out his promise to the Dissenters of having the repeal of the penal laws and the Test Act confirmed by an act of Parliament. Sunderland was asked to make soundings of the members of the oft-prorogued Parliament to see if the necessary cooperation was likely to be forthcoming. The result was decidedly in the negative. Thus in July Parliament was at last dissolved, and plans had to be laid for new elections. The preparations for these new elections were to be unlike anything ever seen before or since in England's long parliamentary history. The end result was to strengthen the opposition to James's policies and to James himself.

Only twice before in history had the crown made a really concerted effort to "pack" the House of Commons with men who would support a particular royal policy. Of course, all members were expected to be loyal in general, but only the Parliaments of 1555 and 1685 were elected for their loyalty to a particular program. Philip II of Spain, husband of Mary I, had tried it in order to undo the Protestant reforms of Edward VI's reign, and was not entirely successful. The election of 1685 was based on Charles II's reorganization of the borough franchises, and as we have seen, even this most Tory of Parliaments had largely frustrated James on everything except money. James now realized that his only hope of securing a Parliament favorable to the repeal of the penal laws and the Test Act was to once again remodel the franchise, to the benefit of Dissenters, Catholics, and truly obedient Anglicans. The mere contemplation of such a remodeling is truly the most stupid thing that James could have done. His brother, Charles, had already alienated the old Whigs from loyalty to the Catholic Stuarts, and now James himself would seek to drive the bulk of the Tories into opposition. All he had done so far had angered the Tory and the Anglican and made them fear for their privileges. A new franchise would spell the death of the Tory/Anglican gentry as the ruling class in England—it would destroy them. The mere suggestion that he might issue a Declaration of Indulgence had been enough to drive many prominent Tories into looking over the sea to William of Orange as a potential savior. The actual issuing of the declaration in conjunction with the attack on Magdalen College had already led many of these prominent Tories to begin a correspondence with William and with his ambassador Dyckfeld. The attempt to reorder the power structure in England would force them to go one step further—to actually begin to plot a *coup d'état*.

In the summer of 1687 a group of "regulators" were appointed to examine the existing corporations and their charters and to suggest reforms, and where that was not possible, outright surrender of the charters. While the regulators were busy with this dangerous task, justices of the peace, lords lieutenants, and judges were sent out in mass into both borough and

county constituencies armed with their famous three
questions, by which they hoped to secure the election
of a Parliament favorable to James and to repeal. The
questions were: (1) Would you as a member of the
Commons support repeal? (2) If you were not a candidate, would you support candidates who would favor
repeal? (3) Do you favor the Declaration of Indulgence? Try as they might for as long as they might,
the inquisitors could not report any massive favorable
response to the questions. A new election, even with
a reformed borough franchise, would be a highly dangerous matter for the king.

In the boroughs the regulators were most active in
introducing new men into positions of power, but they
had to rely upon Presbyterians as well as Catholics,
since there were not in fact enough Catholics to fill
all the new openings. In any case their appointment
fitted in well with the current policy of forging an
alliance between the Dissenters and the Catholics.
Sixty-seven former Whig members of the Commons
who had actually voted for exclusion eight years before
were now readmitted to municipal power.[32] In some
corporations, even those who had been involved in riots
against the original borough reforms in the last days
of Charles II's reign were reinstated. The charter reforms of 1687 were, however, not sufficient to revive
any real hopes that James's allies could win a parliamentary election. The new charters gave the king the
right to remove town councilors, but this was not
enough. During 1688 a new wave of reforms began,
and this time the royal authority to intervene was im-
measurably strengthened. James had in fact acquired
three distinct rights, which he would now be willing
to use to the fullest extent: he could use his removal
powers, which all the new charters since 1681 had
provided for; he could threaten corporations with a

[32] See Sir George Duckett, *Penal Laws and Test Act*, London, 1883.

writ of quo warranto; and he could, finally, force a corporation to surrender its charter altogether.[33] The new councilors and officers, whether Catholic or Dissenter, were specifically appointed on the understanding that the test and the Anglican oaths were not to be administered, and that municipal religious ceremonies no longer had to be according to Anglican rites. These reformed corporations were indeed to enjoy an official religious toleration. The results here must have been both a shock and a disappointment to the king, for in London the new Lord Mayor and the aldermen did take the test, ordered that the celebration of Guy Fawkes Day proceed, refused to invite the new papal nuncio, Count d'Adda, to dinner at the royal command, and did continue to hold Anglican services in the Guildhall chapel.[34]

There seems to have been no significant progress whatsoever in forging that alliance between Dissent and Catholicism that was the king's last hope. The Dissenters and the old Whigs may have been willing to take advantage of the situation to ride into power for their own benefit, but as far as the main issue was concerned, they seem to have become even more wary of the king's motives than before and were in practice allying themselves with the Anglican party. And the Anglicans and Tories themselves were driven almost to the brink of revolt.

It has become popular in recent years as part of the reaction against the extreme Whig interpretation of the events of James II's reign to picture James as a man ahead of his time in his devotion to religious liberty and to paint a picture of the opposition as being both bigoted and unpatriotic in that they opposed their king at home for narrow partisan reasons and were at the same time willing to join the Prince of Orange in his own plot to invade England and secure the crown

[33] Levin, pp. 90–95.
[34] Burnet [A], *History*, III, pp. 191–92.

and kingdom for himself. The validity of the first part of this equation has already been discussed. It is now time to look at the second. Was William the author of the scheme to invade England? And if so, when did the plot jell? Were those in England, almost all of them Tory and Anglican peers, the dupes of William, his willing accomplices, or themselves the true authors of the plot? Those who view James as a man of sincerely tolerant religious principles seem unwilling to blame his downfall on his own subjects, and so the blame is put upon William, albeit with the help and advice of a small cabal of English "traitors." For to admit that England itself was not averse to being invaded means either that most of the English people had lost their patriotism, or that James II had simply lost any further hold upon his subjects and that it was in fact the better part of patriotism to eliminate him with the help not of just any foreigner, but with the help of the husband of the heiress to the throne.

It is wrong, then, to think of William as just a foreign prince. Dutch he may have been, but to large numbers of Englishmen he was one of them, and had been so looked upon by Whigs and Tories, Anglican and Dissenter, ever since the first thought emerged of excluding James from the accession in the mid-1670s. William was no more foreign to English politics than James VI of Scotland had been prior to his own accession, in 1603. Indeed, William was a far more active and natural participant in English affairs than James VI had ever been. And this involvement in England's affairs had on many occasions been with the approval of James II or even at James's own instigation. No, one cannot think of William of Orange as a Dutch Protestant Philip II. In the eyes of James II and his Jesuit cabal, he may have been looked upon this way in 1687 and 1688, but this just proves how far out of touch with true English sentiment James now was.

Any definitive statement as to who first conceived the notion of a Dutch intervention in England is now impossible. However, it does seem to be more than probable that the answer lies in England and not in Holland. The great obsession of William's life was the expansion of Bourbon France. William personally had been deprived of his family inheritance of the principality of Orange, and of the family estates in Franche-Comté and in Luxemburg. Since the revocation of the Edict of Nantes, in 1685, the whole future of Continental Protestantism seemed to be hanging in the balance, and there has never been any doubt about his loyalty to the Protestant faith. The threat to the United Provinces themselves was his greatest worry, although a more complex one, because France was not the sole threat to the Dutch provinces. England, too, had fought three wars against them within the past thirty years. But however complex the defense of the Netherlands might be, there can be no question of William's motives here. The greater enemy of his property, his faith, and his country was France. When he looked to England, there was always the question of whether it was a friend or an enemy. For, to William, England represented a property right just as much as the principality of Orange did, both through his wife and through his own more remote claims to the throne. England also meant a bastion of Protestantism to William. Even though he himself might have been considered a Presbyterian in English terms, still he was not so sectarian as not to appreciate the thoroughly Protestant nature of the Church of England. In fact he was undoubtedly more comfortable with Anglicans than with Dissenters for reasons of foreign policy and politics. The commercial interests that were so important an aspect of the Dissenting classes had historically been a greater threat to the commerical aspirations of his own Dutch state than had the Anglicans, with their more rural and agricultural interests. Dissenters in power would be far more acceptable to him if he himself were on the throne, but not with James II, who was still willing to play a pro-French game. The English merchant Dissenters might have been as thoroughly anti-French as anyone, but they still had the old anti-Dutch tradition as well. As long as William was only an outsider looking in on English affairs, it was better to keep England Anglican. In any case, ever since the days of Danby's hegemony under Charles II, in the 1670s, the Tory Anglicans had had an anti-French and pro-Dutch policy. It was, after all, Danby himself who had been so influential in arranging William's marriage to Mary.

William's political interest in England was intimately linked with the religious. However fearful William may have been of James's pro-French inclinations and of his Catholicism, the Dissenters were potentially dangerous as well, not only because of their anti-Dutch traditions but also because of aspects of their political philosophy. The Independents among them had had a long tradition of republicanism—a republicanism that showed signs not only of lingering on, but of actually growing stronger because of the new alliance between a strong royal prerogative and Catholicism. Better the potentially still-royalist philosophy of the Anglicans than any flirting with Independent and Whiggish republicanism.

So William, then, had many reasons to be intimately concerned with and involved in English affairs. But the nature of this involvement and the factions to be supported or opposed constituted an exceedingly complex problem. A united England under James II, with religious toleration for all, a neutral foreign policy, and with Mary retaining her rights unimpaired to a throne which in turn was buttressed with strong prerogative powers, was of course the ideal for William. But this was an ideal that was proving impossible to achieve. To give all-out support to James meant seeing him push Catholics into positions of power and the total and dangerous alienation of the Anglican majority. This would force James to seek support from France, both financial and diplomatic. James's religious, political, and diplomatic policies in turn appeared to be raising the specter of civil war. The outcome of such a war could mean nothing more than the enforced neutrality of England in the European struggle. This would not necessarily have been a bad thing, but the civil struggle in England might not lead to a perpetual stalemate. It could result in victory for one side or the other. A victorious James would undoubtedly have relied upon French support and thus would be able to pursue his Catholic and pro-French policies to their logical conclusion—a conclusion that would not be to the benefit of the United Provinces or of William personally. At the least, he and his wife would undoubtedly be stripped of their rights of inheritance. A royal defeat in a civil war raised the specter of the 1650s all over again. If it actually did come to armed conflict in England, even the Anglicans would be driven to anti-monarchical sentiments, as had happened with many in the earlier civil war. The conclusion could be another anti-Dutch republic, again a result no less distasteful to William than a triumph for the king. The only thing for it, then, was for William to play his hand very carefully and try to guide wherever and whenever possible the forces of opposition into a pattern that would be of the greatest benefit to himself, his wife, and the anti-French cause.

If this analysis of the situation is accurate, it would seem unlikely that William would seek to stir up the possibility of rebellion in England. It is also extremely unlikely that he would contemplate invasion on his own. If he did attempt an invasion and it failed, he would be worse off than ever. The most probable answer is that he watched events closely, kept in touch with all factions, including the court, hoped for the maintenance of the status quo, and was preparing to intervene if and when it was not only necessary to prevent utter chaos in England but would also have a good chance of success. William was not so much the schemer as the interested observer and practical opportunist. In the end England would have to take the lead in solving its own affairs. William could not control those affairs, he could only capitalize on the opportunities presented to him by others. It was a matter of knowing everything and everyone and being able to judge accurately the differences between appearances and realities. William may not have been a great or even a daring man, but he was shrewd and realistic. The last thing in the world that he wanted was an ill-timed and ill-conceived invasion of England, with James II being in a position to wrap the mantle of patriotism around himself. William, not James, had to become the symbol of English patriotism, and only Englishmen themselves could provide him with that mantle. If they provided the mantle, he would know how to wear it.

The possibility that William would intervene in English affairs had been there from the time of the Exclusion Crisis. But the real question is, what does his intervention mean? If it means only that he was in touch with various political leaders, then it has no special significance. All governments maintain contacts with political leaders in other countries. And it goes without saying that such contact is not always limited simply to the gathering of information, but that influence is sought and exerted. With Louis XIV serving as the paymaster for so many in England, one would have to expect some activity from William. If, on the other hand, we mean by intervention an armed intrusion, then the question is more complex, as we have shown. Those who sought William's intervention during the Exclusion Crisis do not seem to have had military intervention in mind. But at some point prior to November 1688 he must have made up his mind. When? Why? For what purpose? According to Bishop Burnet, nothing was settled until the spring of 1688.[85] Lucile Pinkham[86] dates it from 1686, as the result of a meet-

[85] Burnet [A], *History*, III, p. 276.
[86] Pinkham, pp. 76 and 100.

ing between William and Burnet himself. But it would seem unlikely that Burnet would play down his own important role, if indeed he had played such a role, when he came, after the Revolution, to write his history. There certainly should have been nothing for him to fear in making the truth known after the event. Because of the failure of any of the actors in the drama to record explicitly the details of the plot, we are forced to rely upon Burnet. Without him we have nothing but surmise and circumstantial evidence.

Dr. Stephen Baxter in his excellent biography of William III has chosen to rely upon a close reading of Burnet, and, Mrs. Pinkham to the contrary notwithstanding, he is probably right in doing so.[37] According to Burnet, the first—in point of time—to urge that William come over was Viscount Mordaunt, who had first come to prominence as one of the excluders and as a petitioner against the holding of a Parliament at Oxford in 1681. This "hot" Whig was associated with plottings and intrigues from then on, but there is no evidence that William showed any particular interest, promising only "that he should have an eye on the affairs of England."[38]

While Dyckfeld was on his embassy to England in the spring of 1687, he seems to have attended a meeting at the home of the Earl of Shrewsbury that was also attended by the Marquis of Halifax; the Earls of Devonshire, Danby, and Nottingham; Viscount Mordaunt; Lords Lumley, Herbert, and Russell; and the Bishop of London. Burnet summed up the fruits of this meeting by saying: ". . . he [Dyckfeld] formed a society of some of the nobility who wished well to their religion and country, who were to consult such advices and advertisements as might be fit for the Prince to know from time to time, that he might govern himself thereby. And it was by their directions that

[37] Stephen Baxter, *William III*, London, 1966, ch. 17.
[38] Burnet [A], *History*, III, pp. 274–75.

the Prince formed all his motions, and by their encouragement that he engaged at last in the great design of delivering the kingdom."[39] The initiative for the meeting does not seem to have come from Dyckfeld himself. And it is clear that the group were anxious to serve William, but that they considered that they served themselves and England best by serving William. Again, it does not seem likely that a group as distinguished as these were merely the tools of a foreign intriguer.

When Dyckfeld finally departed from English shores he carried with him letters addressed to the prince. Among them were those of Danby, Mordaunt, Churchill, Colonel Bellasyse, Nottingham, Clarendon, Rochester, Mr. Fitzpatrick, Halifax, Devonshire, Shrewsbury, Sir George Mackenzie, and the Bishop of London, Bedford. The letters conveyed a general sense of good will toward William and also the request that he listen closely to what Dyckfeld had to report orally. They stressed that he had been thoroughly informed as to their sentiments. The most likely implications were that Dyckfeld was carrying their sentiments and perhaps even their dreams back to William. There was no implication that Dyckfeld came in the first place in order to inform them of William's plans. It is again worth repeating that whatever may have been William's grand European design, as far as England was concerned there were many powerful, distinguished, and thoroughly patriotic men, largely Tories, who wanted William's help in finding a solution to their own and their country's problems.

Following the return of Dyckfeld to his master, the course of events began to quicken, and what had been the separate paths trod by England and the United Provinces, William and James, court and opposition, all came together in preparation for the *annus mirabilis* of 1688.

[39] Burnet [B], *History*, pp. 258–59.

CHAPTER 5

William of Orange and Louis XIV

The last quarter of the seventeenth century in Europe was dominated by one great fact: the determination of Louis XIV to achieve lasting glory for himself and for the France of which he was the personal embodiment and the symbol. Considering that France was almost perpetually at war with the rest of Western Europe from the early days of the Thirty Years' War (1618–48) until the final defeat of Napoleon at Waterloo, in 1815, it is perhaps too simplistic to place such a heavy weight of responsibility upon the shoulders of Louis personally. It might be truer to say that there were many inexorable forces at work in Europe during these two centuries that made of Louis merely a temporary actor in the great drama, and that in fact he was just another puppet in the hands of historical forces beyond his ability to control. While this was undoubtedly true in some grand cosmological sense, still it was also true that Louis considered himself, and was so considered by others, to be the great moving force in European history, a man who picked up the torch first lighted by Richelieu and was to create for himself and his country a status not occupied by any European country since Charlemagne. And like Charlemagne, the role of the individual is essential to an understanding of the time.

What also made this quarter century remarkable was that the opposition to Louis XIV was also to be dominated and symbolized by one man—William of Orange. It wasn't so much Europe against Louis or even the Dutch against Louis as it was William versus Louis. For William conceived of himself and was accepted by others as the almost divine agent commissioned by God to call a halt to the expansion and domination of the political and religious system fashioned and led by Louis. It was precisely because the struggle against Louis was so thoroughly entwined with the personality and interests of William that he was able to be so successful in that opposition, and at the same time it was the cause of so many of the difficulties that beset him on his road to success. The relative standing of the United Provinces in the hierarchy of power in late-seventeenth-century Europe was not such as to make them the natural leader of the opposition on their own merits. The decisive factor was the overwhelming determination, courage, and daring of William, who was eventually able to draw upon a united force of both the Netherlands and England.

William's position as husband to the heiress to the English and Scottish thrones, and a more remote claim of his own, provided the necessary extra weight to make it possible for him to survive within the United Provinces themselves against the opposition of the States-General and the narrow commercial world, fearful of the growing hegemony of the house of Orange within the United Provinces, which they represented. If there had not been the possibility that one day he might be much greater than he was, even greater than the United Provinces put together, he might never have survived at home. England, then, was crucial to William, both as a base for his own personal authority at home and as a potential ally in the greater struggle against Louis. The pro-French proclivities of both Charles II and James II were naturally most unwelcome to William, but as long as his wife was in line to

inherit the throne, he could afford the temporary dis-
comfort, secure in the knowledge that the future would
be his. For this reason he could not help but support
his father-in-law, James, against the efforts of the Whigs
to exclude him in 1679–81. He could not afford to gamble then that the exclusionists would win, with himself and Mary as the sure inheritors of James's rights.
After James had come to the throne and was faced with
the rebellion of his "natural" nephew, the Duke of
Monmouth, William again had to remain true to James.
The retention of Mary's rights as heiress was the one
absolute essential in his policy. Even a Catholic England allied to France was preferable to the chance of
losing Mary's inheritance, for that could well mean the
loss of his power at home as well. And if that were lost,
his whole life's work would turn to ashes.

Fortunately for William, the foreign, political, and
religious inclinations of both Charles II and James II
were so largely opposed by powerful elements within
England that neither king could really feel free to
carry out his desires with sufficient strength and continuity to cause William any great damage. On the
other hand, he could never contemplate the unlimited
success of that opposition, because too many among
them were either republican in their political inclinations or were anti-Dutch. Thus the best that William
could hope for was stalemate in England, which in
turn meant her essential neutrality in foreign policy.
William could afford to be patient, just as the English
opposition could afford to be patient. James had come
to the throne past the prime of life and was not thought
to have too many years left to him. In the end, all
would be well for both William and for England itself.
William was even aided by James's single-minded goal
of establishing Catholicism at home, since the opposition he encountered would help to guarantee that
neutrality in military terms. William was also aided by
the fact that James II was, in spite of his religious and
constitutional views, still a patriotic Englishman. Even
he was not so blind to the international realities as to

fail to see that England's own national interest would
be compromised by a too successful Louis XIV. James's
own interests in English overseas, especially American,
colonial and commercial expansion, made him aware
that the Dutch were not England's only or even most
important rival. France was a growing factor there, too.

In retrospect 1685 appears to have been a remarkable
turning point in the lives of England, France, and the
United Provinces, and in those of William, Louis, and
James. The accession of James II and the revocation
of the Edict of Nantes were to unleash thitherto pent-up
forces that would show the basic unity of the European
struggle and that England was from now on an integral
part of the struggle. It is in William of Orange that we
have the linchpin that holds the whole structure of
England and Europe together. Without William it is
difficult to see any such coming together of all the dy-
nastic, religious, and imperial elements that composed
Europe. No one but William could have brought England into the forefront of the European scene at this
time and made her such a central factor that all had
to concern themselves with her.

Contemporaries, however, were still not as thoroughly aware of the central position that England was
on the verge of playing on the European stage. For
most, the central issue around which all the elements
were revolving was the question of the succession to
the soon (supposedly) vacant Spanish throne. To Louis
XIV the Spanish succession seemed to be the one great
issue. Yet in the long run, the succession of William of
Orange to the throne of England was to have a far
greater impact on the course of European history than
the succession to the throne of Spain of a grandson of
Louis XIV—Philip V. But the demise of the last Spanish Hapsburg was not to take place for many years after
the alliance was forged between England and the
Netherlands by William's skill in being able to correctly
judge the English situation and its link with the broader
European situation.

The revocation of the Edict of Nantes, in 1685, was the other great fact that so mightily influenced the future of late-seventeenth-century Europe. By the revocation, Louis sought not merely to remove the rights of the Huguenots in their own political and military enclaves such as La Rochelle; he also desired the total elimination of the existence of the Protestant "stain" from the face of Catholic, Christian France. The persecution that was now to sweep France and the mass exodus of Huguenot intellectuals, artisans, and merchants was in fact to have a greater impact on Europe in general than on France itself. The traditional view that this Huguenot migration weakened France intellectually and commercially has been challenged in recent years, and it has been pointed out that the real impact was upon opinion in the countries to which the Huguenots migrated.[1] Certainly the terror in France itself and the plight in store for those who arrived in the England of James II had a great deal to do with arousing the fear and the anger of Anglicans and Dissenters alike, contributing to the Dissenters' distrust of James's protestations of religious toleration. It strengthened the position of William within the Netherlands, because his habitual anti-French policy could now be seen in a broader light and the States-General were one with him in their desire to serve the Protestant cause and save it and themselves from meeting with the same fate as their brothers in France. The revocation thus had the effect of helping to create the climate of opinion in which it would be much easier to weld an anti-French alliance. Protestant Germans were to feel this same impulse, and even the Emperor, in Vienna, could not be totally immune to it. Even the Pope realized that the harsh, Jesuitical policies of Louis XIV threatened the unity of Europe, which was necessary to confront the westward movement of the Turks

[1] John B. Wolfe, *Toward a European Balance of Power, 1620–1715*, Chicago, 1970, pp. 87–88.

into the heart of Christian Europe. And of course the Papacy has never liked those who claim to be more dedicated to the Catholic cause than Rome itself.

Thus the year 1685 had ushered onto the European scene two factors—the accession of James II and the revocation of the Edict of Nantes—that were to prepare the way for revolution in England, the forging of an alliance between England and the Netherlands, and the creation of a western alliance against the aggressive programs of Bourbon France. But these factors do not necessarily tell us why Louis decided to bring to an end the peace that had settled upon western Europe in 1678. Naturally the European situation looked much different to Louis sitting in Versailles than it did to William in The Hague, Innocent XI in Rome, or even to James II in London. Early in 1688 the Holy Roman Emperor was on the verge of winning a decisive victory over the Turks at Belgrade, and with this great Christian victory behind him he would be in a very strong position to pressure the Pope to grant the vacant electoral throne in Cologne to his own brother. This potential strengthening of the Hapsburg power in western Germany was not something that any French king, much less a Bourbon, could contemplate with equanimity. The Catholic policies of James II in England were not without their dangers to Louis also. He was aware of the commercial rivalry between England and the Dutch, but he was also aware of the Protestant and anti-French backlash that these policies were generating. Louis, in fact, felt called upon to suggest that James be less precipitate and show more cunning and more patience in the pursuit of the Catholicizing of England. Chaos in England would guarantee her neutrality even more effectively than would any amount of subsidizing of James and his court; but if the result were, rather than chaos, a Protestant republic, or even worse the accession of William of Orange, this would be most dangerous to France. The memory of the Cromwellian republic was not a pleasant one. Even though Crom-

wellian England had fought a war against the Dutch,
Cromwell achieved his greatest overseas successes
against the French in the West Indies and had assumed
the mantle of protector of French Protestants.

The dangers Louis could see on the horizon for
France served to convince him that it would be better
to take the offensive and attempt to control events
rather than wait to see what the future might bring. It
seemed essential to pre-empt the Hapsburg move back
into western Germany by an attack on the Rhineland.
He was also convinced by the Marquis de Louvois, his
military commander, that the most appropriate lesson
from England's past was the decade of civil war in
the 1640s, not the decade of the Cromwellian Protectorate in the 1650s. During the '40s England was
forced to abdicate any foreign role because of the Civil
War. Another civil war in England could have the same
effect; and if William and the Dutch did get involved
in it, then the United Provinces would also be immobilized, thus giving Louis the free hand he wanted in
getting control of Cologne, the Palatinate, and indeed
the whole German Rhineland. This was a fundamental
miscalculation, for which Louis was to pay most dearly.
He failed to credit William with enough sense not to
engage himself in the English domestic scene until he
was quite certain of success. Louis saw only chaos
impending in England. William waited to see the possibilities of bringing order out of that chaos before he
was willing to strike. It was to be Louis who played into
William's hands, not the other way around.

Western Europe had been technically at peace since
the signing of the Treaty of Nymwegen, in July of
1678. This temporary end to the Franco-Dutch war
had created a stalemate that the Dutch, at least, felt
they could live with. In return for economic concessions
that allowed the Dutch merchants to resume their traditional trading patterns, the French were given control over some fortresses on the south side of the
Spanish Netherlands, with the remainder of the Spanish

Netherlands being retained as a buffer between the United Provinces and France. A subsequent treaty between France and Spain served to guarantee the success of the treaty between the Dutch and the French and also had the effect of destroying the alliance against the French. The German states could no longer stand alone, and they, too, were to sign separate treaties within the next months which at last brought peace to the West. The peace was important to England because it freed Charles II from having to play the delicate game of balancing off William and Louis and thus enabled Charles to face the Exclusion Crisis with a freer hand and a clearer conscience. At least it had the effect of temporarily cooling off the anti-French mood that was sweeping England, thus strengthening the king in his relationship with the exclusion Parliaments; and at the same time it allowed Charles to secretly work his way back into French graces, resuming the subsidies that would free him from the necessity of calling Parliament again once the Exclusion Crisis was over. While it may well have been a temporary setback for Charles's foreign policy, it was to be helpful to him and to James II, peace in Europe proving to be healthier for the two brothers than war.

The closing days of 1687 and the first weeks of 1688 saw the whole world of William of Orange reach a most threatening turning point. In December it was announced that James II's queen, Mary Beatrice of Modena, was pregnant. This news came as a bombshell to William and Mary, and to the opposition in England. Among all those who wanted to believe it—and there were many—this was nothing but a fraud and an attempt to deny Mary of her right of accession. For two years the Catholics surrounding James had dropped hints that the succession would be altered unless William showed a willingness to support James's religious policies. At first the prospect was held out that Mary's younger sister, Anne, Princess of Denmark, would be the beneficiary. But Anne was a devout Anglican and devout supporter of the Stuart dynasty. She had let her father and the Catholics know of her determination to remain loyal to her church and was thus barely more acceptable as heiress in the eyes of the Catholic cabal than Mary. In the direct Stuart line after Mary and Anne were the Queen of Spain and the Duchess of Savoy, both Catholics, but the succession being altered in their favor would have been impossible to contemplate, even by one as politically unbalanced as James was now becoming. To both William and Mary the most likely way to alter the succession was by James foisting an infant boy upon the world as his own legitimate son and heir. James's enemies, including his daughters, had come to assume as a simple fact that James was old, sick, and perhaps even dying. They firmly believed that either the queen was not pregnant at all, or that if she were, the child would be sickly and soon die, leaving the situation as it had been before. The birth of a healthy Prince of Wales in June 1688 was a great shock, and the only possible explanation for it was that it was a dastardly trick.

The acceptance of the probability of a supposititious child at the time of the announcement of the queen's pregnancy is an important part of the whole story. One of the problems that have bothered historians in recent years is the attempt to date with some precision William's final determination to invade England. We have already seen that the English opposition was looking for his intervention as a means of securing their own salvation. Yet William, as we have also seen, was well aware of the dangers. It has recently become fashionable to date William's final determination long before the summer of 1688.[2] The assumption back in December of 1687 that the news of the queen's pregnancy was nothing but a hoax might lend credence to the claim that he had at least by then settled upon his plan.

[2] See Lucile Pinkham, *William III and the Respectable Revolution*, Cambridge, Mass., 1954, and Maurice Ashley, *The Glorious Revolution of 1688*, New York, 1966.

But the fact that both Mary and William sincerely doubted that even a real child could be healthy would indicate that William was not yet determined upon military intervention. He would have to wait upon events to see if there really was a pregnancy and if so whether or not the child would live. It would seem that anyone as shrewd and cautious as William would not plan precipitately to invade when there still might be no need for it. And in any case, until Louis XIV's own military dispositions were more clear, William could not possibly consider an intervention seriously.

One of the arguments in favor of a long-range plan by William is based on the historic difficulty of successfully launching a cross-Channel invasion. It had not been done successfully since 1066. It is thus assumed that William would need many months, if not years, in which to gather the forces necessary for the grand attack. But since William had spent most of his adult life in the military and naval preparations necessary to counter the rising power of Bourbon France, he wasn't actually starting from scratch when and if he were to decide on the attack on England. He did, however, appreciate the tremendous task involved, and for that reason he could not make definite dispositions until two things largely beyond his personal control had happened: (1) The opposition in England must be able to give him some real assurance of success, and (2) the mighty forces that Louis XIV was gathering had to be neutralized. And they could not be neutralized by William himself if he were stripping the Netherlands in launching an attack on England. The direction in which Louis was moving militarily in 1688 was hopeful in that he seemed more interested in stopping the growth of Imperial influence in the Rhineland, but he had not yet moved there decisively. Within England itself, the opposition was forced also to wait upon events. Then, too, there was the same need to doubt the authenticity of the queen's pregnancy, and yet there was also the need to wait further upon events. None of the friendly and co-operative letters that Dyckfeld and, a few months later, in the fall of 1687, Zuylestein had transmitted to William constituted a definite invitation or an assurance of success. They wanted William to guarantee *them* success, and William wanted such guarantees from them first. Undoubtedly William spent the first six months of 1688 thinking deeply about the various possibilities, but it does seem doubtful that the final and irrevocable decisions had been taken.

The queen's pregnancy naturally overjoyed the king, and he now felt that his position was much strengthened. On the assumption that the baby would be a boy, the future was bright. No longer would his plans for the establishment of Catholicism in England come to naught at his own death. The boy would be raised as a Catholic and as a firm defender of the royal prerogatives. James now felt much freer to antagonize William and to seek more openly a closer relationship with Louis. During the winter of 1688 James devoted much effort to securing the return of the English garrison from the Netherlands and sought to persuade Louis to pay their expenses. The English had maintained a garrison in the Netherlands since Elizabethan times. While in the pay of the States-General, the troops were still English subjects. After a century, their precise role was almost impossible to define. If the troops were actually loyal to William, it was in the interest of both James and Louis to get them out of Dutch hands. If they were still loyal to their English king, then they could either serve as hostages to William's fortunes or as an opening wedge for English pressure to intimidate William. James's first concern was to remove them from Holland and have Louis care for them in France. This would be a form of assistance from James to Louis at no cost to James himself. But most of the soldiers were Protestant, and Louis could not make any exceptions to his anti-Protestant policy following the revocation of the Edict of Nantes. If the garrisons were merely brought home to England, then

James himself would have to provide for them; in addition, it might be taken amiss by the opposition. The memory of Charles I and Strafford contemplating bringing over the Irish army in 1640 "in order to subdue this kingdom" was surely not forgotten. Even those Anglicans still loyal to James and the moderate Catholics both tried to dissuade him from bringing the garrisons back. James was adamant, however, and commanded the return to England of those of his subjects, both English and Scottish, serving in the Dutch garrisons. Those who were Catholic did, by and large, obey; but the Protestants—and they were the larger part—refused. Louis was eventually persuaded to provide a subsidy for three regiments who did return to England. The result of all this was to further alienate William from James, with the States-General moving closer in sympathy to William. The opposition in England was made even more fearful for the future, and James was again moving closer to Louis, and this time it was being done more openly than before.

The idea of bringing the English and Scottish garrisons back from Holland seems to have originated in the subtle mind of Lord Sunderland. He assumed that it would weaken the Dutch, strengthen the king at home, and prove pleasing enough to Louis to induce him to increase his financial aid to James and to himself personally. The earl was a great spendthrift, never able to live within what were really vast means. Once James had started openly and aggressively on his Catholicizing policy, Sunderland bet on the king's ultimate success in alliance with Louis. For the first time in his long ministerial career he threw all personal caution to the winds and devoted himself completely to the service and, more importantly, to the policies of the king. In fact he appears to have been even more wedded to the notion of an Anglo-French alliance and a break with William than James himself. Like the gambler that he was, Sunderland was now quite knowingly and deliberately playing for the highest stakes. All his chips were now on the table, and it was either total victory or total destruction. The days of balancing off one side against the other, foreign and domestic, were now over. Sunderland had gambled on the king and on Louis. He had no further choice but to use every wile, every subtlety, every influence at his command to commit James himself to what were fast becoming Sunderland's own policies, at least as regards foreign policy. The return of the garrisons from Holland would be at Sunderland's own disposal if anything were to happen to the king. But the whole episode was a failure as far as Sunderland was concerned. It strengthened William rather than weakened him at home. Louis was not at all impressed, since he had little or no need or regard for the English army. Where Sunderland assumed that Louis would be grateful for an alliance with England, all Louis actually wanted was her neutrality. And once it had become obvious that Sunderland was now for all practical purposes a hostage to French fortunes, why waste any more money in subsidizing him? Civil war in England, in fact, would suit Louis's purposes quite effectively. There was far more calculation than sentiment in Louis's policy. It is incredible that a schemer of the caliber of Sunderland might have thought the contrary.

What little England had that might interest Louis was the navy. The French fleet was largely committed to the Mediterranean, and an enlarged English fleet allied to the French would be of great help in challenging Dutch naval supremacy in the North Sea and the Baltic. Louis hoped that James would double the size of his force at sea and enter the North Sea and the Baltic to engage the Dutch. Even Sunderland could not bring himself to advise James to go this far. The navy was thoroughly Protestant and let it be known that "popish" officers would be thrown overboard if the king tried to saddle them upon the navy. And in any case the money to finance such an enlarged fleet could be obtained only from an anti-Dutch, pro-French Parliament. Sunderland knew better than anyone that such a Parliament was not in the cards at any point during the fall of 1687 or the winter of 1688. Thus the circle was nearly complete, and it was to prove to be a vicious one. James could not give Louis the help Louis really wanted and needed unless the Catholic and anti-Anglican policy were first abandoned. But if it were abandoned, then James had no need for his alliance with the French anyway. It was becoming more and more obvious that James was in a trap of his own and Sunderland's design. Their only hope for salvation was the birth of a son.

Throughout all these winter months of 1687–88 the haggling between Sunderland and Barillon went on. Sunderland, who had seemed so set on doing all in his power to help the French, was peculiarly resistant to the idea that England should find a way of putting a large fleet to sea. To Louis there seemed to be much more appearance than substance to Sunderland's commitment to the French cause. He even took the papal side against the French in the affairs in Rome. As Louis thought it all over he grew convinced that Sunderland was merely hoping for personal subsidies and would help France only to the extent to which Louis bought his allegiance, or else he and the king were really patriotic Englishmen at heart. This was a shrewder guess in the case of James than in that of the earl. A darker suspicion arose in Louis's mind that perhaps Sunderland was already preparing the way for the future and was in secret league with William. It is true that the Countess of Sunderland had written to William in her own hand in the previous autumn, and in the letter she shows her loyalty to the Anglican Church. The question remains whether this letter was actually written by her alone, in consultation with her husband, or whether she merely copied what he himself had written. The fact that Sunderland was able to enter William's service after the Revolution is not necessarily proof that he was already secretly working for him, but it does present the possibility.

As spring came to Europe in the year 1688, Louis was planning his expedition into the Rhineland. William was more and more apprehensive of Louis's plans for his newly enlarged army and also of the moderate efforts of the English to strengthen their force at sea. William countered by building up his own fleet, and this in turn created a fear in England that William might be plotting to attack. James II was growing both bolder and more impatient. As the day of the queen's delivery drew near he became bolder, but as the Dutch fleet became more menacing he became fearful that it would be directed toward England. But James was not one to either quit or merely sit back and wait upon events. His "forward" policy had to be pursued at all costs, and those at home who stood in his way would have to be taught a lesson. A king of England does not suffer himself to be dissuaded from doing God's and the nation's good work just because of the stubbornness and intransigence of some of his subjects. James, almost alone at this late date, still assumed that the doctrines of non-resistance which the Anglican Church and the Tory party had so often proclaimed would still prevail and carry him and his soon-to-be-born son through to ultimate victory. Sunderland knew better.

CHAPTER 6

The Invitation

The joyful anticipation of the birth of a son did not exclude for long all lingering doubts as to the future. That the boy would be raised as a Catholic and upholder of the royal prerogative would not alone guarantee the perpetuation of James II's new program. The chance was thought to be very good, even by James himself, that the old king might not live to see his son reach his majority. Since the constitution, as it had evolved over the centuries, contained no automatic machinery by which to provide for the accession of a minor, there was a very real chance that any attempt by Queen Mary of Modena to rule the king and kingdom during her son's minority would meet with armed resistance. The same fate would also lie in store for James's Catholic council. The only effective way to provide for the minority reign of his son was to have his wishes formalized and made legally binding by an act of Parliament. James could not even resort to the use of his own last will and testament in order to provide for the future of the realm, as Henry VIII had done, since Henry VIII had been allowed to do this by a special act of Parliament applicable only to himself. Once again James was faced with the impossible question of how to get a Parliament that would in fact be willing to co-operate with him? For over a year he and Sunderland had been working on the problem. Even though James had a tendency to delude himself about the fundamental loyalty of the

Anglican Tories, he never could completely discount Sunderland's warnings that the time for the election was not yet ripe. But the queen's pregnancy seemed to make the calling of a new Parliament even more essential, and thus James once again renewed his offensive against the Church and the Tory leaders in the counties and boroughs. He still assumed that they could be bludgeoned into co-operation. Of course the real effect of this bludgeoning was to be just the opposite.

The reorganization of the boroughs continued apace, and a wholesale purge of lords lieutenants and justices of the peace was undertaken. Some of the greatest families in England were to feel the ax of dismissal, among them the 20th Earl of Oxford, a De Vere, the scion of the great medieval family that was one of the few that had managed to survive the ravages of the Wars of the Roses and the depredations of Henry VII and Henry VIII. Another of the great names, Talbot, Earl of Shrewsbury, was also to suffer deprivation of all offices. These were merely two of the most prominent men who were forced to bow to the royal will. The shock to the system was naturally the greater because of their very pre-eminence. Sunderland had bowed to the inevitable by announcing his own conversion to the Roman Church; the Lord Chancellor, Jeffreys, was to remain a Protestant, and even this most willing and co-operative of James's agents began to show signs of wavering in his absolute support of the royal program. At least he was perceptive enough to know that James was rocking the boat, and he does not seem to have been anxious to be one of those who would be cast overboard by the tidal wave of the reaction that James's policies was bound to create.[1] Meanwhile, the famous, or infamous, "three questions" were still being put to the potential candidates and to the electors for a new Parliament—all with no favorable result.

[1] T. B. Macaulay, *The History of England from the Accession of James the Second*, Chicago, 1888, Vol. II, p. 288.

As winter drew to a close, and all his hopes for the future except the queen's pregnancy seemed to be coming to naught, James seems to have feared that some further and decisive step had to be taken to dispel any possible suggestion that he had reached the end and was about to moderate his stand on the Catholic issue. The proof of his continued determination was the reissuing of the Declaration of Indulgence, April 27, 1688. The second declaration was in substance a repeat of the first, but to it was added an explanatory note in which he expressed his determination that no one should assume any wavering on his part. He also defended the wholesale changes that had been made in the ranks of the borough and county officeholders. He said that no one should hold such office "who will not contribute towards the peace and greatness of their country." To very many this meant that James should remove his Catholic officeholders, since it was their appointments that were likely to destroy the "peace and greatness" of the kingdom.

As disturbing as the reissuing must have been to the Church, the order in council of May 4, 1688, commanding that the declaration be read aloud in every church in the kingdom on four separate occasions, May 20 and 27 in London and June 3 and 10 elsewhere, was a total shock. Perhaps this order should not be labeled as the cause of the Glorious Revolution, but it certainly initiated a sequence of events that led inexorably to that revolution. The Church was being commanded by the king, under his authority as their supreme governor, to give their sign of approval to his Catholicizing policy by the mere act of reading the declaration. The acquiescence of the clergy was no doubt fully expected. The Church had stressed passive obedience to the crown with such consistency and fervor since the Restoration that James really had every right to assume once more that, regardless of how much muttering under the breath there might be, the tradition of obedience would prevail. The Imperial ambassador, however, seems to have thought that the possibility of disobedience was anticipated and was indeed one reason for the command. Von Ranke summed up the situation thus:

This order was, as it were, double-edged; indeed it was intended to be so. If the clergy complied, they themselves recognised the legality of the step which was directed against them, and gave up their own cause; if they resisted they fell into contradiction with their doctrine of obedience, and seemed likely to estrange the Nonconformists by their conduct.[2]

There was a long-standing tradition that the clergy could be called upon to read public documents in the churches. In this sense James would appear to be within his rights in commanding it this time. On the other hand, in the past the documents that were read were either authorized by statute or they were royal proclamations dealing with purely secular affairs, and the Church was always willing to be co-operative here. But now James was using his authority as head of the Church to command the clergy to do what in the eyes of so many of the clergy was tantamount to the destruction of the Church, which they were commanded by law to protect and defend. The refusal to read the declaration was tantamount to a denial of its legality. Did the Church in fact have the right to pass upon the legality of the use of the royal prerogative? In *Godden* v. *Hales* the court had decided that the king did have a dispensing power. No court had as yet ruled on the legality of the first Declaration of Indulgence, and even though many had refused to recognize it, many others had. In any case, was it within the province of the Church to assume a right of "judicial review" and pass judgment on the declaration's legality? It would certainly seem that it was not. However we interpret the motives of the king—religious toleration or the destruction of the Anglican Church—and however we view

[2] Leopold von Ranke, *History of England Principally in the Seventeenth Century*, Oxford, 1875, Vol. IV, p. 345.

the motives of the Church—the preservation of the law and the constitution or the defense of established privilege—the fact is that this order in council was crucial to both James and the Church. Whatever action the Church took, would violate one or another of the sacred principles it upheld. The whole Tory/Anglican system of thought was based on the assumption that Church and crown were but two aspects to one basic reality: the kingdom of England itself. James had now driven them to the point where it was no longer possible to defend one without the loss of the other. The dilemma was cruel and impossible to reconcile as long as James remained king or persisted in his policy. Since there was now no doubt of the king's determination, the Church really had no way out. The only question was, which of its two loyalties was to take precedence— loyalty to itself or loyalty to the crown? It was not long before the answer was forthcoming: The Church had to come first.

James II, the Earl of Sunderland, and indeed all those who had allied themselves totally with the king, assumed that the Church's opposition to the Declaration of Indulgence was based solely upon bigotry and/ or the preservation of the clerical and political monopoly that the Church had managed to secure since the Restoration. The complete acceptance of this interpretation by some recent historians makes it very difficult, if not impossible, to see much connection between this opposition prior to 1689 and the later passage of the Act of Toleration of 1689 except as something forced upon the Church and the Tories by the victorious Whigs after the completion of the Revolution. What has been overlooked is that the Church and the Dissenters were fast becoming allies, if not friends, ever since the possibility of a suspension of the penal laws and of the test was first hinted at. It would seem that this closing of the gap that separated the two Protestant establishments was to take on a coloration that was neither solely tactical nor merely for the duration of this one particular crisis. Among Anglicans there seems to have been a growing awareness that the defense of Protestantism and of the liberties of Englishmen and of the ruling elite on both the national and the local levels could not be guaranteed without some measure of toleration being granted by the Church to the Dissenters. The Tory/Anglican Sir John Reresby, the old friend of James II and governor of the City of York, commented in his *Memoirs* for May 7, 1688, just three days after the issuance of the infamous Order in Council, "I believed most men were now convinced that liberty of conscience was a thing of advantage to the nation, as it might be setled [sic] with due reguard [sic] to the rights and privileges of the Church of England."[3]

There is good evidence that Reresby was correct in his appreciation of the changing climate among leading Anglicans. At least the clergy were able to convince the Dissenters of their sincerity in this matter. The shock of the Order in Council had barely worn off before the leaders in the Anglican hierarchy approached leading Dissenters to gauge their own possible responses to a variety of Anglican reactions to the order. The response was nearly all that the clergy could hope for. It seems unlikely that the Dissenters were so little concerned with toleration that they would support the Anglicans solely on constitutional grounds. Dr. Edward Fowler, Vicar of St. Giles, representing the hierarchy, approached the ever-available Presbyterian leader, Roger Morrice. Morrice had already prepared a statement listing the reasons why the Church should not obey the order. It said that it was "most heinously criminal to publish the Prince's private will and pleasure against his legal and incontrovertible will." It went on to say that "the dispensing power . . . overthrows the very Constitution of the Government."[4] These were

[3] Sir John Reresby, *Memoirs*, edited by Andrew Browning, Glasgow, 1936, p. 497.

[4] Lacey, p. 210.

the arguments of the classic Whigs, who strove to separate the person of the king from the institution of the crown. The king should speak only the law of the land or keep silent. It was also assumed that neither the king as a person, nor the crown as an institution, could effectively override the will of the nation as expressed through acts of Parliament. The suspending power as exercised in the Declaration of Indulgence was thus assumed to be illegal, since it did have the effect of repealing a whole host of statutory laws. The Dissenters of course wanted religious toleration for themselves, but they wanted it to come through what in their Whiggish eyes were proper constitutional means. They still were mindful of the lessons learned in the Long Parliament in the 1640s. The law and the constitution were the first and foremost guarantees of the rights of all Englishmen. The willingness of the Dissenters to cooperate in this time of crisis for the Church went a long way to assure the success of the Revolution when it would come, and perhaps it actually hastened that day, for without the prior guarantee of Dissenter support, it is possible that the Church would not have stood up to James, but would have had to fall back on the tradition of obedience and read the declaration. For the Anglicans needed allies just as surely as did the king and the Dissenters. They could not afford to alienate both.

Fortified in advance with the knowledge that the Dissenting leaders were with them, William Sancroft, Archbishop of Canterbury, called a meeting of all the leading clergy in London and all the bishops in the kingdom. Several prominent laymen were also consulted, among them being the Earl of Clarendon (the royal brother-in-law) and Sir John Evelyn. The inclusion of prominent laymen in the ensuing discussions serves as proof that the opposition to James realized that they were approaching the Rubicon. Neither Tory statesmen nor Anglican clergy could operate effectively in isolation. Each had a role to play and it was important that each understood the position of the other. The Declaration of Indulgence and the Order in Council also coincided with the first good political news that James had received in a long time. A preliminary report from Sunderland's agents forecast a two-thirds majority for the royal policies if an election were now held. The report represented only seven counties, but it was highly encouraging nonetheless. The possibility of an electoral victory for James, coupled with the approaching birth of what might well be a son, was sufficient incentive to speed up whatever plotting might be at work. In that same month of April, Edward Russell, admiral, Whig, old exclusionist, and son of the Earl of Bedford, had gone to The Hague to sound out William once again. The answer this time was as positive as could be expected. William said that if he were invited by the "most valued" people "in their own name and in the name of others who trusted them," why, he thought he could be ready in September. Five months is a long time in a revolutionary situation, and it was clear that the burden still rested upon the English. William was not pushing them and he still had plenty of time either to prepare for the invasion, or, if conditions did not develop properly, to change his mind. He could be ready; he did not promise to come.[5]

As far back as March, the Earl of Danby had come to the conclusion that resistance to James was the only solution. In May, following the reissuing of the Declaration of Indulgence and the Order in Council, Danby was joined by Lord Lumley, who had given the king military support at the time of Monmouth's Rebellion, and the deprived Bishop of London, Henry Compton. It would seem to be very unlikely that Sancroft could have been totally ignorant of the plot that was brewing among the ranks of the Tory and Whig leaders. It is in fact very likely that Clarendon was aware as well. The Church now had to do its bit and take up the

[5] Feiling, p. 226.

torch of resistance to its king and head. In a significant passage, Von Ranke summed up the prevailing sentiment, if not the actual plotting:

It is a marked feature in the history of the time that the Episcopal Church, the Parliamentary party, the Prince of Orange, and the Pope of Rome himself, shared an opinion that the Catholics should remain excluded from political rights, on the ground that the grant of those rights seemed likely to shake the edifice of the English constitution, while King James, on the other hand, in his Indulgence aimed principally at procuring for his Catholic fellow-believers a complete political equality.

The Church of England men and the Presbyterians had certainly not arrived at a mutual agreement; but nevertheless they held together on the whole against their common antagonist: and that not more against the Catholics than against the Anabaptists and Quakers whom the King strove to unite with the Catholics.[6]

The Order in Council was officially gazetted on May 7, and five days later Sancroft met with those few of the clergy and laymen who had been able to get to London in time. The meeting took place at Lambeth Palace, the archbishop's official residence, just across the river from the Palace of Westminster. The attendance was small, but they were individually important: Sancroft himself; Compton, who was now ready for action; Bishops White of Peterborough and Turner of Ely; Lord Clarendon; and the Vicar of St. Martin's in the Fields. Thomas Cartwright, the Bishop of Chester and one of the few of his rank who was in sympathy with the court, had not been invited but made an unwelcome appearance nonetheless. While he was present, no business of substance could be contracted. But it is surprising that Cartwright had no suspicions of what was afoot. If he did, he evidently was not the royal spy that he was

[6] Ranke, IV, p. 395. (Even the Quakers and Baptists were far from united in their support of James, as has been shown earlier.)

thought to be, since the petition that was eventually sent to the king seems to have taken him by complete surprise. Once they were able to get down to business, they decided that all the ranking clergy in the province of Canterbury should be summoned at once. It was time to act and to act decisively. Numbers were essential to the success of any such action.

Six days later, May 18, another meeting took place, and few such gatherings of bishops in England's history can have been more important in impact than this one. The bishops of Winchester, Norwich, St. Asaph, Bath and Wells, Chichester, and Bristol were joined by several other lesser but eminent clergy. Sancroft, who up to now had not been the strongest of James's opponents, had already worked out a draft of a petition to the king, which was to serve as the basis for the final draft. The petition began by denying all disloyalty to James and any feelings of intolerance toward others. The traditional loyalty of the Church to the crown was unimpaired, and in due time they expected that both in Parliament and in Convocation they would prove both their loyalty to the king and their respect for the tender consciences of the Dissenters. However, they felt called upon to remind the king that the so-called prerogative right to dispense with or suspend ecclesiastical legislation had been denounced in Parliament in 1662 and 1672, and it was thus clear that no such prerogative power existed. Therefore the recent Declarations of Indulgence were strictly illegal. "Your petitioners cannot in prudence, honour or conscience so far make themselves parties to it as the distribution of it all over the nation, and the solemn publication of it once and again even in God's house, and in the time of his divine service."[7]

On that same evening of May 18, six of the seven signers of the petition went to Whitehall to present the petition in person to the king. Sancroft did not accom-

7 Kenyon, *Stuart Constitution*, pp. 441–42.

pany them, ostensibly because he was known to be out of favor at court, but it may well have been because of his lack of enthusiasm for the confrontation. Even though the petition was based on Sancroft's own draft, it has generally been suspected that Compton of London was the real inspiration behind the document, Sancroft merely lending the vast prestige of his office.

James received his bishops and met with them in his closet. The petition combined brevity with clarity and there was no mistaking the meaning on first glance. The king was shocked. He had never expected such a reaction to his direct command from men such as these. He flew into a rage and shouted, "This is a standard of rebellion." The royal temper shocked the bishops as much as their petition had shocked the king. Apparently it never occurred to them that their petition reflected anything more than a just and accurate statement of the law and the constitution, and that a mere reminder to the king might not be sufficient to deflect him from his chosen path. The lack of comprehension of the other, on each side, was truly amazing. It does tend to cast doubt upon the likelihood that the bishops were involved in any of the plotting to bring over William. What is most likely is that the bishops, including Sancroft, had sincerely felt that the Declaration of Indulgence and the Order in Council were unconstitutional and that the king would be willing to face this fact when confronted with it. On the other hand, Compton, of London, and Clarendon may very well have played their hands subtly and carefully, leading the bishops further into opposition than they either knew or wanted. If they had known what was in store for them personally, some might have refused their signatures.

In spite of the king's violent loss of temper, he did proceed quite coolly and deliberately during the next four weeks. The day after receiving the petition, he summoned his judges for consultation. On Sunday the twentieth, the day appointed for the first reading of the declaration in the London churches, several clergy absented themselves, others failed to read the declaration, and in only four parishes in the whole metropolis was the Order in Council complied with. This widespread refusal to obey cannot be explained as a deliberate plot or conspiracy. It was a spontaneous reaction to what in the eyes of any good Anglican was an illegal and unconstitutional attack upon them and their Church. It was the spontaneity of the refusal that proves how far removed from reality James was. It can't even be thought of as an act of rebellion. On the contrary, it was an act of defense. It was an unconscious and spontaneous declaration of what John Locke would be publishing in his *Second Treatise on Government*, namely, that the king, not the Church, had broken the compact (contract) that bound king and Church together. It was not the clergy but the king who was engaged in rebellion against the commonwealth. As Charles I had declared at his trial and execution in 1649 that he was the surest guarantor of the rights of Englishmen, so now the clergy of the Church of England were to step forth, unknowingly and spontaneously, in the same role. That this was true is demonstrated by the reaction of the ordinary Londoner throughout the next four weeks.

On June 8, the offending clergy, including Sancroft, were brought before the Privy Council and asked to confirm that the petition was in fact theirs. Conscious of their common-law rights against self-incrimination, Sancroft retorted that the king knew very well what petition had been given to him. They did not have to convict themselves out of their own mouths. That evening, the seven found themselves in the Tower of London, to which a large mob of ordinary Londoners proceeded the next day to show their solidarity. The significance of this and similar proepiscopal demonstrations in the following days and weeks cannot be overestimated. When, in the long course of English, or even European, history can a time be recalled when the bishops of the established church were cast in the role of popular heroes? Even Thomas à Becket achieved popular adulation only as an individual, and that because of his death. That the populace should cheer the bishops proves to what extent the king had destroyed himself. Only the most irresponsible and foolish of monarchs could have reached such a nadir. James was certainly out of his time, but not, therefore, necessarily ahead of it.

While the London mob was at the Tower demonstrating their support of the bishops, the queen went into labor and the next day was delivered of the son that she and James had prayed for and expected and that William and the English nation had feared. The timing of the birth and the sex of the child were too much for the opposition to accept. James of course was ecstatic. Clarendon first went to St. James's Palace to kiss the king's hand by way of congratulations, and then he was off to the Tower to visit the bishops, joining the throngs that were going in and out.[8] That the birth and the imprisonment were political events and were linked one to the other was to become accepted fact as far as the opposition and the public were concerned. Adding to the inevitable doubts as to the true parentage of the child was the fact that the baby was a month premature and that of the queen's three previous pregnancies one had culminated in the birth of a daughter and the other two had ended in miscarriages. All through this pregnancy there had been rumors of a miscarriage, and the queen herself, undoubtedly out of a sense of delicacy, had been most reluctant to discuss her pregnancy. Such delicacy was uncommon among English women of the time and so it, too, added to the atmosphere of suspicion.

The birth had been witnessed by the usual galaxy of court officials, male and female, and normally their testimony would have been sufficient to allay any

[8] *State Trials*, XII, p. 195.

doubts. But the chasm that had opened between the nation and the court was too wide. No testament of Jeffreys or Sunderland, of the Duchesses of Mazarin or Portsmouth, could bridge the gap. Those who either wanted to or had to believe in a conspiracy would not be put off. Unlike the Popish Plot of the 1670s, there was now no small band of intriguers cooking up a story that would then be sold to a gullible public. The belief that James had worked a fraud was spontaneous and well-nigh universally accepted.

Burnet's account of the birth of the prince gives us an insight into how and why men of intelligence and sophistication were in all honesty to accept the notion of a conspiracy:

The child was not heard to cry, nor was he shown to any in the room; but the under-dresser huddled away something in her arms, pretending more air was necessary, into a dressing-room hard by, that had communication with other apartments; and the King, delaying some minutes to follow her, made it seem as if he had been minded to give time for some clandestine management. No satisfaction, in the meantime, was given to the ladies who came in that the birth was real: the Princess [Anne], when she returned from Bath, had no sure conviction of it; and Chamberlain, the man-midwife, not having been called in to the labour, as usual, heightened the probability of an imposture. If there was no imposture, the matter, in short, was so unaccountably managed as to give sufficient grounds of suspicion, and might therefore excuse the nation for being so cold in their expressions of joy, and so formal in their congratulatory addresses upon this occasion.[9]

To counter the almost universally accepted rumors of a fraud, the king sought and obtained signed depositions from several of those present at St. James's on the happy day. Among those who deposed for James was Lord Chancellor Jeffreys, who swore that he had seen the queen in labor and had seen the baby within seconds of its birth. Jeffreys' testimony carried little weight at the time, although, since he had already expressed

9 Burnet [B], *History*, p. 270.

to Clarendon his grave doubts about the wisdom of
trying the bishops, he was no longer so obviously tied
to the king as to perjure himself. But these depositions
came too late to undo the harm done by the initial
reaction, and in any event fact and reason now counted
for so little that there was probably nothing that anyone could have done or said that would have convinced
even the most disinterested.[10] Beyond a handful of
Jacobites, it would be years before anyone could bring
himself to admit that perhaps the new Prince of Wales
was legitimate after all. Because there was no conspiracy
to defame James, there was really nothing that he could
do to counter the refusal of the nation to accept his
son. His standing in the nation and among his own
Protestant family was destroyed and his position was
irremediable. The king himself, however, was still filled
with joy and hope for the future.[11]

Jeffreys had his doubts about the political wisdom
of trying the bishops, and he was a good enough lawyer
to have doubts about the possibility of making the
charges of seditious libel stand up in law. To try the
case in the Ecclesiastical Commission would merely
have compounded the political complications, and so
the common law was to be invoked and the case went
before King's Bench with a carefully picked jury. Among
them were one baronet and one knight, and the remainder were all esquires. The whole of the testimony
was heard in one long day, with the jury being locked
up for the night without heat or light, to consider their
verdict. The arguments of the two sides are particularly
interesting since it was the prosecution that dealt primarily in technicalities, and the defense that was willing
to face the grand questions. The bench itself was most
scrupulous throughout the whole proceedings. The Lord
Chief Justice himself presided, and on the innumer-
able occasions of his own interventions it was obvious

[10] P. J. Helm, *Jeffreys*, London, 1966, p. 171.
[11] Turner, p. 405.

that he would leave no stone of law or logic unturned that would drive the prosecution almost to distraction in trying to present their case. When it was the turn of the defense, the latitude given was far greater.

The prosecution case was not, first of all, founded on the libelous nature of the petition but on the question of whether the seven bishops had signed it in the first place, whether it in fact had been delivered by them to the king, and only thirdly was the matter of its libelous nature raised. The bishops had been ushered into James's closet by Sunderland, but the Lord President had then absented himself. The only witnesses to the delivery were the bishops, who could not be made to testify against themselves, and the king, who could not in any circumstances appear in court anyway. When the bishops were brought before the Privy Council they had been asked if the signatures on a petition produced by the king were theirs, to which they reluctantly said yes; but at the meeting they were never asked if that was the same petition they had previously delivered to the king. The prosecution, then, could prove in court that the bishops had signed the petition, but they could not prove that they had ever delivered it to the king. The only evidence they could present in court was purely circumstantial. The prosecution's contention that the petition was libelous was based essentially on the reaction in London the next day, when it was printed and circulated, but there was never any proof as to who did the printing or how a copy of the petition came into the printer's hands in the first place. The bishops were not even charged with this responsibility. Since the prosecution could never prove the delivery of the petition either to the king or to the printer, the defense could well have let it rest here and claim that it was merely a private expression of their own opinions. The prosecution hoped that the jury would have enough common sense not to be taken in by these technicalities.

During cross-examination the defense stressed the

inability of the prosecution to prove the delivery of
the petition into the king's hands, but when it came
time to present their own case they relied almost
completely on the substance of the petition and the
motives that lay behind it. In so doing they in fact were
tacitly admitting that the document had been delivered to James by the bishops themselves, although all
readily admitted that Sancroft, the archbishop, was not
one of them. The appeal was made to the Parliaments
of 1663, 1673, and 1685 to the effect that the dispensing power in matters of religion had no standing in law.
They were allowed to quote from the journals of the
Lords and of the Commons even though their use as
evidence was not without legal flaw, and in fact when
the decision was made that the jury could be supplied
with the written evidence when they went to deliberate,
the journals were specifically excepted, with no com-
plaint from the defense. (James may have discussed
the case in general with his judges after receiving the
petition, but from the transcript of the trial there is
certainly no indication that the judges were in any way
prejudiced against the defendants or their counsel.

The main line of defense was thus exactly the same
as the principle upon which the bishops had decided
to write the petition in the first place. They were not
merely fighting to avoid conviction. They were fighting
for the principle that the king had exceeded the bounds
of his prerogative in issuing the Declaration of Indulgence and that the Order in Council commanding them
to read the declaration was an order without standing
because their obedience would make them parties to an
illegal act. The century-old question of responsibility
was again to raise its head. Since in law the king can do
no wrong, and since the declaration was deemed to be
illegal, then the king himself could not be held responsible for it, either in law or in logic. Consequently
the declaration and the order had to be the work
(responsibility) of the king's "evil" advisers. Ever since
the reign of James I this issue of responsibility

had been like a Greek chorus, always in the background but on occasion in the forefront of political struggle.

The problem never was a purely theoretical one; rather it was at the heart of the constitutional crisis. For some, unwillingness to cast blame upon the person of the king was merely a question of good manners. For some it may have been a nice device of legal logic, which would facilitate criticism of government policy without the overt risks of charges of treason or slander. But the real question was one of power: who was to be held responsible for the government of the realm, and to whom was this responsibility owed? The issue incorporates, but it also transcends, the simple struggle between crown and Parliament. Whether Parliament was thought of as just the two Houses, of Lords and Commons, or as the three-branch institution of king-in-parliament (king, Lords, and Commons) really made little practical difference. The only final solution to the problem of the relationship between crown and Parliament required an answer to the question, who is the crown, the king personally or his ministers? If the king personally is the crown incarnate, then his ministers are responsible to him, and he in turn is not responsible to anyone or anything. Of course a denial of the king's personality and the bestowal of the mantle of monarchy upon the minister or the ministers collectively would have been a denial of the traditional constitution and would in fact lead to the creation of a "crowned republic." The Whigs of the seventeenth century might be perfectly willing to accept such a solution to the problem, but the Whigs were not England, and such a willingness to have a "crowned republic" merely tended to delay the Tories' acceptance of the possibility that someone other than the king personally was to be responsible. The ultimate solution to the problem was, of course, to be in the classic tradition of medieval political theory that the king had two bodies—public and private. The ministers are to be answerable to the king on a personal basis but are responsible to the nation represented in Parliament for their public acts. Eventually the day was to come when the ministers would owe their office to Parliament but their loyalty to the king. Once that day arrived the king would wear the crown in theory and his ministers would wear it in fact, and Parliament would ultimately decide who those ministers would be. It would take another century following the Glorious Revolution before the solution would be refined in all its parts, but a giant step in this direction was to be taken in 1688 and 1689. The attack upon the Church in general, and the trial of the seven bishops in particular, was a part of this giant step. Even the Tory and Anglican leaders were now being forced by events to move in the Whig direction. The only way they could both oppose the king and salve their obedient consciences was to accept the principle of the "king's two bodies." Therefore, in this case they would deny they were libeling the king by accusing him of exceeding the bounds of his prerogative. He could not personally wish to do such a thing. His advisers were responsible for that. Thus there could not be a libel against the king.

An indication as to just how far things had now gone is seen when this line of argument was being used by those most bound morally, spiritually, and legally to the person of the king. The Whigs were already at the point where the king personally was to be attacked and assigned the blame for the crown's illegal actions. The Revolution settlement, and the Declaration of Rights of 1689 in particular, would concern itself primarily with restricting the rights of a king, not just his ministers. James was to be held to blame personally because he was in fact the guilty party and everyone knew it. No king since Richard II, in the fourteenth century, had run such a personal government. No power of decision was delegated to anyone, and no advice was sought or received from any holders of office under the crown on any topics of real consequence. The ministers did his bidding or were sacked. The Privy

Council and the Cabinet council barely functioned. If there were any who spoke to James and whose advice he took, it was the secret Catholic junta, and he was responsible for them, not they for him. Thus in the context of June 1688 the bishops were loyal and obedient almost to a fault. Putting such men on trial in a fit of passionate rage was truly criminal in its folly. One might almost say that those whom the gods will destroy they first make mad.

The dispensing power was the heart of the case for the defense. The bishops again felt they were remaining true to their consciences of non-resistance and passive obedience, because if the king had no dispensing power, then they were not attacking his prerogative. One cannot attack what does not exist. The defense went even further in their protestations of loyalty and denied that they wanted the king to revoke the declaration. They merely claimed the right to refuse to obey the Order in Council because it had no standing in law. The king, even on the advice of his councilors, could not command the performance of an illegal act. To bring these facts to the attention of the king personally could not be a libel, but a right and a duty owed to the sovereign by his loyal subjects.

The Lord Chief Justice summed up all the evidence and the law for the benefit of the jury. In his summation he sought to undermine the defense's case by stating that the issue of the dispensing power was not an issue for the jury to consider. The rights of a common-law jury do not and did not extend into the realm of "judicial review." They were to determine the facts within the law, not to rule on the law itself. The factual issues were two in number, and he stated them thus for the jury's consideration:

The truth of it is, the dispensing power is out of the case, it is only a word used in the petition; but truly, I will not take upon me to give my opinion in the question, to determine that now, for it is not before me: the only question before me is, and so it is before you, gentlemen, it being a question of fact, whether here be a certain proof of publication [of the petition]? And then the next question is a question of law indeed, whether if there be a publication proved, it be a libel?

He proceeded to say that if the jury believed that the petition before them was the one delivered to the king, then the bishops were guilty of publication:

Now, gentlemen, any thing that shall disturb the government, or make mischief and a stir among the people, is certainly within the case of "Libellis Famosis"; and I must in short give you my opinion, I do take it to be a libel.[12]

After fortifying themselves with wine, the jury retired, deliberating through the night in the dark and chill. The next morning, Saturday, June 30, the verdict was rendered: NOT GUILTY. "At which there were several great shouts in court, and throughout the hall."[13]

There were immediately very loud acclamations through Westminster-hall, and the words "Not guilty," "Not guilty," went round with such shouts and huzzas, that the king's Solicitor moved very earnestly that such as had shouted in the court might be committed. But the shouts were carried on through the cities of Westminster and London, and flew presently to Hounslow-heath, where the soldiers in the camp echoed them so loud that it startled the king, who was that day entertained in the earl of Feversham's tent: insomuch that his majesty sent him out to know what was the matter. The earl came back and told the king, "It was nothing but the soldiers shouting upon the news of the bishops being acquited." The king replied, "And do you call that nothing? but so much the worse for them." What his majesty meant by the last words he had not much time to interpret: he could only show some indignation, that the bishops had escaped a legal penalty, and he threatened to deliver them up to the ecclesiastical commissioners.[14]

[12] *State Trials*, XII, pp. 425–26.
[13] Ibid., p. 430.
[14] Ibid., pp. 431–32.

If James now felt dependent upon his Ecclesiastical Commission, he was depending upon a weak reed indeed. The commission did meet and duly ordered the declaration to be read and even ordered ecclesiastical authorities to make visitations and to report on the churches that failed of compliance, but in fact nothing was done to either punish the seven bishops or to follow up the new order to publish the declaration. The commission was "drifting," and the Bishop of Rochester sent in his resignation, declaring that he "thought it inconsistent with his profession and character to act any longer in it. . . ."[15] In the autumn the king made the futile gesture of dissolving the commission.

During this miraculous month of June 1688 a third event of vast importance was to join the list that included the trial of the bishops and the birth of the Prince of Wales: the formal invitation to William of Orange, which was sent by "the immortal seven." The seven who put their signatures to the letter were but a small part of the ever-growing throng who were willing to align themselves to such an extreme, and possibly dangerous, commitment. The list of those who were willing to provide bail for the imprisoned bishops shows this, and it also shows the wide variety of political and religious views they represented: they were the Marquis of Halifax, not given to making rash or idle gestures of protest; the Earls of Bedford, Danby, Ossory, Clarendon, Carbery, Burlington, Manchester, Carlisle, Clare, Shrewsbury, Dorset, Kent, Nottingham, Radnor, Worcester, Devonshire, and Scarsdale; Viscounts Fauconberg and Newport; and Lords Bolingbroke, Grey, Paget, North, Crewe, Chandos, and Lumley.

Following the birth of the prince, William sent Zuylestein over to London, ostensibly to congratulate the king on the birth of his heir. But William had a more important task in mind for his emissary; he was to make further contact with Edward Russell to see

15 Ibid., p. 432.

if the invitation that William had earlier indicated he was willing to entertain was soon to be forthcoming. Russell had worked for months to get William to agree to support with arms an English rebellion against James. In this he had worked closely with Henry Sidney, who was William's principal agent in England. Whether these men would have instigated a rebellion in England if William would not or could not promise help will never be known. But it is highly unlikely that William would have invaded England without a prior guarantee of support from leading Englishmen of both parties and of both the Anglican and Dissenting religions. William's hopes and fears for an English rebellion and for his own intervention have already been examined. In brief, England was ripe for rebellion. William feared the outcome if he did not intervene, and once he had decided that he would intervene he was determined that the English should play their part in such a way that he, not they, would be the masters of the situation, and that the rebellion would not only succeed but he would be the principal beneficiary. His insistence upon prior support from prominent men, Whig and Tory, Anglican and Dissenter, both ensured success for his enterprise and meant that he personally would emerge victorious, because he alone would be able to hold the conspirators together. Furthermore, by playing upon the hopes and fears of each faction among them, he would be the arbiter of the final solution—the crown of England would be his. While he showed great skill in revealing at any one time only that part of his plan that it was in his interest to show, there can be no question but that it was the crown itself that he wanted for himself. He would be no regent for the Prince of Wales, who could now be raised as a Protestant, nor for his wife, Mary. Not only would he not be a regent, he would not be a king consort either. He must have remembered how unhappily that arrangement had worked out for Philip II in the 1550s. If he were to invade England, the prize was his own assumption of the crown. England would be his, saved from itself, and allied with the Netherlands in the great crusade against Louis XIV, which always had been and always would be the driving force of William's very existence.

Ever since returning to England in May, Russell, assisted by Henry Sidney, was busy making contacts and trying to put together the combination that might prove acceptable to William. The arrest of the bishops, the birth of the Prince of Wales, and the royal determination to bring the bishops to trial proved sufficient to bring their efforts to a successful conclusion. Among the many leading figures in Church and state who were approached, there was not one who failed to keep the secret and reported the conspiracy to the court. Many of the Tories, such as Clarendon, Rochester, Halifax, and Nottingham, demurred when it came to putting their signatures to the letter; but they gave immeasurable support merely by keeping silent. In any case, they had all been in contact with William at one time or another during the previous months, and so their fundamental sympathy to the cause could largely be taken on faith.

The "immortal seven" who did sign the invitation, on June 30, the day the bishops were found not guilty, were the Earls of Danby, Devonshire, and Shrewsbury, Lord Lumley, Bishop Compton of London, Admiral Edward Russell, and Henry Sidney. Danby, Lumley, and Compton were the Tories, the rest being Whigs. If only seven could be brought to sign, the list was as balanced as could be. The ardor of Russell and Sidney on the Whig side was certainly evenly matched by the ardor of Danby, Lumley, and Compton. Danby may well have been in continuing disgrace with the political nation for his role in the 1670s in the court of Charles II, Lumley may have been a "nobody," and Compton had been barred from exercising his office as Bishop of London; but their signatures were not without significance. Compton's role in getting the seven bishops to sign the petition against the reading of the declaration is proof of the influence he had over Sancroft of Canterbury and the majority of the bench of bishops. Danby was without question committed to Anglicanism and an anti-French foreign policy. He had been a major factor in the arrangement for the marriage of William and Mary, and his great experience and ability as a minister of the crown would make him a welcome addition to any new administration that might be established. It has also been suggested that none of the Whig signatories represented any of the major figures in the nation. Russell was a professional sailor; Sidney, a member of a family known more for rebellion and republicanism than for its status as a family of substance; Devonshire was wealthy but had a reputation as a frivolous grandee, given to dueling (more like a French nobleman at Versailles); and Shrewsbury was young and in perpetual poor health. Collectively they did not have the weight to carry England, or even the aristocracy, with them. But they proved to be both able and determined to see their schemes succeed—indeed they now had no choice. And in any case they were but the tip of the iceberg. A list of 161 peers, temporal and spiritual, has been found among the Bentinck papers in The Hague. The list divides the peers into groups, depending upon their support or not of the opposition. Eighty-five of them were listed as definitely among the opposition, with another thirty-five being in the probable category. The seven did not stand alone, and William knew it. They merely provided the means by which William could now justify to himself and to England his decision to indeed come over. The role of the seven may have had little practical significance, but the symbolic significance was decisive.

The letter itself sets out the reasons why the signatories were convinced that the time had come to act. But the action had to come from William. There was no hint in the letter that they themselves would com-

mence a rebellion without him. On the contrary, they
expected that the situation would deteriorate during
the following year, with the king securing an army and
an officer corps more loyal to himself and his cause
than the existing army camped at Hounslow Heath.
Without William, the prospects for England seemed
dark indeed. With him, all appeared to be bright. The
signatories assured him that 95 per cent of the common
people would support him and that a large portion of
the aristocracy would do so, too. They had to admit,
though, that the percentage of support among the
nobility was less than among the ordinary people, but
that more peers were sympathetic than felt free to say
so at the moment. Since the king did have an army,
the people of England and their natural leaders
feared to rise up against the tyrant without a Dutch
army to secure their success. But if a sizable Dutch
army did land, they were convinced, masses of Englishmen would rally to it and their combined forces would
be able to overwhelm the royal forces. They urged a
speedy decision from William, not only because the
future was dark without his help, but because there
was already afloat a vague sense of doubt as to where
William stood on the future of England. The speed
with which William had sent his congratulations upon
the birth of the prince had shocked some people,
especially since not one Englishman in a thousand believed in the legitimacy of the baby. If William were
to retain his position as the "leader of the opposition"
he must declare himself quickly and decisively. And
once the positive decision was taken he was urged to
land his forces within two weeks; otherwise the news
of his preparations would undoubtedly leak out and
the "immortal" seven would surely be arrested. Now
that they had gone this far and had issued the invitation, William must not let them down. It was now
or never for them and for William.

During the next few weeks many follow-up letters
were sent to William by some of the seven and by

others informed of the secret. Not only did Nottingham show great reluctance to see the project go forth, but even Sidney began to have his doubts about the final outcome of any landing. He took it upon himself to suggest that William would do well to bring Marshal Schomberg into his service. His great reputation as a soldier and a lover of England would be of much value to William and the cause, militarily and psychologically. A more positive tone was adopted by the two Hydes, Clarendon and Rochester, who were anxious to assure William of their total loyalty to him, hinting that he should not be misled by their failure to add their names to the invitation. Lord Churchill, a great soldier, a Tory, and a principal supporter of James II at the time of Monmouth's Rebellion, came out even more unequivocally, albeit cryptically, for William in his letter. Since he and his wife were so close personally to Princess Anne, this letter carried great significance.

The tone of the letters, including the invitation itself, must have amused as well as reassured William. For at least the past six months he had feared a rebellion in England that would get out of hand and lead either to a victory for James and his French policy, or else to a Whig/republican triumph. But in the summer of 1688 it was clear that there would be no rebellion without him, but that with him there was an excellent chance of success. Circumstances had conspired, with his own deft handling, to create a situation in which he alone was the key and the master. There was to be no question as to how he should react. The time had come to strike, or more accurately, the time had come to make the definite decision to strike. Once the decision was made, the timing would depend less upon events in England and the wishes of his fellow conspirators than upon his flanks in the Netherlands and in France. The States-General had to be dealt with and so did the new army that Louis XIV had raised. To some extent he still had to wait upon events and upon the decisions that others were about to take, but he also knew that he must become more active in helping to determine these events.

One further indication of the prospects for the future in England itself was the peculiar twisting and turning indulged in by the Earl of Sunderland. Upon the birth of the Prince of Wales he had formally announced his conversion to the Roman Church. Rather than being a total commitment to James (at a time when nearly everyone else was deserting him), it in fact gave Sunderland a freedom of maneuver that was to assist both William and himself in the long run. James could hardly turn his back on Sunderland now, and so the wily and experienced old intriguer was able to urge a modification of the king's forward religious policy on one hand, hoping to stave off the possibility of a rebellion and/or a Dutch invasion; and on the other hand he was able to negotiate more freely with Louis XIV while at the same time keeping in touch with William. His conversion represented his awareness that the crisis was fast approaching and that James must be led into a more moderate policy. He felt freer to do this within the Catholic fold than without. In the end, he couldn't save James or the baby prince, but he did manage to save himself, which was Sunderland's chief aim throughout his life anyway.

So by midsummer both England and William were to wait upon events. Each was aware of the one crucial fact: William was going to invade England. For William the problem was when and how to protect his continental flanks in the process. For James and Sunderland the question was how to stop the invasion or how to make it fail if it were launched. This in turn could be done by diplomacy or war, by alliance with or against France, or a combination of them all. But as far as England was concerned, it was William, not James, who was to be the principal determining force. James was not even the master of his own fate, much less that of his country. It is now time to look once again at the complicated situation on the Continent and how William was able to put all the pieces together in preparation for his assault on England.

CHAPTER 7

The Invasion

With Louis XIV armed once again, the crucial question was when and where he would resume the offensive. For William there were two questions: how to protect the Netherlands from France, and how to carry out the successful invasion of England. As regards the struggle against Louis there was a further question that William had to answer. Given the fact that France could be stopped only by an alliance, hopefully under William's guidance if not leadership, what should be the unifying spirit of this alliance—a positive theme of Protestantism or the purely negative theme of stopping France? To William, these two may have been one and the same thing, but this was not manifestly the case with the Holy Roman Emperor, the Pope, or the German Catholic princes. If he were to get a modicum of help from these Catholic powers, he must obviously stress the anti-French theme while exhibiting sufficient toleration for Catholicism to win the trust of the Catholic powers and yet not frighten his fellow Protestants in the Netherlands and in England. The task would not be simple, but it would be accomplished, with a good assist from Louis himself and James. But it would take more months of hard work and patience on William's part, for Louis was slow to tip his own hand as to whether he would actually launch his new attack, and if so, where. In the meantime, every overture of peace in the Rhineland that emanated from Paris would tend to disarm the Emperor, who was more immediately concerned with the Turks and the Danube, and make it necessary for William to use every trick to twist Louis's overtures so as to make them seem as nothing more than a cover for his aggressive designs.

William had worked hard since the fall of 1687 to weld an alliance, and had sent two separate embassies into the North German states to assist in this. Mrs. Pinkham has asserted that this proves that William was already determined to invade England and needed these alliances for his protection. It is more likely that he needed these alliances to protect himself against Louis, whether he were to invade England or not. William had assumed almost from birth that he was in the direct line of inheritance of the English crown. By Continental standards, the claims of his wife, Mary, and of his sister-in-law, Anne, were meaningless. It was only with reluctance that he accepted English law, which allowed inheritance of property by a woman. But as much as William coveted the English throne, he coveted control of England's foreign policy even more. Louis XIV was satisfied with a neutral England; William of Orange demanded an England that would further the interests of the United Provinces. Desirous as he was of the English crown, William would make no move until he was quite certain that the English wanted him to and that it was consistent with his policy of opposition to Louis XIV. Therefore these negotiations may well have been conducted with the thought that their successful conclusion would help make possible an invasion of England, but that is still no proof that William had already definitely determined on the invasion at such an early date.

Just as events in England in June of 1688 had finally determined William to invade England, so an event in Germany in the same month precipitated a chain of events that was to make the invasion possible. On June 3, the Electoral Archbishop of Cologne died. Several months earlier, Louis XIV had managed to secure the election of one of his puppets, Cardinal von Fürstenberg, Bishop of Strassburg, as archbishop coadjutor and probable successor as Electoral Archbishop. A vote for France in the Imperial Electoral College was something the Emperor and the Pope could not tolerate. The Rhineland Germans feared Louis, but would not take the lead in standing up to him. The Emperor and the Pope were needed to buttress their opposition to France. Luckily for William, when the required election for archbishop elector took place, Von Fürstenburg received a majority of the votes but not the necessary two-thirds majority. Thus the election was thrown into the lap of the Pope, who chose Prince Joseph Clement of Bavaria, whose selection Louis XIV refused to recognize. The lines were now being drawn favorably to William. He could now oppose Louis without appearing to be anti-Catholic. The role that James II now chose to play was to complete William's diplomatic triumph, for James sought the role of mediator between the Pope and the Emperor on one hand, and the Pope and Louis on the other. Whatever may have been the sincerity of his motives, they were taken as nothing more than proof that he was in fact just another of Louis's puppets. And William no longer needed to fear that his designs on England would seem to be founded on anti-Catholicism.

James's offer to serve as a mediator in the Cologne affair was readily taken as proof of his subservience to Louis for reasons that may well have been based on false suspicions rather than fact; but it must always be remembered that at any point in history, the general public no less than political leaders are forced to make decisions and to take actions based upon what the facts appear to be. They cannot be expected to have the knowledge that only hindsight and a study of the sources can provide. That is why the image presented by a government to its own people and to the world is really more important in the short run than the true facts themselves. And the image presented by the gov-

ernment of James II was one that could not but be
looked upon with fear by any Protestant in England
or on the Continent, and by anyone who considered
the might of Louis XIV to be the greatest threat to
the peace and independence of Western Europe and
the cause of toleration. In June, James had sent his
fleet of twenty ships into The Downs as a show of force
to impress his opponents at home and also as a warning to the Dutch. The French fleet was in the Mediterranean, engaged with the Algerians. But Louis was
said to have informed James that the French fleet
would join the English in the Channel if it were necessary to protect James from his enemies. Whether
James and Louis were in fact working in such close
concert is highly unlikely. It was just a gesture of friendship on Louis's part, but the news was looked upon as
thoroughly menacing by the States-General, in Amsterdam. It served to convince these sturdy Dutch burghers
that William's struggle with France and his meddling
in English affairs was not just a personal peculiarity of
his own. They now realized that a joining of the two
fleets would be disastrous for Dutch commerce and
that France and Jacobean England were indeed deadly
enemies. This was a great victory for William. He now
was to have the moral support of the Amsterdam
burghers and, what was perhaps of even greater value
at this time, their financial backing.

The appearance of an English-French alliance, and
it was to have reality only in appearance, totally con-
verted the Elector of Brandenburg to William's cause.
He had been briefed nearly a year earlier as to William's hopes for intervention in England. Throughout
the first half of 1688 he had been kept informed. (It
was this early briefing of Brandenburg that has been
used as evidence that William had definitely determined to invade England as far back as the autumn
of 1687. It is more likely, however, that William expected that it would eventually happen, than that he
actively sought to make it happen. Ever since the fall

of Clarendon and the parliamentary hassle over the passage of the first Test Act, the possibility of William's having to actively intervene in England had been there. But the weight of the evidence still points in the direction that no final decision was taken until June of 1688. And it also still seems more likely that it was the course of events in England that brought William to his final decision rather than William's decision that influenced the course adopted by the opposition in England. Danby, Devonshire, and Compton were certainly not mere pawns in the hands of William of Orange.) The Elector was a thoroughly committed Protestant and a thoroughly loyal German who was committed to the integrity of the Holy Roman Empire as it then existed, which meant that he favored the present system, whereby the North German states could retain their political and religious freedom under the Imperial umbrella and the Rhineland was German, not French. Brandenburg looked upon the Dutch as his natural allies just as much as William looked upon the German princes as his natural allies. To both, a Franco-English alliance could spell disaster politically and religiously. To the Dutch burghers it also meant economic disaster. The pieces were falling nicely into place. What was now necessary was to convert the diplomatic alliance into a military alliance with adequate financial backing.

With money, ships, and men at his disposal and with the assurance that the drain on his own resources occasioned by the impending invasion of England would be made good by the contributions of his new German allies, the problems facing William were largely brought about by the English. Those who issued the invitation, together with their friends, were not happy at the prospect of a large army of foreigners descending upon their island. The ostensible reason, and the one conveyed to William, was that a large Dutch army might well provoke a patriotic reaction in England that would redound to the benefit of the government. The real reason undoubtedly was that they did not want to lose complete control of the situation to William. They wanted William to serve their interests; they did not want to serve his. Therefore, it was suggested that a small Dutch army and a large Dutch fleet were what was wanted. William, on the other hand, favored a large army and a small fleet. By putting Admiral Russell on board a Dutch ship and giving him a Dutch naval title, it was hoped that the English fleet he had so recently commanded would either not fight or would even come over to the opposition. This indeed was what happened.

William had greater confidence in the English fleet than he did in the English army and militia. He knew that the army was riven by political and religious antagonisms, and that while it might not prove to be a useful instrument for James, it might not prove to be useful to William either. As for local levies that might be raised by the opposition landed magnates, he both doubted how effective they might be in this endeavor and at the same time feared that if they were successful these levies might not be completely loyal to William himself. Thus he had no choice but to put his fate in the hands of his own army under his own command. If it was possible to master the situation, he intended to do so.

Part and parcel of this struggle, albeit a muted one, for the control of the enterprise was the disagreement as to where the invading army should land. All the great landowners among the "immortal seven" who had issued the invitation had their estates in the North of England. They therefore urged William to land on the North Sea coast, thus preserving them from the wrath of James and at the same time giving them a political hold over William. It was in their interest to appear to be as helpful to him as possible if he should triumph, and to use his army to protect themselves if all should fail. For both political and military reasons they were against William's decision to land on the

Channel coast in the West of England. Not only would the conspirators be largely left out of the action, but they feared, and rightly so, that the work of James and Jeffreys in the West following the defeat of Monmouth had broken the back of any potential opposition in the West country and William would be solely dependent upon his own forces in what could actually turn out to be hostile country. In this estimate they were quite correct. But William had his own interests to care for. He did not want to depend upon the English conspirators for the success of his enterprise, and by landing in the West he knew that he would be on his own. He had also been warned by his admirals that an autumn invasion launched across the North Sea was far more dangerous than one launched across the relatively calmer and narrower Channel. Thus, for both reasons the landing was to be in the West, and with a sizable army directly under William's personal command. There was nothing for the English to do but acquiesce. Their fate now rested with William. All that they could now do was to adjust their own actions to his. If the North were to be secured they would have to do it themselves, but they could not necessarily expect any help from William, or even thanks from him, for that matter.

By September of 1688, time was running out for Louis. He had his mighty grievances against the Pope and the Emperor, and the impending fall of Belgrade to Imperial forces meant that if he were to attack the Rhineland and the Palatinate at all, he must do it quickly. Marshal Vauban had promised that a lightning strike was possible and it would all be over soon. The large army that William had finally been able to gather, financed by the States-General, and the large German contingents made available through the help of Brandenburg and the newly formed League of Augsburg (Spain, the Empire, the Netherlands, Sweden), determined Louis to waste no more time. But where should he attack? If he were to strike directly at Hol-

land, England not France would be the primary beneficiary. And in any case it has already been pointed
out that Vauban had suggested to Louis that a Dutch-
English war might so debilitate both that France need
not worry about either. The affair of the archbishopric
of Cologne and the supposed claims that Louis's
brother, Orléans, had to the Palatinate were to take
precedence in Louis's mind. So the great army he had
assembled was to be hurled into the Rhineland and
into North Germany, Philippsburg being the principal
target. Unfortunately for Louis, Philippsburg was very
well fortified and was able to withstand the siege until
the autumn rains turned the ground into a sea of mud.
But Louis maintained the seige and also pushed on
and around, deeper into the heart of western Germany.

William was now a free man and James II was
doomed. The States-General now agreed that Holland
was safe at least until the following spring. Thus, they
were willing to let William use the men and money
they had provided, and he could launch the invasion
of England. James made a gesture toward an alliance
with William against Louis, but no one paid any attention to him. At last he seemed to realize the really
great danger he was in and that William did indeed
intend to attack him. He also realized that he had
little hope of rallying support to repel the invasion
unless he made concessions to the opposition. For a
man who had always felt that his father had lost his
throne and his life because he had made concessions
to his opposition, this was a tragic situation indeed.

Still confident of the future, James had announced
in late August that the writs for the long-awaited new
parliamentary elections would soon be issued, bearing
the date of September 5. The writs were to be accompanied by a list of exact instructions, which the borough
regulators were ordered to read over and over again so
as to ensure the election of men loyal to the policies
of the court. The French invasion of Germany, in September, changed all of this, however, and the writs

never were issued. The invasion inaugurated two
months of furious activity on James's part, in which
he tried to undo all the damage of the past three years.
By the end of the month Sunderland had lost all hope
and was finally able to get James himself to realize the
full extent of the danger. It was Sunderland again who
took the lead in attempting the switch of gears. He who
had guided the king's Catholic policy for the past year,
now urged an alliance with the Church. James was now
prevailed upon to promise the holding of a new Parliament that would be freely elected, and he accompanied
this announcement with a statement declaring that the
rights and privileges of the Church would be defended,
providing always that universal freedom of worship be
guaranteed. On September 28 an order in council was
issued declaring that England was in imminent danger
of invasion. The writs for this new election were canceled and it was clear that while the emergency lasted
there would be no new elections. Other steps, however,
were to be taken in the attempt to win back the support of the Church and through it of the Anglican/Tory
establishment.

James held a conference at the end of September
with all the bishops then resident in London, with
Sancroft serving as their leader. The archbishop did
his best to convince James that all was not yet lost,
but that to salvage anything he must be prepared to
make concessions to both the Church and the local
authorities. There seems to be no doubt that Sancroft
sincerely hoped that there was still time to effect a
reconciliation between the king and his realm. The
arguments put forward had some effect upon James,
and he did announce the abolition of the Court of
High Commission. He restored the old charter to the
City of London and to the other deprived boroughs,
quashing the quo warranto proceedings that were still
outstanding. The Fellows of Magdalen College, Oxford, were restored to their rightful places, and a promise was made to reinstate those justices of the peace

and lords lieutenants who had earlier been replaced.
The promise of a new and free election to Parliament
was also made. Nothing of any consequence came of
any of these concessions; it was much too late.

Very few of the old gentry and aristocracy were willing to resume their old positions in the administration
of local government. The failure of the concessions to
have the desired effect was due primarily to two causes,
one foreign and one domestic: Too many, now aware
that William was planning an invasion of England,
realized that it was best to lie low and wait upon
events. A reconciliation with James might merely have
led to their compromising themselves with William
if he were to invade successfully. But perhaps even
more important was the total collapse of any trust in
James or in his concessions. At the end of August he
had begun to bring his Irish army over to England.
It is impossible to imagine anything more shocking or
humiliating to England. To the Englishman of the
seventeenth century the Irish were subhuman savages,
destined to be the perpetual serfs of freeborn Englishmen. As Macaulay said, "They did not belong to our
branch of the great human family."[1] James's willingness to rely for support upon an Irish-Papist army was
consistent with his refusal to make the one concession
that might have saved him—the renunciation of his
suspending and dispensing powers. The refusal to make
this concession, coupled with the arrival of the Irish,
convinced nearly all Englishmen that James was not
now, or ever, to be trusted. Trevelyan has pointed out
that in this respect James II was as much a man of
principle as his father, Charles I.[2] Neither would concede what they considered to be the true heart of the
royal patrimony—their prerogative powers. On the contrary, both were willing to go to any length, including
deception, guile, and force if need be, to defend that

[1] Macaulay, II, p. 385.
[2] Trevelyan, p. 130.

prerogative. Charles I was willing to give up his life rather than concede his prerogatives. The son was willing in the end to flee into exile rather than make this ultimate concession. Men of principle they were, but their principles were totally unacceptable to the bulk of the nation. Since they were determined to win all, the only alternative was that they lose all.

James seemed destined to lose all. What did William hope to win? Did he actually seek to overthrow James and win the crown for himself, or did he merely intend to "intervene" in English affairs in order to secure the election of a free Parliament? Princess Mary, in her *Memoire*, said that William did indeed hope to dethrone James II.[3] Did this mean, however, that he would seize the vacant throne for himself? Probably not. In any case, there was a long tradition in England that he who dethroned one king was accepted as the new king, assuming that he had some royal blood in his own veins. Thus William's desire to dethrone James was thoroughly compatible with his announced intention of securing the election of a free Parliament. If he dethroned James, there would be a good chance that such a free Parliament would then vote him the crown. He was certainly not interested in serving as regent to James or to the baby Prince of Wales. He had already rejected the offer of the regency that Charles II had proposed back in the days of the Exclusion Crisis. But the deposition of James and his own selection as king depended upon his ability to maintain an effective alliance between the Tories and the Whigs. The Tories may have been his closest allies up to the point of invasion, but there was always the doubt as to whether they would go all the way with him and offer him the crown. The Whigs, on the other hand, would not jib at deposing a king, but some of them at least were too willing to contemplate the establishment of a republic, crowned or uncrowned. The Tories

[3] Baxter, p. 233.

represented the bulk of the effective leadership in Church and state, and William needed their support. He needed the Whigs in order to effect the deposition of James. The formula was really quite simple, then: the Whigs would be willing to change the dynasty by act of Parliament, and the Tories would be willing to maintain a strong monarchy with the prerogative remaining largely unimpaired. He wanted a Whig revolution based on Tory principles. To effect this meant that he had to be clearly in league with both parties and had to keep them from falling out with each other. To do otherwise might still lead to the creation of a king's party, as the Grand Remonstrance had done in 1641.

At the end of September William was ready to sail, but the winds were not. Not until the end of October were conditions right. Bishop Burnet was on board ship and had stated that the fleet intended to sail to the North of England, when in fact it went into the Channel and headed for the coast of Devon. Baxter is convinced that this was William's aim all along (and we have already discussed William's motives). In advance of the arrival of the Dutch fleet, ships were sent ahead with copies of William's declaration in which he stated his reasons for coming and what he expected from all loyal Englishmen. The declaration was the work of Grand Pensionary Fagel and was carefully constructed to win friends and to make no enemies either in England or on the Continent. It was a revolutionary document in that it made the distinction between the king and the nation as the object of supreme loyalty. In this respect it was closer to the social-contract theory of John Locke than to the Statute of Treasons of 1352. As had always been the case with English revolutionary documents, so with this one: it was not the king but his evil advisers who were blamed for the whole catalogue of evil deeds that had been perpetrated upon England ever since the accession of James II. The essence of the document is that the king through his

evil advisers had subverted the laws and thereby the
rights of Englishmen. It rehearsed all the attacks that
had been made on the Church, the boroughs, the justices of the peace, the lords lieutenants, and the judiciary. It denounced the introduction of Papists into the
royal service, and most of all, the exercise of the supposed prerogative of dispensation and suspension. William stated that this was the worst of all because by
these devices the crown was arrogating to itself the
supreme legislative power of the realm that rightfully
and lawfully did and does belong to Parliament. The
last straw, however, was the pretended birth of a Prince
of Wales, a fraud that could result only in the further
subjection of the English people and the denial of the
right of succession to the Princess Mary, his wife.
Therefore, because of his own and his wife's great love
for England and the rights of all its people, because
of their own rights to the succession, and because of
the invitation from several of the lords spiritual and
temporal and of gentlemen from all ranks, he had determined to enter into England with sufficient force
to subdue the evil counselors of the king and to secure
the election of a free Parliament according to the franchise as it existed prior to the innovations of the present reign. This meant the restoration to office of all
those deprived by James II and the restoration of all
the old borough charters that had been revoked or
modified during the reign. "So the two houses may
concur in the preparing of such Laws as they, upon
full and free debate, shall judge necessary and convenient, both for the confirming and executing the law
concerning the Test, and such other laws as are necessary for the security and maintenance of the Protestant Religion; as likewise for making such Laws as
may establish a good agreement between the Church
of England and all Protestant Dissenters; as also, for
the covering and securing of all such who would live
peaceably under the government as becomes good subjects, from all persecution upon the account of their

Religion, even Papists themselves not excepted. . . ."[4]

In the furtherance of this good and mighty task, William called upon all Englishmen who had regard for their liberties to offer their assistance to him. And with the liberties of England once again secure it would then be possible to do the same in Scotland and in Ireland, where it would be necessary to once again secure the Protestant and British ascendancy. In Scotland the good work would be done with the assistance of a freely elected Parliament, as in England. The implication was that Ireland would have to be saved by William alone; that kingdom could not be left to its own devices.

Since the English court had gotten wind of what was in the declaration prior to its formal arrival in England, James had begun his hasty attempts to undermine it by making the concessions discussed above. To counter whatever effect those concessions might have had, William added a supplement to his original declaration in which he warned the English that concessions made in haste and in fear by the same arbitrary power that had earlier taken away the English liberties could not be trusted. They could be snatched away again just as quickly as they had been granted. William really need not have feared the effects of James's concessions—there were none of any use to the king. The English may not have thought of the concessions in quite the way William suggested they should, but at least the country was in a state of suspended animation or numbness by the time William set sail. David Ogg has summed up the atmosphere prevailing in England that autumn and has captured the mood exactly: there was no spiritual excitation, as there had been in June and July; "on the contrary, it reflected that listlessness which comes from having to choose between two evils . . ."—the Papist king and the Dutch.[5]

[4] Cobbett, V, p. 10.
[5] Ogg, *James II and William III*, p. 211.

Perhaps it was just as well that England was in this mood. Any great expression of excitement in anticipation of William's arrival might well have generated a spiritual revival in favor of James. As it was, England was in no mood to do other than wait upon events. This attitude of listlessness undoubtedly goes a long way to explain the bloodlessness of the revolution that was soon to be worked in the land. The Tory and Whig leaders may have worked deliberately to prevent enthusiasm from carrying the country into a replay of the civil war of the 1640s, but a few leaders at the top could not control or dictate the mood of the masses. The coming months were bloodless by act of policy as regards the leaders and by sheer emotional ambivalence as regards their fellow countrymen. In any case, England was to be spared all the horrors and failures of a civil war. Any other benefits that were to come from the Dutch invasion can be looked upon as a gratuitous gift, with the credit going to the Whig and Tory leaders, but also to William and to James II himself.

The ultimate destination of the Dutch fleet remained a secret and a mystery to the English, the French, and seemingly even to Admiral Herbert, who sailed with the Dutch. Even he seems to have assumed that the invasion was to take place somewhere along the east, or North Sea, coast. In any case, that is where James had sent his fleet, under Admiral Dartmouth. But whether due to higher and more secret orders, or because of the strong east wind—to which most participants assigned the decision—the fleet sailed on into the Channel and headed west, finally putting into Torbay on November 5, with Dartmouth's fleet following. As the Dutch fleet passed between Dover and Calais, the prince in the van, the ships were strung out in a line formation extending to within a league of either shore. The spectacle was viewed by throngs on both shores, and the fleet endeavored to portray an image both of invincibility and of the noblest of intentions. English, not Dutch, colors were flown, and the prince's

flag bore the motto THE PROTESTANT RELIGION AND
LIBERTIES OF ENGLAND. William, however, did not dis-
play the royal standard—in place of DIEU ET MON DROIT
he proclaimed JE MAINTIENDRAI. The bands on board
were playing martial airs.

Whatever mystery there may still be as to William's
immediate and ultimate goals, there was none surrounding the stand the king was to take. Relying on his own
best judgment and the unanimous advice of his English
and French advisers, he was convinced that the Dutch
would strike on the east coast and that the combination
of the lateness of the year, the weather, and the undoubted loyalty of the mass of his subjects would see
him through to a resounding victory. He did not even
feel impelled to declare war on the Dutch until after
the landing. The landing in the West threw all into
disarray, psychologically even more than militarily. That
William would land in the West was a surprise, and
that the English fleet could do nothing to stop it was
also barely understandable. But the suspicion arose that
the fleet had little stomach for a fight anyway. If William had sailed into the North Sea and into the waiting
arms of the English fleet, why, then, it is possible that
the fleet might have put up a defense; but Dartmouth's
shock at seeing the Dutch sail up the Channel seems
to have unnerved him. His fleet was smaller than the
Dutch, a point he was constantly to stress in his dispatches to the court, and William had already landed
by the time Dartmouth caught up with the enemy.
The tactical excuse was thus available to him to do
nothing; the real motivation, however, may well have
been political. Dartmouth and his fleet were to join
the mass of Englishmen, Louis XIV, and William himself in waiting upon events. Never had "watchful waiting" become the guiding principle for so many in such
a momentous circumstance. It was now up to James
to save himself if he could. Even Portsmouth, his final
point of departure if all else failed, was now in immediate danger of being taken from him. All now de-

pended upon the king himself, and he was his own worst enemy. As the Marquis of Halifax was to write: "That a people may let a King fall, yet still remain a people; but if a King let his people slip from him, he is no longer King."[6]

The city of Exeter was quickly seized without opposition, and William sat down to wait. A few, and only a few, of the leading citizens came to pay their respects or to offer their assistance. But while the rush to join William was less than overwhelming, none showed the slightest disposition to oppose him. Among those who did come was Sir Edward Seymour, the "king of the West," who had first raised the flag of opposition against James's policies in the early months of his one and only Parliament, 'way back in 1685. His support and that of Lord Mordaunt served to guarantee that there would be no resistance forthcoming in the Southwest. It had long been assumed that the furies of the reaction to Monmouth's landing had destroyed all anti-loyalist tendencies in the region. That may have been so, but it had certainly not created any new spirit of loyalty to the king and the court. As a device to assure ultimate victory, or at least survival, the English who had joined the prince's camp drew up an "Association," composed by Bishop Burnet, who had sailed over with William. The declaration asserted their determination to assist the prince in achieving his declared goals —the calling of a free Parliament and the restoration of the fundamental laws. It also committed them to a pledge of their own lives and fortunes if any attacks were made upon the person of the prince. So William's overt support was small but influential. They realized that the stakes were high, but the goal was still supposedly no more than arranging for James and William to clasp hands and see to the election of a free Parliament according to the old franchise. Given James's

[6] George Savile, Marquis of Halifax, "Maxims of State," *The Complete Works of George Savile, First Marquess of Halifax*, ed. by Walter Raleigh, Oxford, 1912, p. 183.

adamant refusal since the fall of 1685 to have anything
more to do with a freely elected Parliament—even Sunderland had at last been dismissed over this concession
—the achievement of the goal was certainly highly unlikely. William's English friends may still have considered it realistic. That William did is unlikely. If
he did have his eye on the crown, nothing was yet said
to indicate it. But once he had gambled so much and
was now actually encamped on English soil, it would
seem likely that his own goal, if not plans, was far more
advanced than those stated in his declaration.

Since Lord Dartmouth had been either unwilling or
unable to prevent William's landing, the only possibility of stopping William rested with the king's army.
Turner has suggested that if James had been inclined
to move quickly he might well have succeeded in ex-
pelling the invaders, who were in poor condition to
fight after the rigors of the sea voyage.[7] However, the
evident reluctance of the populace to rally spontaneously to the king's cause spelled doom to James's political and religious policies whether he succeeded in ex-
pelling William or not. William was no Monmouth,
and the political climate in England had changed almost beyond recognition since the spring of 1685.
Where there was general support for the destruction
of the Monmouth rising, there would have been only
a sullen acquiescence in a royal victory on this occasion. Unless James were able to hold the country down
by force and govern by martial law—assuming that Louis
XIV would provide the money and perhaps even the
men, which was now highly unlikely—he would have to
seek a political reconciliation, which meant the calling
of a Parliament. It is impossible to believe that after
all the hopes, dreams, plots, and intrigues of the previous year, the country would just settle back and see
James triumph over all. William's defeat could well
have led to a civil war, which James could not win in

[7] Turner, p. 429.

the long run without subjecting England to a French-style and perhaps even a French-run monarchy. He would need autocratic power to win such a war, and victory would cement this new power. The calling of a free Parliament before the invasion had been too much for James to accept. He could hardly expect to profit from free elections after crushing William, since the country would be completely alienated. But whatever the possibilities for the future may have been, in the crucial hours of his life and reign James lost his ability to act decisively and may even have lost his nerve. Whatever may have been his principles of monarchy and government in the past—and he was, after all, a high prerogative man and had always believed that his father's downfall had been caused by vacillation and too great a willingness to compromise—James II in fact was not made of the stuff of tyrants. Whether it was a desire to spare his people, his wife and young son, and himself; a premonition of impending doom; or the want of a backbone, is impossible to say.

More likely than any of these explanations is the evidence of rapidly advancing senility. Prior to the invasion, James personally had been the dominating and driving intelligence in the court. He had come closer to being his own chief minister than any king had since Charles I had been stripped of Laud and Strafford. But with the landing of William, all was chaos at court and seemingly in James's mind as well. His Privy Council and his Catholic council were as confused as he was—the former because they were not dedicated to him, the latter because they had never had experience of government or decision making, their role having always been that of inspiring James in the pursuit of his Catholicizing policy, leaving the tactics and strategy to the king himself. James had taken all the reins into his own hands, and now that the crisis had come he had no idea what to do with them; and there was no one of any substance to whom he could turn. His own response to the crisis was a decline into apathy and a paternal concern for the welfare of his wife and son. On board ship to France later on, and all during the long years of his exile, he was always happy in his apathetic unconcern at his own fate and of his dreams for his country, to which he was devoted. It may even be possible that his response, or lack of it, to the invasion and his subsequent flight into exile were in fact motivated by his sense of duty and patriotism. Turner himself has suggested that senility was unlikely in a man still so young and physically vigorous.[8] In any case and whatever the reasons, James did manage to spare his country a great tragedy, even though he was never to earn any compliments for himself in the process.

After approving of Dartmouth's handling of the fleet and partially recovering from the shock of hearing that William had landed in the West, James finally, after several days of confusion and indecision, decided that he should personally take command of his army, which was now encamped at Salisbury, still sixty miles distant from William's force, which had moved up to Axminster. James was accompanied to Salisbury by a host of his relatives and officers, almost all of whom had already made elaborate and presumably definite plans as to how and when to desert the king for the prince. Clarendon's son, Lord Cornbury, had already deserted from Salisbury but had not been able to induce any significant number of his troops to follow him. This was thus an encouraging sign for James. However, the desertions that were to follow were so grand in terms of the persons concerned that the effect would be shattering, no matter what the troops themselves chose to do.

John Churchill, now Lord Churchill, who had played a major role on behalf of the king in crushing the Monmouth rebellion, had spent years in the service of James both as Duke of York and as king. Churchill's wife, Sarah, had been a lady in waiting to Mary of

8 Turner, p. 456.

Modena, both as duchess and as queen, and was a close companion of the Duke's daughters, Mary and Anne. Once again James was to put his confidence in Churchill, promoting him to the rank of Lieutenant-General. Accompanying James to Salisbury, Churchill was to play a role that shocked both his contemporaries and posterity. Early in August Churchill had written to William renewing his pledge of loyalty, which he had first made over a year before. This letter served to condemn his future actions in the eyes not only of James II's friends, but even in the eyes of those who wholeheartedly approved of the Glorious Revolution.

Mr Sydney will let you know how I intend to behave myself: I think it is what I owe to God and my country. My honour I take leave to put into your royal highness's hands, in which I think it safe. If you think there is anything else that I ought to do, you have but to command me, and I shall pay an entire obedience to it, being resolved to die in that religion that it has pleased God to give you both the will and the power to protect.[9]

To have written this letter, the meaning of which is not really in doubt, and then to join the king and assume the command of his forces at Salisbury, was to cast a shadow over his personal honor and integrity that shocked the world until his great descendant, Winston Churchill, succeeded, at least partially, in righting the balance nearly two hundred fifty years later. While at Salisbury, Churchill urged the king to take the offensive and press the attack against William. James, either because of indecision, apathy, or a keen appreciation of the risks involved, did not heed the advice. While the king planned his retreat to London, Churchill deserted the royal camp, accompanied by the king's nephew, the Duke of Grafton. To have spent his adult life in the service of James, to have joined his command at Salisbury, to have urged an advance upon

[9] Sir Winston S. Churchill, *Marlborough: His Life and Times*, New York, 1933, Vol. I, p. 272.

the Dutch army, and then to desert to the enemy was indeed a cruel and, as it proved, decisive blow to James.

Churchill's great abilities as a soldier and statesman were to enable him to survive this episode, but he was to carry with him to his grave the reputation of being a man without basic integrity of character. To the English, a man's principles are not as important as his willingness to abide by his principles, and a pledge once given cannot be taken back. The problem, of course, was that Churchill had made conflicting pledges—to James and to William. Since it was William's declared purpose to do no more than secure the election of a free Parliament, which in turn would require the cooperation of the king, the conflict could have been resolved if William and James had come together. An advance by the royal army need not necessarily have resulted in battle. As the two armies approached, there would be the possibility, at least, that James and William would agree to avoid the final resort to arms and that the reconciliation could be effected. James's refusal to advance and his subsequent decision to retreat meant that the reconciliation was doomed. Therefore, the pledge to William, which in turn meant a pledge to the Protestant religion by law established, had to take precedence over the pledge to the king. As involved and casuistical as this justification may be, it is that offered by Winston Churchill, and after two and one half centuries it has begun to carry weight.

As James progressed back to his capital, he discovered that Prince George of Denmark, his son-in-law, had gone over to William, and upon reaching London he found to his ultimate dismay that his daughter, the Princess Anne, had left to join her husband. These two crucial defections were rightly attributed to the work of Churchill. Once he made the decision to desert his king and friend, he had to guarantee the success of the rebellion or lose all. He did his work well, and the success was his. There was little left for the king to do but arrange for the departure of his queen

and his son and then of his own person. All the efforts
the king made during the last week of November
and the first week of December to negotiate with William appear in retrospect to have been nothing more
than another bout of indecision or merely a smoke
screen while he thought through his final plans for
escape. If the efforts to reach a compromise with William were sincere, they were singularly unsuccessful.

William remained at Exeter, receiving the deserters,
but not succumbing to them. He was as determined
as ever to play his own game and to wait upon events.
Since all was going so smoothly, there was no need
whatsoever for William to allow himself to become the
pawn of any of those who had come over to him, no
matter how strong or influential. Danby, in the North,
had sent a steady stream of letters to William but had
received no answers. In the end, the North had to fend
for itself. Either it had to rebel and submit itself to
William or it could wait upon events and see William
triumph without its help. Danby chose to act, and with
the help of Lord Derby the North rose against the
royalist forces and delivered itself over to William's
cause. William received word of the northern rising
before leaving Exeter, and therefore, when he did finally break camp and begin to move east at a leisurely
pace, he was secure in his own command of the situation, North and South. Danby could help William but
he would be in no position to dictate to William. The
king, in turn, was reluctant even in the face of these
disasters to call upon the aid of Louis XIV. After all,
William had not as yet formally attacked James's forces,
and he was therefore reluctant to provoke him need-
lessly. Louis was quite content to remain cautious. All
along, he had gambled that the invasion would serve
to immobilize both England and Holland at no cost to
himself. So far, his strategy was working. And it should
again be said on James's behalf that as little as he understood England, he was still a patriot.

As James entered London after his retreat from Salisbury, the capital itself was in turmoil for fear that if the rival armies were to actually engage in battle, it might be within the city itself. This fear that London itself might become a battleground was compounded by the furious comings and goings of all those men of consequence who were personally concerned with the fate of the dynasty. During the king's absence Whitehall was besieged by these people seeking news, burning papers, covering their tracks, and in general trying to arrange their affairs so that they would at least survive regardless of the final outcome of the battle of wills between William and James. The return of the king, who immediately summoned a council of peers, soon put a stop to the fears and the agitations. James needed advice, and for once he seemed bent upon following the advice that was offered. Since his plans for escape were already laid, this was undoubtedly just a "smoke screen," as Dr. Ashley had called it.[10] Among the peers were the Earl of Bedford, the father of Admiral Russell; and the Earl of Clarendon, the royal brother-in-law. James already knew that Derby had failed to obey his commands to secure Lancashire, and that Danby had instigated the northern rebellion. Under the circumstances, the advice that could be rendered was obvious and the king had no choice but to accept it, or flee. They therefore proposed "To issue a pardon to the Prince's adherents, to remove papists from offices, to assemble a Parliament, and to send a deputation for a treaty to the Prince."[11] James agreed to all these proposals, and the news served immediately to restore tranquillity to the metropolis. Those who attended the conference were shocked by the king's demeanor. It was said that his mental powers seemed to have gone from him. "Where were the looks, and where the spirit, which had made three kingdoms to

[10] Ashley, p. 169.
[11] Dalrymple, I, p. 168.

tremble?"[12] Dalrymple suggested that the greater change was in the minds of the observers, not the king. James had never made three kingdoms tremble; his councilors, however, no longer looked upon him as their sovereign, but as a pitiful, broken old man. Their advice was the counsel of despair if not defeat. In effect, they told him that he could save his throne only by repudiating everything for which he had stood as a man and as a king.

A commission consisting of Lords Nottingham, Halifax, and Godolphin was sent to William with a draft treaty. The first two peers had long been in communication with William, although neither had signed the invitation. Godolphin was a close friend of both Sunderland, who had recently been dismissed from office, and Lord Churchill, who had already defected to William. By the time the commissioners reached William's camp, the Earl of Clarendon had also defected. James's fate was thus placed in the hands of men who were far more concerned with their own and England's fate than with that of the king or of the dynasty. It was probably true, though, even at this late date, that they were more interested in using William to get concessions from James than they were in effecting a change of dynasty, which William had not as yet called for anyway. The letter the commissioners bore stated simply that the king had agreed to the calling of a Parliament on January 15, at which time the various grievances to which William had referred in his declaration could be aired, and that both armies should keep a safe distance from London so that the Parliament could carry on its deliberations free from coercion from either side. Naturally a few security guards would be provided.

William was in no hurry to receive the delegation. They got lost along the way because of a drunken guide; the prince delayed in issuing passes for them to proceed behind his lines; and when they finally did get to

the Dutch camp at Hungerford, William refused to
see them personally, sending William Bentinck and
Lords Oxford and Shrewsbury instead. Rather than re-
plying to the commission's letter, William's emissaries
informed them of the prince's terms. He demanded
the removal of all Papists from office and the withdrawal of all proclamations directed against William;
the Tower and the fort at Tilbury were to be turned
over to the jurisdiction of the City of London, and
monies were to be provided for the maintenance of
William's army while it was in England. Also, no more
foreign troops were to be allowed into the kingdom,
Portsmouth was to be in the custody of those chosen
by both William and James acting in concert, and if
James were to reside in London during the meeting of
the new Parliament, then William was to be allowed
to do so too.

These demands—and they *were* presented to the
commissioners as demands, not as points for further
discussion—were actually drawn up by those Englishmen who were in attendance upon the prince. He only
exercised a veto over them. William and the English
defectors disagreed on one point. William wanted the
writs for an election, which James had prepared, to
stand. The defectors wanted them canceled. Because
of their attendance upon William, many of the English
feared that a sudden election would catch them out of
their local communities and thus they would not secure election for themselves. William heard them out,
but did not give in. Thus we can assume that the English defectors wrote the answer to James's letter, but
the contents thoroughly represented William's own
stand. The old writs were to stand.[13] It is important
to bear this in mind. William, as always, had to play
his cards most carefully. As we shall see, he had by now
clearly determined to acquire the crown. This meant
the removal of James. But James had to be seen as the

[13] Ibid., p. 170.

author of his own doom, and if he appeared to be pushed to the brink, then it was better that the English themselves should appear to have done it. Therefore, the English were allowed to frame William's answer, but in words that he himself could approve. The final result was, on paper, liberal and something that most fair-minded observers could see to be fair and natural, given the circumstances of the two sides. In fact the terms seemed more acceptable to Halifax, the moderate Tory and royal commissioner, than they did to many of the Whigs who had thrown in with William. What they wanted at this point was the removal of James and the installation of William. Having deserted their king, they could not rest comfortably with any settlement short of total victory.

William saw it differently, however. He was not greatly concerned with either the fate or the honor of the defectors. He was merely content to use them for his own purposes. One way or another, James would have to remove himself. William was still gambling that, given time, the victory would fall to him; he would not in the end be forced to seize it. But the apparent willingness of the prince to play for time and to comtemplate negotiations with the king did not sit well with some of the English. For those with William a Parliament called under the writs issued by James II was far from their definition of a victory. The brilliance of William's strategy was already becoming clear. The English, at least the Whigs, now wanted a change in dynasty, and they had come to this position on their own. William would not have to seize the throne; they would give it to him. The throne would be vacant by James's own doing, not by his. William's own hands would be as clean and as unfettered as they could possibly be in such circumstances. Never was a *coup d'-état* so cleverly planned, nor so easily accomplished. There may well have been a good deal of luck involved in all of this, but William trusted in his own reading of the situation, and since he played his hand consistently from the start, it seems wrong to assign his final triumph to luck alone.

The prince's answer was delivered to Halifax, but since the commissioners were not empowered to negotiate with William, no formal answer on the king's behalf was forthcoming. Halifax did, however, take the opportunity to have a private conversation with Bishop Burnet. Since Burnet was garrulous and even a bit flighty, it appears that his presence at the meeting with the commissioners was part of William's strategy. He knew that Burnet would talk, but perhaps Halifax would reply in turn. And so it was. Halifax asked Burnet, "What is it that you want? Do you wish to get the king into your power?" Burnet replied, "Not at all, we would not do the least harm to his person." Thus Halifax: "And if he were to go away?" To which crucial question Burnet answered, "There is nothing so much to be wished." Burnet repeated the conversation to William, who expressed his approval. William's strategy was now exposed. Would the king co-operate? It was Macaulay's view that even at this late date James could have stopped his enemies from forcibly overthrowing him, even if all the disparate forces were to unite against him.[14] He may have been right. Perhaps William realized it. If so, his strategy was not only brilliant, but forced upon him by circumstances. The end of the drama was to come quicker than anyone had the right to expect.

The commissioners received the prince's answer on December 8 and set off again for London. The king received the answer to his letter on the tenth and promised that he would in turn reply the next day. No reply was ever forthcoming. Instead James spent the night burning the writs for the Parliamentary election, ordered the disbandment of his army, and early the next morning fled Whitehall for Sheerness to take ship for France. The decision to flee had been taken on the

14 Macaulay, II, p. 488.

ninth, the day the first news of the prince's answer
had been forwarded to him. He packed the queen and
the Prince of Wales off and promised to join them
within twenty-four hours. In his letter to Feversham
calling for the disbandment of his army, the king
summed up the situation:

Things being come to that extremity that I have been forced
to send away the Queen and my son the Prince of Wales that
they might not fall into my enemy's hands, which they
must have done had they stayed, I am obliged to do the same
thing, and endeavour to secure myself the best I can, in hopes
it will please God, out of His infinite mercy to this unhappy
nation, to touch their hearts with true loyalty and honour.
If I could have relied upon all my troops I might not have
been put to this extremity I am in, and would at least have
had one blow for it; but, though I know there are many loyal
and brave men amongst you, yet you know you yourself, and
several of the general officers told me, it was no ways advisable
to venture myself at their head. There remains nothing more
for me to do but to thank you and all those officers and
soldiers who have stuck to me and been truly loyal; I hope
you will still have the same fidelity to me and, though I do
not expect you should expose yourselves by resisting a foreign
army and poisoned nation, yet I hope your former principles
are so rooted in you that you will keep yourselves free from
associations and such pernicious things.[15]

This was not the letter of a man in a fit of panic. It
is the letter of a man resigned to fate, not in fear of
his life. His failure to give instructions as to the disposition of his troops or to their future relations with
William, would indicate that James had completely
washed his hands of his former kingdom. The future
was not for him to determine, to influence, or even to
contemplate. There was no hint that the flight was
merely a temporary expedient, until time and circumstances were more propitious. This letter had the tone
of finality about it.

The flight to the coast and its denouement was a

15 Turner, p. 442.

comedy of errors, James being captured and returned to London, much to his own and William's annoyance. But the flight and its failure did in the end serve to convince one and all that the reign of James II was at an end. James took the Great Seal with him. Why he did so and what he did with it was conceivably fraught with significance, but what that significance was has never really been determined. Before his departure from Whitehall he had burned the writs for the election that had not yet been posted, and ordered the cancellation of those that had been sent. It is possible that by taking the Great Seal with him, he hoped to prevent anyone acting in his name from calling a valid Parliament. By retaining the Seal he retained the ultimate symbol of his royal authority. When Charles I had fled to Oxford in 1641 the Great Seal soon followed him and Charles was able to use it as a symbol that the legal government was still his and was in Oxford with him. A reign does not end by moving the Seal, but by smashing it to bits. Thus James fled with the full determination that he was the king and would remain so. But as he was rowed across the Thames he deliberately threw it overboard. Why? Was this a way of hiding it from his enemies, so that he was still king but neither he nor they could exercise the authority of the crown? Or did dropping it in the river serve as a substitute for the smashing of the Seal and thus signify the end of his reign? No one knows, and, really, no one cared. Whatever the motives, James II had given even an ardent Royalist/Anglican a good excuse, if one were wanted, for believing that his reign had ended voluntarily, by "abdication." At any rate, James told Barillon that if William seized the throne, he would not be able to call a legal Parliament without the Great Seal. James's hope of denying the symbol of legality to those who were now to assume the responsibilities for the kingdom were dashed. A fisherman caught the Great Seal in his net off Lambeth Pier and delivered it to the Privy Council. "Heaven seemed by this accident to declare that the laws, the constitution, and the sovereignty of Great Britain were not to depend on the frailty of man. . . ."[16]

The news got out the next morning that the king had fled, and the whole day of December 11 saw the Protestant mob looting and damaging Catholic chapels and homes and insulting or roughing up those unpopular figures who were associated in the public mind with the court policy. Among them was Lord Jeffreys, the Chancellor, who was arrested and sent to the Tower, which had already defected to William. The Lord Mayor feared for his own and the City's safety, and he hastily called a meeting of those peers and privy councilors resident in the City to a meeting at Guildhall. If the king had truly abandoned his kingdom, it was essential that law and order be maintained as best as possible and that the vacuum be filled immediately. Consequently, the assembled peers and councilors agreed to inform the prince at once of the state of the crown and the City, and to urge him to hasten to the capital. The message was duly delivered to William, who was by now at Abingdon, in Berkshire, still disinclined to proceed faster than events could carry him.

Before the prince could fully make up his mind about the message from London, word came that the situation had once again changed and was even more confusing than before. Fishermen on the lookout for priests had captured James, and upon discovering the true identity of their prisoner, had treated him with all proper respect. When news of the capture reached London, the Privy Council met again and decided to invite James to return, and sent Lord Feversham with a coach with which to deliver him. Where the royal flight had been greeted with anti-Catholic rioting, news of his capture and imminent return evoked expressions of

[16] Campbell, John, Lord, *The Lives of the Lord Chancellors of England*, London, 1845, III, p. 576.

pity and concern for his fate. While his journey back to London was not exactly a triumphal progress, still he was met with a limited enthusiasm. Forced once again to contemplate the state of his and the kingdom's affairs, he saw the situation to be hopeless and so took no other action than to send Feversham as an emissary to William, inviting him to St. James's to confer as to what the future should be.

Some of the prince's advisers suggested that he should indeed proceed to London and make the king a prisoner, but William was not to be dissuaded from his original strategy. James had fled once rather than face either a fight or a conference with William that could only result in the calling of a Parliament. William gambled on the likelihood that James would do exactly the same thing again if the opportunity were presented. The strategy had been sound, as far as William could see. It had failed in its execution only by a stroke of ill fortune. So that he would not become the hostage of fate again, things would just have to be better arranged next time. Consequently, Lords Halifax and Shrewsbury were ordered to see that all English guards were removed from the royal precincts in London and Westminster and that Dutch guards be substituted for them. This task was accomplished without incident. A message was then sent to James stating that William felt called upon to enter London, but that it would be safer for both the City and for James if he would first remove himself to the town of Ham, with suitable guards for his own personal safety. James's reply to this offer is final proof, if still more proof were needed, that James had ceased to think of himself as king. He was willing to leave London but hoped that he would be allowed to go to Rochester rather than Ham. Since Rochester was a port, the meaning was clear, and so the next day saw William enter London from the west as James exited to the east and proceeded to Rochester. James spent a week in Rochester, under the protection of Dutch Catholic guards, in a fit of indecision and being advised by many that a stand was still possible. A message from his wife in France recalled him to his promise to follow her, and so his mind was made up for him and he sailed away into exile.

William avoided all publicity as he entered London, and it was not until the next day that he was greeted by a delegation of bishops and masters of the City companies. William was urged, especially by the lawyers then present, to assume the crown immediately, as Henry VII had done after Bosworth, and to issue writs for the election of a new Parliament. Nothing, however, was to sway the prince from his basic strategy. Instead of assuming the crown and calling a Parliament, he agreed to assume the administration of the military, with the peers administering the government, and to issue letters resembling writs calling for the election of a convention. "Thus was the Revolution brought about in England, with the general applause of the nation."[17]

Actually there was more apathy than applause, and what applause there was, was more out of relief that England had passed through the night peacefully than that there had been a revolution. Even Bishop Burnet had to record that basic sense of fair play that once again manifested itself:

. . . only some few steps in the latter part of it were not so well approved. The waking the King out of his sleep in his own palace, and ordering him to be gone, when he was ready to submit to anything; the placing a strange guard about him, dismounting his own, and posting the Dutch where the English used to stand, looking like a compulsion upon his person, gave some disgust, and furnished an excuse for his going away.[18]

[17] Burnet [B], *History,* pp. 286–89.
[18] Ibid., p. 289.

PART III

The Revolution Settlement

CHAPTER 8

Parliament and Crown

During the interregnum between the flight of James II and the offer of the crown to William and Mary, the crucial decision as to the nature of the settlement was made by William himself. While appearing to remain secluded at St. James's Palace, he was actually continuing to watch the course of events most closely. Now that James was gone, we can see the rapid return of the leading politicians to the political views and principles they had held in the days of Charles II and the first two years of James II. The Tories/Anglicans showed tendencies to return to the old hereditary principle and to passive obedience. The Whigs looked forward to a parliamentary, not a hereditary, settlement of the crown and to securing the long-dreamed-of revenge upon those who had co-operated with both Charles II and James II in the crushing of the Whigs after the failure of exclusion. William now saw that it was no longer practicable to let events take their own course. He must actively seek to control those events or all would be lost. He had not abandoned the Continent to an aggressive Louis XIV, at great expense to himself and the Dutch estates, just to further the interests of one or another English faction. As far as possible, he had to control the settlement, but in doing so, he had to make it appear that England was securing her own destiny and that the proper forms were respected. But he had almost all the cards in his own hands, and the strongest card of all was that he was there and James was gone. If he were to pack up and go home, the English would be at each other's throats, and he and they both knew it. While he would not seize the throne, he was determined that it would be given to him. The conscience, or honor, of the Whig or the Tory meant not a thing to William. How the offer was arranged was their business, but arrange it they must. As he told those in attendance upon him, he would not tolerate the return of James II, he would not serve as his regent, nor would he be his wife's "gentleman usher" if the crown were to be given to her. Under any of these circumstances he would return to Holland.

So the interregnum was spent with the government practically in limbo and with the air being filled with the issuance of pamphlets debating the fundamental issues to be settled by the Convention Parliament. The Whigs were ready to move directly to the election of William as king, thus achieving both revenge on the house of Stuart and the triumph of the principle that the monarchy was a public, not a private, institution, at the disposal of the nation. The Anglican clergy now felt great pangs of conscience over their near desertion of the principle of passive obedience. For them and for the Tories in general the question was either a regency in the name of James II, or if he could be seen to have abdicated, then the crown should descend directly to Mary. Indeed, for the clergy, the thought of even a regency was too much at first. For at least the first two weeks after William's arrival in London, they were still hoping for the restoration of James. Their retreat into the folds of their old doctrine of divine right, hereditary monarchy, and passive obedience to it merely served to remove the bishops from any key role in fashioning the final settlement. If anything was to be salvaged from the old Tory/Anglican tradition, it would be the task of pragmatic politicians such as Halifax and Danby who would accomplish it, and they were far more concerned with the realities of power than with logical consistency or niceties of conscience, for which William cared not a fig anyway.

The Convention was duly elected, and met on January 22, 1689, in a setting and under rules representing those of as true a Parliament as the circumstances would allow. Of course there was no speech from the throne and no Lord Chancellor who could preside over the Lords. The leading candidates for the leadership of the two Houses at first appeared to be two of the men who had consistently opposed James and had assisted William in the invasion: Danby and Sir Edward Seymour. The designations, however, went to two men who represented a tendency to "trim"—Halifax and Sir Henry Powle.

The Convention was in a truly unique position in English history. In circumstances and in opportunities it resembled both the meeting of the Long Parliament, in the fall of 1640, and the meeting of the Convention in the spring of 1660. As in the spring of 1660, there was in fact if not in theory a vacancy on the throne, and thus the Convention had the task of "restoring" a valid and viable government. As in the fall of 1640, the crisis of government and of the constitution provided the opportunity and the need to reform the traditional constitution. The question was, which of the two precedents would carry the greater weight? Would 1640 and all that followed be re-enacted in a major, perhaps wholesale and even violent, change in the whole structure of Church and state? Or would 1660 be the model and lead to no change of any substance and merely see the "restoration" of the old system in the person of William, either as king or as regent? This book began with a discussion of the Restoration of 1660 and showed how it had totally failed to solve those fundamental problems in Church and state that had led to the Long Parliament and the Civil War in the first place. The use of either 1640 or 1660 as a model for the new settlement could only help lead to failure again in the not too distant future. As it turned out, the Convention of 1689 was to combine reform with restoration. Whether this was sheer luck or whether it was a conscious decision on the part of William and the Convention leadership is the question that confronts us. That the result was, indeed, both reform and restoration cannot be denied, however. The next thirty to forty years have been described as a period of political instability in England,[1] but that is not the same as saying that it was a period of constitutional instability. The distinction between constitutional and political stability may well be a fine one, but nonetheless there is such a distinction. The settlement worked out in the Convention and in the later Parliaments of the new reign provided a framework within which the new political battles could be fought and eventually achieve what Professor Plumb has called the "adamantine" stability of the eighteenth century.

Throughout seventeenth-century Europe there was a conscious effort being made to create conditions of political and social stability, so as to make the turmoil that had plagued Europe since the Reformation a thing of the past. Where this stability was achieved on the Continent it was invariably the work of the monarch or, as in Germany, of the ruling nobility. The result was the creation of the highly centralized monarchical state in which government administered society, but with little or no room for the free play of political forces or personalities, except at court and then only in the pursuit of office. The France of Louis XIV was the exemplar of the seventeenth-century European achievement of stability. Politics was denied a role, and the nation was administered. Considering the horrors of the wars of religion in sixteenth-century France and of the Thirty Years' War in Germany, it is understandable that politics was condemned as being allied with fanaticism, which could lead not only to the destruction

[1] See J. H. Plumb, *The Growth of Political Stability in England*, 1675–1725, London, 1967.

of the state but of the very fabric of society itself. Something not unlike this was seen in Tudor England, where, for long, historians had seen the development of "Tudor despotism." In fact the Tudors, especially Henry VIII and Elizabeth I, were themselves too political and too wise to seek, much less to hope to achieve, anything comparable to that which Louis XIV eventually acquired.

The Stuarts were another matter altogether. Coming to the English throne quite ignorant of English laws and customs, and being inclined to a sympathy with the Continent, especially France, they sought to recreate in England what seemed to be the new European ideal—a stable and prosperous nation administered by and through the agency of the royal prerogative. The Protectorate of Oliver Cromwell, whatever his conscience may have told him, was just another example of this same centralizing and administrative tendency; the Restoration and the reigns of Charles II and of James II saw the further extension of the same trend.

Unlike Charles I and Cromwell, Charles II was both too secure on his throne and too wise politically to push his dreams beyond the brink. The Exclusion Crisis had played right into his hands, however, and during the last four years of his reign and the three years of James II's, the Continental way was being vigorously extended. James II, however, was either too principled or too stupid to realize that he was going too far and too fast. His religion provided the excuse for his policy and the excuse for those who would oppose him, but his religion was not the basic or even the real issue. The real issue was a struggle for power, as it had been in 1640 and in the Cromwellian interregnum. It has already been pointed out that this struggle was fought on two levels —who would exercise the powers of the central government, the king or ministers responsible to Parliament, and secondly, what powers should the central government exercise in the first place? The Restoration had

simply restored the system of Charles I, minus the prerogative courts. Both Charles II and James II had been
able to demonstrate that in the absence of a Parliament
they were able to stretch the prerogative very far indeed, and James II even managed to re-create one of
those prerogative courts that had been abolished by
statute in 1640—the High Commission. Ever since the
Addled Parliament, of 1614, the "country" was determined to find a means of clipping the wings of the
prerogative, with the monarchy if possible, without it if
necessary. A solution to this problem would have to be
found in 1689 or within the next few years, or the likelihood of revolution and civil war could not be dispelled. The Convention of 1689 did indeed take the
first vital step in this direction. The rest was to be accomplished in the remaining years of the new reign.
Of course, the French wars and the personality and
character of William III were also to play important
parts.

Clipping the wings of the royal prerogative was only
half the task and half the story. A decision also had to
be reached as to what powers would reside with the
central government and what powers would devolve
upon the country itself and its ruling class in the boroughs and provinces. In some ways, this was the more
important issue. An all-powerful central government,
even if exercised by men answerable to Parliament, still
offered limited opportunities for the mass of the gentry
and aristocracy and their colleagues in the boroughs.
Only a few men could ever hope to achieve sufficient
office and influence on a national level to slake their
thirst for power. By halting the march of centralization
and actually returning power to the localities, a far
larger number would be able to achieve and exercise
power and responsibility and to see that their own and
their clients' and neighbors' interests were protected.

Dr. Plumb has likened the position of the gentry in
the later-seventeenth century to the barons in the late-

twelfth and early-thirteenth centuries.[2] Where the latter secured their rights in Magna Carta, the former were to consolidate theirs in the Bill of Rights. Even if the full and complete Revolution settlement was not the work of the Convention alone, but was being forged throughout the reign of William III, still it was true that by their disposition of the crown and by the drawing up of the Bill of Rights the basic foundation was laid. A king bent more on foreign war than on the administration of England was to facilitate the accomplishment of the remainder before his reign was over. As we relate the story of the Convention, the names Whig and Tory, Dissenter and Anglican come into frequent usage; however, it must be remembered that, meaningful as these designations are—and they are meaningful indeed—there was still an underlying unity between the groups. The reign of James II had shown quite clearly that Whig and Tory and Anglican and Dissenter could work together with a high degree of amity when they could see that the enemy of one was also the enemy of the other. James's effort to establish Catholicism by means of the royal prerogative had succeeded in reminding the ruling classes of England as to just how much they did have in common. Once James was gone and the new dispensation was settled, then the old factional fights could begin again, as fiercely as ever. But the new fights were within the basic system, not against it. At least until after the accession of the Hanoverians, in 1714, the game of politics was a vicious one, with little concern either for the rules or for the losers. It was a game to see who would control the center; the center itself was clearly located in Parliament, and the center was increasingly inclined to let the localities alone. This would be the achievement of the Glorious Revolution, and within two generations even the form of conflict at the center would be regularized and England would settle into the classic

[2] Plumb, p. 22.

eighteenth-century stability in which politics was largely a struggle for office or place, waged more by families and patron/client factions than by party itself. The England of Sir Lewis Namier was not created in 1689, but the foundation was laid, and the first few floors were constructed by the time William died.

Historians have long been interested in the interaction of ideas and events and of the relative importance of the man of ideas and the man of action. Put most simply, does the idea generate the action or does the action generate the idea? Does the thinker and writer have a creative role to play in the world of reality, or does he merely rationalize the status quo and its practical alternatives? The greatest names in English political theory have been men who combined both roles —thought and action—to a greater extent than has been true on the Continent. Undoubtedly the two outstanding political thinkers of the seventeenth century in England were Thomas Hobbes and John Locke. Of the two, Hobbes was the pure intellectual while Locke was both an intellectual and a man of affairs; Hobbes was more in the Continental stream of political thought, while Locke was more typically English. It may be faulty logic to base a generalization as to the role of ideas in relation to action upon a sample of just two men; but for whatever it is worth, it is a fact that Hobbes and his writings carried precious little political weight in the seventeenth century. The *Leviathan* made hardly a ripple on the waters of politics when it first appeared, in the 1650s. In fact it carried little weight even in intellectual circles until the emergence of the utilitarians, in the early-nineteenth century. Locke, on the other hand, was a man who had worked closely with the Earl of Shaftesbury in the '70s and had been assigned the task of drawing up a system of government for the Carolinas. He was not a participant in the Glorious Revolution, but he was aware of the practicalities of political life and of the difference between a theory of government and a constitution that would have to be put into use. The question is, to what extent did the ideas of Locke, or of anyone else, have a vital role to play in the Convention? The publication of Locke's two treatises on government did not occur until 1690, but they were written before the Revolution, although his attacks on Filmer were already extant.

Put simply, seventeenth-century political theory was not creative in any true sense. Where its tenets could be seen in action, it could be seen to follow rather than precede that action. But the political thinker was then, as he is now, a useful adjunct to the men of action, in that he could take affairs out of the realm of pure interest and link them with the gods or with nature or with the eternal verities. This is not to suggest that men of action do not have principles, or that they do not read and quote and take seriously the work of the political theorist. But there was nothing in the seventeenth century comparable to modern ideological politics, where the ideas of a single man or group of men take on religious significance and provide a substitute for one or another of the traditional other-worldly religions. We see no Filmerians, Hobbesians, or Lockians in the world of Parliament or of the court.

Just as the modern Conservative and Liberal party traditions can be traced back through the centuries, encompassing Tory and Whig and on to the Royalist and the Parliamentarian, so we can also trace back two fundamental streams of political theory: There is the Tory stream, which began with Bishop Hooker and passes on down through Filmer, Clarendon, Bolingbroke, Burke, and Disraeli. The Whig tradition can be traced through Eliot, Pym, Sydney, Shaftesbury, Locke, Charles James Fox, and Lord John Russell. In 1688 and 1689 the traditions were alive, but the weight of events was to pull them together, never to be fully separated again. What separated the parties was the view of the nature and origin of the state. Both were monarchical, but to the Tory the monarch was God's vicar on earth. The right of accession to the throne was itself by an act of God—in other words, the accident of birth. The office of king was of divine origin; the occupier of that office was not necessarily divine, but his selection was an act of God and could not be challenged. Thus the Tory was wedded to the principle of hereditary monarchy, and to the principle that loyalty and obedience were owed politically and morally to the office and to its occupier. For the Whigs, on the other hand, there was ever since the early-seventeenth century the growing tendency to think in terms of what Locke finally called the social contract. The office of king was the ultimate creation of the society itself, for its own ultimate good. As long as all went well and the interest of society was defended, then hereditary succession and obedience were right and necessary. But if and when the time ever came that the existence of a free and healthy society were threatened, then those who represented that society were free to take appropriate action. Locke's second treatise, which was written prior to the flight of James II, goes a long way in justifying the right of rebellion. Actually both these theories are products of the medieval world and its adaptation of Aristotelian politics. For Aristotle, St. Thomas Aquinas, and Bishop Hooker the form that government took was dependent upon the goal that government and society were to achieve. For Aristotle the goal was to develop and give vent to the virtues of citizenship—thus a middle-class polity. For St. Thomas the goal was salvation for the souls of men; therefore a unified monarchical state taking its guidance from the Church was the preferred form. This Thomistic solution was essentially that which Hooker defended as right and natural for England.[8] For the early-seventeenth-century precursors of Whiggery, the goal was the health and safety of the people, thought of largely in a secular context in spite of the fact that we call them Puritans. Henry Parker

[8] *Of the Laws of Ecclesiastical Polity*. Books i–viii, London, 1594–1662.

had in the early debates in the Long Parliament come to the conclusion that government by king, Lords, and Commons was all well and good when the three were in unison; but if king and Parliament differed on fundamentals, then Parliament was supreme. Going one step further, he suggested that by "Lords" only the temporal peers should be meant. If the king differed from Parliament, he was to be eliminated. If the spiritual peers differed from the temporal, then the bishops were to be eliminated. And last of all, if the temporal peers differed from the Commons, then the temporal peers were also to be excluded. The result was the sovereignty of the House of Commons, for the public good.

But 1689 was not 1640, much less the Middle Ages. In spite of the constant use of religious and historical precedents in the rhetoric of the Glorious Revolution, a new day was in fact dawning in England. The modern world was being born. The fact was that the Anglican Church had since the reign of James I talked as much about obedience to the "powers that be" as it had about divine and hereditary monarchy. The Whigs talked about the supremacy of Parliament within the governmental structure, but they were not really republicans at all. They might declare that the crown was basically the gift of the nation, but once the gift had been bestowed the king was not to be denied all prerogative rights. They did not anticipate government by Parliament, but government by the king, through ministers accountable to Parliament. Even then, it was up to the king to choose the ministers. Parliament would have the right of veto over their works, and if necessary over their tenure in office.

By 1689 both Tory and Whig, Anglican and Dissenter were not all that far apart from the social-contract theory enshrined in the *Second Treatise on Government*, by John Locke. The rhetoric differed, but the substance was essentially the same. What Locke did was to expose that fundamental issue upon which the English governing classes, rural and urban, really stood—private property. It was not necessary to follow Locke's logic in developing the labor theory of value as the origin of property or the logic of the state of nature in order to arrive at the notion of the social contract. Reduced to its simplest, Locke said that men had a right to life, liberty, and property, and that it was the task of government to protect these rights. Any government that had effectively ceased to govern had broken the contract and, therefore, society would have to constitute a new one. There was certainly nothing new, at least as far as England was concerned, in assuming that the task of government was to defend the lives, liberties, and properties of the subjects. This had been the basis of common law since the twelfth century. Since that time, powerful factions of peasants or aristocrats who felt threatened in their rights had frequently rebelled. Edward II, Richard II, and Richard III had all been eliminated under such circumstances. These successful medieval rebellions, however, had not been waged in the name of new theories of life or government. They did not seek to remake the system, but merely excised from it that person or office which was felt to be the destroyer of their rights.

The decades of the Puritan Revolution had witnessed something unique. The system itself had been torn asunder and new models devised, and the men of 1689 were most careful not to let this experience become a precedent for them. The Long Parliament started out in general agreement as to who and what were wrong within the system. The intractability and deceit of Charles I, combined with the penchant for devising new forms of government by reinterpreting and even misinterpreting England's past, led to the destruction of the old system; but it was soon found impossible to impose any new one upon a people who were at best largely apathetic or even downright hostile. When all the attempts to devise and impose a new system merely led to even greater attacks upon the rights of Englishmen, the effort was abandoned. In 1689 a medieval-

style rebellion took place, but, thanks to the co-
operation of James II and the wisdom of the rebels,
without the violence. This time the changes would be
limited to the exclusion of only those persons and institutions that could be seen to have clearly failed the
nation in the task of protecting its rights. No wholesale
scrapping of the system was either wanted or attempted.
The Prince of Orange's fears that a rebellion in England without his guiding hand might lead to republicanism prove to be groundless. It is very possible that
they would have been groundless even if he had not
intervened. The lessons of the 1640s and 1650s were
not to be forgotten so easily, or so quickly.

The election to the Convention returned a majority
of Whigs, but also a large number of Tories. While it
is necessary to use party labels, it must be remembered
that neither party, before, during, or after the Convention, had any exact membership, organization, or program. The parties were there, but not in the formal
sense that could be observed in the exclusion Parliaments of Charles II. And even then, the split between
court and country was more real than that between
Tory and Whig. In the Convention, almost all the members were country, so it was the Tory and Whig traditions that served to divide the members one from the
other.

The Marquis of Halifax was elected "Speaker" of the
Lords and Henry Powle Speaker of the Commons. In
lieu of an opening speech from the throne, the Prince
of Orange sent a letter which was read to both houses.
It was short and to the point: He had confidence in
their ability to devise a just settlement, but it was ur-
gent that it be done quickly. Second only in importance
to a speedy and amicable settlement of the English
government was the need to protect the Protestant interest in Ireland, which had come under attack. To
make this point, he warned them that Holland had
gone to great expense on England's behalf, and had
exposed herself to great danger in the process. The

Dutch troops could not stay in England indefinitely. The Houses then proceeded to thank William for his intervention and his administration of affairs, and urged him to continue his administration during the days of their deliberations. Unlike the reluctance he showed in December to take on both civil and military administration, he now readily consented, again urging speed upon them. The foreign situation was pressing for decisive action.

Before the Convention could get down to serious business, a letter arrived from James, who was now established at St. Germain. In it he showed that he still recognized himself as king, and once again offered the nation a freely elected Parliament that could provide for the safety of the Protestant establishment and the properties of the subject; those who had worked for his removal would be protected by the passage of an act of indemnity and oblivion. When the Commons learned that the letter that Lord Preston offered to the Speaker was from the pen of James, the House refused to receive it, and it remained unopened. This should have been sufficient warning to those who sought to settle the government by creating William regent, that this cause was hopeless. If they would not even acknowledge receipt of a letter from James, they were hardly likely to continue to regard him as their king.

On January 28, the Commons went into a grand committee, and the decisive business of the Convention was at last begun. A son of the late Archbishop of York, Mr. Dolben, set the tone of the debate and its final conclusion when he moved "That king James 2. [sic] having voluntarily forsaken the Government, and abandoned the kingdom, it is a voluntary demise in him."[4] This seemingly simple one-sentence motion was actually fraught with many conflicting interpretations, and in the course of the debate a broad and far-ranging opportunity was provided for the lawyer, the philosopher,

4 Cobbett, V, p. 36.

the linguist, and the simple man of affairs to tickle his fancy and expound upon the nature of society and government, the relationship between Protestantism and Catholicism, freedom and tyranny, and the meaning of such words as "abdicate" and "desert," and even to discuss what was meant by the "people" and by "representation." The fact that the kingdom was without a king, at least temporarily, was indisputable, and the fear of his return was balanced by the fears of anarchy if a settlement was not reached. The times called for an honest examination of the fundamental nature of society and government. The memories of the Long Parliament made them aware that the debate must deal with the fundamentals, but it also created an atmosphere in which each participant spoke only in such a way as to facilitate a settlement, not to disrupt or to prevent arrival at a quick decision. Never could there have been such a momentous debate with so much good will and willingness to listen as well as to expound. The debate in the Commons and the subsequent debate in the Lords, as well as in the joint parliamentary committee that followed, must certainly rank as one of the finest hours in parliamentary history. The times called for the best that Parliament could offer, and the members rose to the occasion.

As the debate progressed on the state of the nation in general and on Mr. Dolben's motion in particular, the one obvious fact that all could agree upon was that the king was gone and the nation was without an effective and legal government. Once this fact was agreed upon, it was necessary to define the nature of the "vacancy." Was there a mere "vacancy" on the throne, or had James's flight resulted in the removal of government, including the crown itself? Was the throne vacant or did England cease to have a throne? Sir Robert Sawyer, who had served as legal counsel to the seven bishops during their trial back in June, posed the question that Locke was to imply in his *Second Treatise*. If the government itself had come to an end, then didn't the task of reconstituting government devolve upon the people of England themselves? A convention composed of those same people who would in normal circumstances sit in a Parliament did not constitute "the people," nor were they the representatives of the people. They merely represented three estates of the realm—the lords spiritual and temporal, and the free-holders and burgesses. What Sawyer called the "fourth estate"—the mass of peasants and workers—was not represented in Parliament or in the Convention, but they were "people," and if the government itself had been dissolved, they, too, should be consulted in the task of reconstituting a government. By posing the problem in these terms, only one answer could be forth-coming. The throne was still there, but it was vacant. The Convention's task was to fill the throne, and they had the competence to do so. Obviously, no one relished the notion of carrying the good of the people to the point of actually consulting the people. Even republican Whigs were not prepared to go so far.

There was the further question of whether or not James's flight was to be considered as the normal demise of the crown. If James were to be thought of as dead in the eyes of the law, then the crown should devolve by heredity to the heir. Who was the heir? The baby "Prince of Wales" or the Princess of Orange? While some were willing to face the fact that James was still alive and therefore should still be regarded as the king, they were few indeed who were willing to accept as a fact that James Francis Edward was the true Prince of Wales and consequently the new king because of the "demise" of the crown. Therefore, if there was a demise, then Mary should be the queen. But it was by now no secret that Mary would not accept the crown at her husband's expense, and of course William would not co-operate in such an arrangement anyway. To de-clare William the king would violate the hereditary tra-dition and indicate that something more than a mere demise of the crown was at issue. What was indeed at issue, however, would have to be less than the total dissolution of the institution of government. The Tories wanted to stay as close to the hereditary principle as possible. The Whigs were anxious to prove once and for all that the three estates of the realm had the power to violate that principle when the occasion called for it. There had always been a republican streak in Whiggery, and now was the opportunity to put it to work. Both sides realized intuitively, however, that they had better agree on something, and quickly.

After allowing the original motion to be amended and refusing to postpone a decision to another day, the Commons adopted the following resolution:

That King James the Second, having endeavoured to subvert the Constitution of the Kingdom, by breaking the original Contract between king and people, and, by the advice of Jesuits, and other wicked persons, having violated the fundamental Laws, and having withdrawn himself out of this Kingdom, has *abdicated* the Government, and that the Throne is thereby become vacant.[5]

The resolution now went to the Lords, who had been waiting for the Commons to take the lead. The choice of the word "abdicate," seemingly simple and a precise statement of the facts, was a very divisive word, indeed, fraught with politics. The use of the word in the Commons' resolution was a victory for the Whig policy. The Lords was by and large the refuge of the Tory interest, and the word was to become the center of their grand debate. Eventually it would take a joint parliamentary committee to resolve the issues.

In an opening effort to avoid dividing on the issue, however, the House went into committee, with Danby presiding. A motion was made to disagree with the Commons that the throne was "vacant." The House should agree as to how to fill the vacancy before admitting that there was one. Should the non-existing "vacancy" be filled by a king or by a regent? The second

[5] Cobbett, V, p. 50. Italics added—*SEP*.

Earl of Nottingham, the son of Charles II's Lord Chancellor, and soon to be one of William's secretaries of state, argued both forcibly and persuasively for the declaring of a regency as long as James should live. The precedent of Don Pedro, in Portugal, seemed to carry weight with the House. Danby and Halifax, both of whom had earlier hoped for no more than this, were perfectly aware of the realities of the situation and had to extend themselves to the utmost to prevent the Lords from following Nottingham. Their efforts succeeded by the narrowest of margins: 51 for filling the "vacancy" with a king, 49 for filling it with a regent. Among the minority were the Tory old guard, including some from among the bishops whom James had tried. Clarendon, Rochester, and Godolphin voted for the regency, and thus were able to salve their tender consciences for their past efforts to undermine James. Archbishop Sancroft and Lord Churchill were absent, presumably for "diplomatic" reasons.[6]

By avoiding the issue of the "vacancy," and by rejecting the alternative of a regency, the Lords were sticking to strict hereditary constitutionalism. The throne was incapable of being "vacant" under the hereditary system. Either James II was still the king or his daughter Mary was queen, or the baby prince was king. Halifax was already committed to William's assuming the throne. Danby still hoped that Mary would assume the throne alone.[7] The course of the debates in and between the two Houses was not only influenced by party and principle, but by jockeying for position and place in the new administration. Naturally this was especially true among the Lords.

The day after the defeat of the regency, January 30, the Lords resumed the grand debate on a series of motions that carried their lordships into the highest realms of abstract political theory. Locke's still-unpublished

[6] Ibid., V, p. 59.

[7] Andrew Browning, *Thomas, Earl of Danby*, Glasgow, 1951, Vol. I, p. 421.

second treatise was for all practical purposes dissected and put to the vote item by item. On a motion calling for a vote as to whether the English monarchy existed by divine right or by an "original contract" between the king and the people, the principle of the "original contract" won by a larger margin than had the principle of kingship the day before—53–46. The high Tory position had reached its peak at the beginning and was now clearly in retreat. With the Commons clearly inclined toward the Whig position, it was now becoming clear that the Tories could not expect to salvage anything except by compromise. On the next question—whether James II had broken the original contract—the affirmative won with almost no opposition. Thus on the fundamental theoretical issues, the Lords were as Whiggish as the Commons.

The next day, January 31, the Lords finally got down to the issues of fact: had James II "abdicated," as the Commons had resolved? Without much ado, the Tories were able to carry the matter and the word "deserted" was substituted for "abdicated." As many in the Commons were to point out later, the two words were seemingly synonymous, and therefore of no great consequence. But there was a most serious point of consequence at stake. As Mr. Hampden pointed out, "abdication" was a legally binding and irrevocable act. "Desertion" implied no more than that James had sailed away from Rochester and could return again some day. Since the Lords had so far failed to declare the throne vacant, and since they had also resolved that there was to be a king and not a regent, without specifying the name of the king, it was conceivable that the Lords meant to imply that upon his return James would still be the king. It was obvious that the Lords did not want James to return, but the Tories, nonetheless, had won a point that could be very useful later on in the final effort to arrive at a compromise and to save something from the wreckage of their hereditary principles.

The most bitter fight of the day was on the question
of the "vacancy." To the upholders of the hereditary
principle the throne can never be vacant, and so it was
resolved. It was now clear that even though the Tories
had been beaten on the regency question, they were
still capable of upholding the principle of a hereditary
monarchy. At this point the Lords were on record that
James had broken the original contract with his people,
that the government should be in the hands of a king
and not a regent, that James had deserted (although it
was not clear whether he had deserted the throne or the
country or both), and that the throne was not vacant.
The one missing point was the crucial one. Who, then,
now occupied the throne? A motion calling for the proclamation of William and Mary as king and queen was
now introduced, and lost by five votes.

Danby's role in these early debates in both Houses
was to maintain the principle of hereditary monarchy
and to secure the accession of the Princess of Orange.
He also wanted to eliminate Halifax from future influence and to consolidate his own position. He knew as
well as Halifax and Shrewsbury did that William
wanted the throne for life or nothing. The only practical
choice facing Parliament was James II or William III.
But Danby played his hand as though he did not know
this. Since he had greater influence in the Lords than
any other peer, and since he also commanded the
greatest block of Tory votes in the House of Commons,
he was not without power and influence. If he hoped
to force William's hand, however, the hope was a for-
lorn one, and was probably doomed from the beginning.
As has been pointed out several times above, even the
princess was unwilling to play Danby's game. While
Danby was undoubtedly a man of certain principles,
yet he was also a proud and ambitious man who
sensed earlier and more fully than most of his contemporaries that the ability to control votes in the two
Houses was one road to power and influence. If one was
not a personal favorite of the sovereign, it was the only

road. By sticking to his principles, when even he knew the result was largely forgone, Danby was being loyal to his own conscience and at the same time was maintaining his personal control over the high Tories, who constituted about half the Lords and a sizable minority of the Commons. By sticking to principle he could hope to win a few points in the final compromise and at the same time manage to hold his followers together under his own leadership. For himself personally, he was to receive the Lord Presidency of the Council for the next ten years, although largely denied any major role in practical affairs. Danby, who worked the hardest to deny William the throne, was, at the last, the one who proposed the dual monarchy of William and Mary. He not only secured his own future but, by playing a devious middle-of-the-road game, was able to salvage something for his own conscience and the consciences of Whig and Tory alike. Danby, the high Tory, should get the major share of the credit for the ease and bloodlessness of the Glorious Revolution.

Now that the Lords had passed their various resolutions in response to the one grand resolution passed by the Commons, the scene moved back to the Commons. What were they to make of the ambiguous, not to say contradictory, resolutions that their Lordships had devised? The Commons resolution was open to dispute in the Lords because of the wording, although the meaning and intent were quite clear. The Lords' resolution was clearer as to the wording, but far from clear as to meaning and intent. The Commons could now make of them what they willed, and Danby and his followers were not in a position to control events.

The Commons began by debating the substitution of the word "desert" for "abdicate." We have already seen that Mr. John Hampden thought that this left an opening for the return of James II. But this was the extreme Whig interpretation. Wiser and cleverer councils were to prevail. Heneage Finch, a son of the first Earl of Nottingham and one of the few in the Commons who had first stood out for a regency, now suggested that the choice of words meant little. The Commons could accede to the Lords' word—"desert"—and then make it mean what they chose. Danby's conduct in the Lords was now seen to have led to a new willingness on the part of Tory commoners to express themselves and at the same time prepare the way for compromise. When the question was put to agree with the Lords that the king had "deserted" and that the throne was not vacant, the motion was lost and the Commons were left with the choice of either pushing ahead to fill the throne according to their own lights, thus defying the Lords, or proceeding to a conference between the two Houses. The decision was quickly made to go to conference, and John Hampden was selected to present the reasons why the Commons could not accept the Lords' amendments. He shrewdly pointed out that if James II had deserted, the throne must be vacant since no one else was recognized as occupying it. The Lords themselves had joined the Commons in asking William to administer the kingdom. Thus they themselves had tacitly admitted that neither James II was king nor was anyone else on the throne by heredity. If the throne were not vacant, why had William, who was not a direct heir, been asked to administer the kingdom? That was a function to be fulfilled by a king or queen, if there was one. The point was well taken and was to prove decisive.[8]

At the ensuing conference, the Lords held their ground and so Hampden had to report to the Commons. When the Lords' amendments were again put to the vote, they were again decisively beaten. Compromise might have been in the air, but each side expected the other to make the first break. When the conference resumed, and resume it did since neither House was willing to bring affairs to a crisis, John Somers, later the Lord Chancellor, and Sergeant Holt,

[8] Cobbett, V, p. 64.

a lawyer, went on at great length over the history of England and of Rome, detailing the history of the word "abdicate," all the while admitting that they were debating a "mere word." The Earl of Nottingham explained the Lords' reason for the word "desert" by saying that the crucial issue was neither "desert" nor "abdicate," but the "vacancy" of the throne. The Commons had linked "abdication" with "vacancy," and the Lords meant to link "desertion" with "no vacancy." That was the issue—was the crown hereditary or elective? At least both sides had reached the point that they were debating words, but what they should have been debating was the constitution of England. Was the throne descended by heredity or was it an elective office to be freely disposed of by the will of Parliament?

The willingness of the Commons to move toward compromise could be seen by the choice of representatives to the conference. Even though John Hampden, an extreme Whig, was the Commons' reporter, their spokesmen were lawyers such as Somers and Holt. Surely their selection was not to be mere chance. That two Whig lawyers would find much in common with the high-Tory Anglicans Nottingham, Clarendon, and the Bishop of Ely was not to be unexpected. When Nottingham suggested that the debate over "abdicate" be postponed and that they proceed to debate "vacancy," much further discussion took place, but in the end it was John Hampden who seized the opportunity to put aside the less important issue and proceed with the discussion of the "vacancy." It was clear that James II was gone, and a solution to the problem must soon be found.

The new debate began with a powerful and persuasive statement from Mr. Sacheverel, who summed up the situation as it stood if the Lords' amendments were to be adopted by the Commons: James II had deserted the administration of the government, but was king still. This meant that England was in a *de facto* state of civil war, since even the Lords had voted to offer the administration to the Prince of Orange. Since James II was still king and had not called them into session and had not approved of transferring the administration of the state to William, everything they had done was illegal and unconstitutional. But since the Lords agreed with the Commons that James II should not be allowed to return, the only way to avoid the fact of unconstitutionality and possible civil war was to declare the throne to be vacant. *Both law and practicality required that the throne be filled by someone other than James.* Thus it was necessary first to admit it was vacant, so they could then proceed to fill it. The Commons were quite correct as to their reading of the situation. But in return for demolishing the logic of the Lords' amendments and the danger they posed for the peace and safety of the realm, the Commons, said Mr. Sacheverel, were willing to deny that a declaration that the throne was vacant in any way implied that the throne was to be considered elective. Thus if the Lords would admit that the throne was vacant, then the Commons would concede that it was a non-elective office.[9]

Clarendon was faced with a difficult situation, both as a representative of the House of Lords and because of his own peculiar conscience and family connection with the dynasty. Without going so far as to admit of a vacancy, he did inquire as to exactly what the Commons meant by a vacancy. Was the throne vacant as to James II personally or as to heirs as well? The Lords could not admit that a father could either abdicate or desert anything beyond his own rights. The rights of his heirs were not to be thought of as being touched. Otherwise, the kingdom would be without a royal family and the throne would *ipso facto* become elective. For Clarendon, and without doubt most of the peers, the issue was not James II personally, but a hereditary monarchy versus a commonwealth. Even the most Whiggish of peers could not be unaware that the denial

[9] Ibid., V, pp. 85–86.

of hereditary monarchy could be but an opening wedge to a denial of the hereditary principle in general. Sergeant Maynard had to throw in a legal caveat at this point. While agreeing that the monarchy was hereditary and not elective, Clarendon's argument did not meet the existing situation, since James was still alive and therefore his heirs could not yet come into his estate by heredity. The Commons were thus willing to accept hereditary monarchy as a general principle, but circumstances could require an election nonetheless. The Earl of Pembroke replied that the debate in both Houses had stressed that "desertion" and/or "abdication" were in law the equivalents of a "demise" (the legal death of a king). Consequently, Lord Clarendon's point was in fact well taken and fully appropriate under the circumstances.

Mr. Sergeant Maynard summed up the Commons dilemma:

But your lordship will neither agree it [the throne] is vacant, nor tell us how it is full. King James is gone, we hear or know of no other; what shall the nation do in this uncertainty? When will you tell us who is king, if King James be not? Shall we everlastingly be in this doubtful condition?[10]

Lord Nottingham was as fully versed in the intricacies of the law as was Sergeant Maynard. He summed up the Lords' position in a long and tightly reasoned statement in which he said that James could be considered dead in the eyes of the law. If they admitted that the crown was hereditary and that the heirs could not accede until the natural death of the father, then they would have to elect a king, which in itself was a dangerous precedent for the future. Even more troublesome, however, was the fact that the elected king could serve only until the death of James and not until his own death. Since they were in fact willing to admit that the new king should serve for his own natural life, then it was necessary to consider James lawfully dead now

[10] Ibid., V, p. 90.

and to proceed to fill the throne with his rightful heir. After a rebuttal by Mr. Sacheverel, Lord Nottingham said that the Lords would be willing to admit that the throne was indeed vacant, but only as it concerned James II.

An impasse appeared to be at hand. Yet real progress had been made and both sides knew it. The Lords were ready to admit that the throne was indeed "vacant" as regards James II, and the Commons were ready to admit that the throne was not an elective office, at least in ordinary circumstances. The basis for the final compromise was much closer at hand than either would admit. The Commons' representatives took the lead in warning of the impending breakdown in the negotiations by stressing that their commission limited them to a discussion of the reasons for the Lords' amendments, not to the filling of the vacancy. The Earl of Rochester said that the conferees should assume full authority to debate any and all matters relevant to the settlement of the state of the realm. He then went on to throw in a warning of his own. What effect would the altering of the English succession have upon Scotland? What guarantee was there that Scotland would accede to this? And he hardly needed to stress the dangerous consequences that had always ensued for England when England and Scotland went their separate ways. He didn't even bother to remind them that Scotland, which was the first of his kingdoms to rise against Charles I, was also the first to return to its allegiance, and that was while the English were still proceeding to defeat him. The loyalty of Scotland to the Stuart dynasty was indeed a most important factor for the English to consider.

As the debate proceeded, the peers began to move in the direction of an election. They admitted that a Parliament was fully free to alter the succession at any time. Even on this present occasion, the Lords were willing to admit that the succession should be altered to eliminate the possibility of a Papist coming to the throne. But the crucial point was that a "Parliament" could do this, not a "convention." Therefore, the Convention should admit that Mary was queen by hereditary succession, and then after the assembly of a proper Parliament, the necessary adjustments to the succession could be made. At least the Tory peers were now willing to put more emphasis upon the sovereignty of Parliament than they were upon the divine rights of heredity. The Earl of Nottingham wound up the debate in the conference, for all practical purposes, by imploring the Commons to admit that the throne was vacant only as to James II and that the rights of his heirs could be altered, but only by a Parliament. This could not be done by James's own abdication or by a Convention. He pleaded for the Commons to meet the Lords halfway so that the nation could once again be secure in its government, and so that the settlement would be as close to the traditional constitution as possible. After a few more speeches from the commoners that merely went over the old ground once again, the conference ended, seemingly in failure.

During the first week of February, as the conference wended its way through the legal and constitutional history of England and through the English and Latin legal dictionaries, the Prince of Orange began to grow impatient. For nigh unto two months he had kept his own counsel at St. James's Palace, supervising the administration of the government but reluctant to push the Convention into a settlement. The contact that Danby maintained with the Princess Mary, and the tone and course of the debates in the Lords and in the conference, forced him to face certain facts and to in turn make the Convention face one overwhelming fact. It was clear that there was strong sentiment in the Lords for a regency, either for James II or for Mary. It was also becoming obvious that the weight of the arguments presented by the peers in the conference was beginning to be felt in the Commons, and that Danby's men were again coming into the open and gaining strength. In turn the Whigs, especially in the Commons, were digging in their heels, and a stalemate appeared likely. On the other hand the possibility of a stalemate was just as frightening to the Convention as it was to William. Therefore, the time was ripe for him to intervene, and intervene he did—decisively. Mary wrote a letter to Danby rebuking him for his efforts on her behalf, and then William summoned a meeting attended by Danby, Halifax, and Shrewsbury, and made the following statement:

Some, he heard, proposed to settle the government in the hands of a regent, during the King's [James's] life. He had no objection: It might be a wise project: But, if he was the person intended for the office, he thought proper to let them know, he would accept of no dignity dependent upon the life of another. Others, he understood, proposed to settle the Princess alone on the throne, and admit him to a participation of power through her courtesy. Her rights he would not oppose: Her virtues he respected: No one knew them better than he did: Crowns to others had charms: To him they had none: But he thought it proper also to let them know, that he would hold no power dependent upon the will of a woman. Therefore, if either of these schemes were adopted, he could give them no assistance in the settlement of the nation; but would return to his own country, happy in the consciousness of the services he had endeavoured, though in vain, to do to theirs.[11]

William's conference with the leaders of the Lords was not the only pressure now brought to bear. Petitions were being presented by the mobs that were gathering in the streets of Westminster, petitions that called for settling William and Mary on the throne and for doing it quickly. Fear of the mob was a powerful inducement to make haste. The last thing in the world they wanted was to give the Whigs an excuse to effect an alliance with the people in the streets, as had been done during the early days of the Long Parliament. So on February 6 the conference broke up, and the same

[11] Dalrymple, Appendix, pp. 203–4.

day the Lords voted to accept the original resolutions of the Commons that the throne was vacant because of the abdication of James II. Was this a defeat for the Lords and for the Tories? Not really. The stand the Lords had taken in their own House and at the conference had had its effect upon the Commons. The Commons' conferees had admitted that the crown was hereditary and not elective. They came to realize the necessity of recognizing the rights of Princess Mary just as much as the Lords had to recognize the necessity of "electing" William king in an emergency situation. Not only did both Houses now want to compromise, they both realized the necessity for it.

It was Danby who took the lead in the Lords and literally forced his followers to throw in their lot with the Whigs in accepting the resolution of the Commons. By a majority of three the Lords voted to accept that James II had abdicated the throne, and by a majority of twenty they agreed that the throne was vacant. When the whole package was put to a final vote it carried, 65 to 45. Thus Danby and the House had agreed that the monarchy was elective, at least in this particular emergency. He then proceeded to introduce the resolution offering the crown jointly to William and Mary. By personally taking charge of the compromise in the Lords, Danby was able to put pressure on the Commons and force them to go along with his compromise. Once he and the Lords had agreed to "elect" William king, the Commons could hardly refuse to admit that Mary had the right of inheritance. The Lords' decision was taken on February 6, and the Commons followed two days later.[12]

Once the momentous decision had been taken to offer the crown jointly to William and Mary, a new and highly significant issue arose. If the prince and the princess were to accept the offer and become king and queen, those who held office in Church and state would

[12] Browning, I, p. 431.

be required to take the oath of allegiance. But would the traditional oath be acceptable? Could they swear that William and Mary "are and by right ought to be" King and Queen of England? Were they indeed to accede to the throne by right? For the Tories, Mary succeeded by right, William did not. The high Tories, with Danby's support, now dug in their heels. Nottingham and Danby proposed that a new oath be devised that would meet the present situation. It was felt to be of the highest importance that what was just done in "electing" a monarch not be passed off as being within the limits of the traditional constitution. William was *de facto* king, but no one but God could make a *de jure* king. This incident was not to become a precedent.

While the Lords debated the matter of the oath, the Commons had selected a committee under Sir John Somers, a Whig, that was empowered to draw up a declaration offering the crown to William and Mary and stating the reasons for so doing. Out of their deliberations came the Declaration of Rights, which was later framed as a bill in Parliament and formally enacted into law. As approved by the two Houses in the Convention, the declaration created a new oath of allegiance which totally avoided the issue as to the right by which William and Mary were king and queen. It merely said that they were. The declaration rehearsed the long litany of crimes committed by James II in his effort to undermine the liberties of the subject and the religion that was by law established. It was the traditional list of grievances that always appeared in the beginning of any great constitutional document. It was the custom, after the statement of grievances, to state the form that the redress would take:

1. The royal power to suspend laws or the execution of the laws was null and void without the consent of Parliament;

2. The dispensing power, "as it hath been assumed

and exercised of late, is illegal," but the implication was that a limited right to dispense remained with the crown (every attempt to define the limits of its use came to nought);

3. The establishment of the Court of Commissioners for Ecclesiastical Causes was illegal, as were all other courts and commissions of a similar nature;

4. No money could be levied from the subject except as provided by Parliament, both as to manner and time;

5. The subject had the right to petition the king, and no one could be penalized for so doing;

6. A standing army in peacetime without the consent of Parliament was illegal;

7. Protestants could bear the arms to which they had the traditional right;

8. The election of members of the House of Commons should be free of royal interference;

9. No member of Parliament could be held to account outside of Parliament for anything said or for any vote cast;

10. No excessive bail was to be charged, no excess fines levied, and no cruel or unusual punishments inflicted;

11. Juries were to be impaneled according to law, and in treason trials the jurors were to be freeholders;

12. No fines or grants of forfeitures of estates were to be allowed prior to a lawful trial and conviction;

13. Parliament should meet frequently;

14. All of the above were the undoubted rights of Englishmen;

15. The above rights could not be questioned or impugned in future.[13]

On the understanding that the Prince and Princess of Orange wholeheartedly agreed with the above provisions, and since William in his own declaration had promised to intervene in England in order to restore

[13] See appendix G in this book.

and defend the rights of Englishmen, the Convention resolved that

William and Mary, Prince and Princess of Orange, be, and be declared King and Queen of England, France and Ireland, and the Dominions thereunto belonging, to hold the Crown and Royal Dignity of the said Kingdoms and Dominions, to them the said Prince and Princess during their lives, and the life of the Survivor of them; and that the sole and full exercise of the Regal Power be only in, and executed by the said Prince of Orange, in the names of the said Prince and Princess during their joint lives. . . .[14]

The succession was to be in the heirs of Mary's body. If she had no heirs, then the succession was to go to Princess Anne of Denmark, the younger daughter of James II, and if she had no heirs of her body, then the crown was to descend to the heirs of William's body. (By 1701 it was clear that none of these conditions could or would be met and thus the Act of Settlement providing for the Hanoverian succession was necessary.) This last provision made it quite clear that the English crown was a hereditary one and not elective. The accession of William was not to constitute a precedent.

There then followed the new oath of allegiance, which merely stated that William and Mary were king and queen. How and why were not mentioned. A second oath required the taker to deny as impious and heretical that the Pope could exercise any authority whatsoever in respect to the legitimacy of the kings or queens of England. No foreign potentate could exercise any jurisdiction whatsoever within the realm of England or release the subject from his allegiance to his lawful sovereign.

Both Houses of the Convention proceeded to the palace of Whitehall on February 13, and Lord Halifax read out the Declaration of Rights to the prince and princess. The prince responded:

[14] Cobbett, V, pp. 110–11.

My lords and gentlemen; This is certainly the greatest proof of the trust you have in us, that can be given; which is the thing which makes us value it the more; and we thankfully accept what you have offered to us.—And as I had no other intention in coming hither, than to preserve your Religion, Laws and Liberties, so you may be sure, that I shall endeavour to support them, and shall be willing to concur in any thing that shall be for the good of the kingdom; and to do all that is in my power to advance the welfare and glory of the nation.[15]

Later that day the heralds proclaimed William and Mary to be the King and Queen of England, France, and Ireland at the usual places in London and Westminster. The "revolution" was done. But was it a "revolution" and was it "glorious"? The next few months were as vitally important as the previous year had been and would show to what extent a new order had indeed been established. If this had indeed been a revolution, who besides William was the winner and who besides James was the loser? This latter question is easier to answer than the former.

[15] Ibid., V, p. 111.

CHAPTER 9

Epilogue

Although we do not have the transcripts of the debates of the committee that drew up the Declaration of Rights, we do know that the Whigs and the Dissenters made efforts to make the declaration into a forward-looking document as well as a conservative one. Two points that were urged were toleration of religious dissent and security of tenure for judges. In the long run the committee was probably very wise not to go beyond a catalogue of the "crimes" of James II and a restatement of the fundamental principles of good government under a mixed monarchy. Since the Convention was technically illegal, it was wise to fill the throne and then let a legal Parliament make the desired reforms in the system. So the first act of the new administration was to convert the Convention into a legal Parliament. The newly designated Parliament then was obliged to get down to business and begin the real task of reform and of solving the problems that had plagued England since the death of Elizabeth I.

It was pointed out earlier that the Convention played a role comparable in many ways to that of the Long Parliament as well as that of the Convention of the Restoration. But the differences were just as profound as the similarities. Unlike the opening session of the Long Parliament, this Convention was not concerned with the "evil" advisers of the king. This time there was no reason to resort to euphemisms. James II himself was the "evil" perpetrator of events. Therefore, there was no need to clean out the old administration along with the king. Even though there was to be no rash of impeachments of court officials, it was assumed that a new administration would need and desire a new team of administrators. The Whigs naturally assumed that their day had come. It would not be long before they were sorely disillusioned. King William III may have been the Whig darling since Charles II first attempted to get around the penal laws with his proclamation of the Declaration of Indulgence. But all along it had been the Whigs who needed William more than he needed them. When the crisis finally did come, William found almost as much support from the Tories as he did from the Whigs. And it was this Tory support that made his peaceful succession possible. Thus, if anything, William owed more to the Tories than he did to the Whigs. However, William was not a man who tended to rely upon sentiments of gratitude. He was always coldly realistic in assessing any particular situation. He had always had a deep fear of being dependent upon anyone besides himself, and he had no intention of allowing his newly won crown to become the prisoner of any one faction within England. But there was another reason why he was loath to place himself in the hands of the Whigs. He had a basic and profound distrust of their political philosophy. He may have used their theories of elective monarchy in order to secure the crown, but once it was secured he intended to rule with all the prerogative powers that any of his divine-right predecessors had. His behavior during the Exclusion Crisis is proof that he was unwilling to accept any derogation of the principles of hereditary English monarchy beyond the limited compromise necessary to get the crown for himself. He was not going to be a gentleman usher to James II or Queen Mary while serving as a regent, and he was not going to be the gentleman usher to any faction of English politicians while serving as the king.

Before Parliament could draw up its first legislative acts, William selected his Privy Council and his new officers of state, and the result was a victory for no one but William himself, and perhaps England as well. Danby (now Marquis of Carmarthen) came back into office after ten years as Lord President of the Council. Since he had wanted the lord treasurership, this was no victory for him, and, although he retained the office for the next ten years, he never actually played a major role again. Halifax was made Lord Privy Seal, which really put him on a par with his bitter rival, Danby. The treasury was put into commission, with Godolphin being one of the commissioners. Of all the men who had served James II, it was Godolphin who had been most unswerving in his loyalty and had not defected until after James had fled to France. Of course his selection as a commissioner was not based upon this, but upon the need to have a man of experience in the treasury, yet without the freedom to act independently. James II had so decimated the bench of judges, filling the vacancies with his own lackeys, that there was no one of great judicial experience who could be trusted. So the chancellorship was also put into commission, all the commissioners being commoners. The two secretaryships of state were given to Nottingham and Shrewsbury. The first was a high Tory and the other a maverick who often toyed with Whiggery. It was thus made manifestly clear right at the beginning that the principle victor of the Glorious Revolution was the new king himself. Throughout his reign William fought to retain his freedom to control his own administration and to become the prisoner of no man and no faction.

If the events of 1688–89 are to be thought of as a revolution, it was not in this area that the change was to be found. Ever since the Restoration, the opposition in Parliament had sought to make the administration responsible to Parliament, but Parliament had always shied away from the ultimate responsibility of actually making the appointments to office. They had always agreed that the king would make the appointments and Parliament would then sit in judgment of their works. This was not altered by any formal change in the constitution, because neither the king nor Parliament wished for such a change. The achievement of responsible government was to be advanced during William's reign, but not by any conscious or deliberate act or statute. We will have to look elsewhere for the solution of this problem.

The Declaration of Rights did not solve the problem of the responsibilities of ministers. It did not solve the problem of the tenure of judges. It did not solve the problem of religious comprehension or toleration. All it did was provide a cure for those particular crimes committed by James II. Thus the suspending power was outlawed and the dispensing power was circumscribed. Frequent Parliaments were called for, but no machinery to effect this was provided. The Convention in and of itself, therefore, did precious little that could be called revolutionary. But it did set into motion a chain of events that would through proper parliamentary action effect a revolution in practice, even if not in theory.

Once the Convention had been turned into a lawful Parliament, the two Houses turned to the matter of religion. The failure of the Restoration settlement had to a great extent been caused by the refusal of the Cavalier Parliament to create a comprehensive church. The success of the Glorious Revolution was largely made possible by the willingness of the Dissenters to seek relief through strictly constitutional means and to put their trust in the word of the Anglican Tories that toleration would be achieved through the preservation of the Church, not through its destruction. The Tories had committed themselves to toleration of dissent, and now the time had arrived to make good the promise. But, naturally, it was far harder for the good Anglican to contemplate the loss of his special privileges once the threat posed by James II had been removed than it had been a year earlier, with the publication of James's Declaration of Indulgence. One of the new Secretaries of State, Lord Nottingham, reintroduced the bill for comprehension that had first been proffered in 1680. This bill gave so little to the Dissenters that it had no chance of passage. In the Commons John Hampden proposed a comprehension bill that went so far that it had no chance of passage. The only hope for the Dissenter was a compromise that Dissenters could live with and that also had a chance to pass through a Parliament which was becoming far more Tory in its leanings than could have been expected from a body that had just "elected" the Presbyterian William as its king. The compromise was designed to preserve the integrity of the Church of England as it had been reestablished at the Restoration and to protect the monopoly of office that had been secured through the Clarendon Code. The final solution was toleration conceived as narrowly as possible and still consistent with the moral commitment that had been made to the Dissenters. The new act was, however, to meet with the grudging acceptance of the Dissenting leaders and was to remain the religious settlement for England for the next 140 years. Its great success in the long run was due, however, less to the actual provisions of the bill than to the willingness to compromise over its enforcement in later generations.

The new act did not in fact ever mention the word toleration. It did not repeal any of the Thirty-nine Articles of the Anglican Church, and it did not repeal any part of the Clarendon Code. It also specifically did not apply to Catholics or to Catholicism. What, then, did it do? "An Act for Exempting Their Majesties' Protestant Subjects, Differing from the Church of England, from the Penalties of Certain Laws" allowed all those who took the Oath of Allegiance and Supremacy and the declaration against transubstantiation to absent themselves from the services of the Church of England

and to hold services in their own conventicles. Dissenting clergy could gain exemption from the penal laws by subscribing to thirty-four of the Thirty-nine Articles. Those articles exempted dealt with homilies, rites, traditions of the Church, infant baptism, and the consecration of bishops. For both Dissenting clergy and laymen, the law was most explicit that these "privileges" required that all Dissenting services *not* be conducted behind locked doors. Where previously the facts of life had forced the Dissenter to hold his services behind locked doors, now the law barred him from locking the door and even provided him with the obligation to register with the local bishop. So the Dissenter and the Dissenting service were now legal. But a price was still to be paid. All parliamentary efforts to remove or amend any or all of the Clarendon Code as it affected the holding of office under the crown or any other political rights in local government were rejected during the spring and summer session. The Dissenting clergy were bitter, and felt cheated, but the majority in Parliament would not give in. The Whigs may have resented the Tory reaction in the last years of Charles II, but the interference in local government in James II's reign was too fresh in the mind to admit of any renunciation of the Tories' newly reclaimed positions of power in the boroughs. The "Toleration" Act of 1689 was the bare minimum required to fulfill the Tory promise of relief and that was all. If this act is to be considered a Whig victory, it was only because many Whigs had rallied to the Tory/Anglican banner.

Frequent meetings of Parliament had also been one of the perennial requests of the political nation since the years of Charles I's personal rule. The Triennial Act of 1641 and its updated version of 1664 had proved of no practical value in forcing a reluctant monarch to call a session of Parliament when he didn't want to, much less make him confide in Parliament or allow it a share in the decision-making process. The Declaration of Rights once again sounded the cry for frequent Parliaments, but no provisions for its enforcement were included. In 1694 a new Triennial Act was passed, which said that there must be a session at least every three years and that no Parliament could last longer than three years. This meant that there had to be an election at least every three years.

It was the Mutiny Act that guaranteed the enforcement of the Triennial Act. Since the maintenance of a standing army in peacetime was outlawed by the Declaration of Rights, it was necessary for the new Parliament to make legal provision for the existence of William's army. The act provided for the funding of an army and for its governance under martial law in peacetime for a period of seven months, until the new Parliament would meet. Ever since that first Mutiny Act the authorization for the existence and the governance of a peacetime army has been by the continual reenactment of an annual authorization. This required that there be a session of Parliament every year, and this in turn meant that the crown would be forced to rule according to the law of the land as laid down in statutes, among which was the new Triennial Act. Since early monarchs had often ruled for years without the existence of a standing army, even the Mutiny Act was of crucial importance largely because of the problems of war which William faced almost continually throughout his reign and because of the revolutionary basis of the new administration. Almost perpetual war abroad and the fear of the Jacobites at home required that the new regime and the nation itself have continuous military protection. If the new monarchy had entered into office in an era of peace, it is highly unlikely that the traditions of continual Parliaments and triennial elections would have been so easily and so thoroughly instituted. As a further guarantee that the king would be dependent upon Parliament for his future revenue, there was no permanent revenue settled upon him as had been done in the beginning for Charles II and James II. The ability of the crown to find its own sources of finance during the personal rule of Charles I, and the success of Charles II and James II in securing funds from France had finally brought home the lesson. A good king is one who cannot finance the government of his realm or even the maintenance of his court without taxation. A king financially dependent upon Parliament will in turn be a parliamentary king.

But keeping the king dependent upon Parliament for his finances does not in and of itself guarantee that the king will always rule according to the law. The vast bulk of the law was already there by either statute or custom and there was little that Parliament could do to control the day-to-day administration of the realm. In the last analysis the bench was the guardian of the law. The ability and the willingness of the Stuarts to interfere with the working of the bench, and the occasional dismissal of unco-operative judges, had become a scandal by James II's reign. The Revolution would not be complete without some provision for the integrity of the bench and security of tenure for the judges. William III himself took the lead here. Before he became king and while still serving as the administrator of the government, he issued orders that judges would no longer serve at the royal pleasure but upon their own good behavior. This finally received statutory status in the Act of Settlement of 1701. This act provided for the removal of judges only upon an address to the king being passed by both Houses of Parliament.

There was one other significant statute affecting the judicial process that can be considered part of the Revolution settlement, although it certainly cannot be said to have settled a problem that had ever been of such weight as to endanger the peace of the realm. Soon after the Restoration the peers began a long and sometimes acrimonious campaign to change the methods by which peers were tried for treason and felonies. The tradition was that a peer so charged was tried in the court of the Lord High Steward before a jury of thirty peers. Such a body could be stacked against a peer.

What the peers wanted was a trial before the entire
body of adult peers. The Commons were always most
reluctant to do anything that might add even more
"privileges" to the great number they thought the peers
already enjoyed. Almost every session of Parliament in
William's reign saw the introduction of a new treasons
bill in one or the other House. Not until 1696 could the
two houses finally agree. The new act did grant the
peers a trial before the full House of Lords, but it also
extended greatly the rights of all defendants in subsequent trials for treason. The defendant was to receive a
copy of the indictment at least five days before his trial,
he was to have legal counsel, and there must be depositions from at least two witnesses to the same act or one
deposition each to two separate but similar acts. Except
when charged with an attempt to assassinate the king,
the charge had to be brought by a grand jury no later
than three years after the alleged act or acts. Impeachment for treason was not affected by this act; therefore
the hold that Parliament might have over members of
the king's ministry was not impaired. But the king's
ability to destroy purely political enemies was largely,
if not totally, abolished.

The relationship between the two Houses of Parliament was not directly affected by the Revolution, yet
the behavior of the two Houses during the weeks of
the Convention does illuminate the growing tendency
of the Lords to defer to the Commons. At least they
were tending to defer in the sense that they let the
Commons take the lead. The Lords debated the general
state of the realm while the Commons debated specific
resolutions. The Lords then addressed themselves to
these resolutions. The final compromise over the occu-
pancy of the throne found the Lords accepting the
wording of the Commons. This tendency to allow the
Commons to take the initiative could be seen throughout the post-Restoration era. Both times, the Exclusion
Bill had originated in the Commons, with the Lords
acting very much like a modern second chamber, either

revising or rejecting the work of the lower House. The ultimate failure of William III to choose his ministers on the basis of his own estimate of their abilities or usefulness rather than their party affiliation was largely due to the efforts of the Commons to embarrass or even to impeach his ministers in the Commons. Responsible government was Parliament's goal, but it was increasingly to be the House of Commons that assumed the initiative in achieving this goal. Even though it had been becoming apparent since the days of Elizabeth I that the opposition to royal policy was largely centered in the Commons, the Lords had always assumed that they were at least a coequal branch, if not the superior branch. The role of the Commons in the earliest days of the Long Parliament was making it increasingly clear that to the bulk of the country opposition, Parliament meant the House of Commons. The fact that only a tiny minority of the Lords supported the parliamentary cause during the Civil War, which in turn led to the abolition of the Lords in 1649, created a precedent that was never to be forgotten. After 1697, when William was forced to rely upon a Whig administration in order to secure the financing of his program, it was because the ability to control a majority in the Commons was unquestionably the key to control of the administration. That this was a result of the Glorious Revolution was mere happenstance. The crucial factor was that the Commons controlled the purse strings, and the new king could not finance his wars and conduct his diplomacy with any hope of success unless he shared office, if not power, with those who in turn controlled those purse strings.

The final proof that the accession of William and Mary constituted a revolution is found in the passage of the Act of Settlement of 1701. All the provisions for the future succession to the throne specified in the Bill of Rights had come to naught with the death of Princess Anne's last child, the Duke of Gloucester. Unless a further statutory delimitation of the succession were

enacted, the crown would pass on to the Catholic line
of Stuarts in the Rhineland Palatinate. It fell to the
lot of a Tory House of Commons to provide the remedy.
That the Whigs would resort to a statute was to be
expected; that the Tories would is proof that, regardless of the large number of Tories, lay and clerical, who
considered themselves Jacobites, the bulk of the party
had long since faced reality. The eclipse of the Tory
party after the accession of George I and the notorious
conspiracies at the end of Anne's reign by Bolingbroke
(Henry St. John) and Oxford (Robert Harley) cannot
refute the fact that the bulk of the old Tory and Anglican alliance had come to grips with the facts of English
life and the needs of the country. To allow a Catholic
to accede to the throne in the name of the hereditary
principle was absolutely unacceptable after all that had
transpired since 1685. Just as the Tories had made the
accession of William and Mary possible, and the truth
is that they not only guaranteed that it would be bloodless but that it would happen at all, it was now essential
that they take the lead once again. In the long run it
would be better for England and for the Tories if the
inevitable were to be accomplished with themselves
having as large a hand in the operation as possible. Just
as the granting of the throne to William and Mary was
done in such a way as to salvage something for the Tory
conscience and interest, so the Act of Settlement must
also be used to salvage something.

The Act as passed provided that, upon the death of
Anne, the succession would go to the nearest Protestant
heir, the Electress Sophia of Hanover, and the heirs of
her body forever. The principle of an elective monarchy
was openly admitted. But in return the Tories were
to achieve a great victory that would make a half century in the political wilderness palatable, if not desira-
ble. The new dynasty was to be bound around with
Tory and Anglican chains that the Whigs would never
bring themselves to undo. Any future monarch must be
a Protestant at his succession and must then enter into

communion with the Church of England, if not already
a member of the Church. Any foreigner acceding to
the English throne could not encumber England with
foreign obligations resulting from any of his own foreign possessions without the consent of the English Parliament. No monarch was to go abroad, except to Scotland or Ireland, without the consent of Parliament.
These three provisions were significant victories for the
Tory/Anglican cause. The new dynasty would be forced
to identify itself with the Established Church in particular and not just with Protestantism in general, as
William had done. And no new dynasty would be able
to automatically involve England in its own foreign en-
tanglements, as William had also done. The Tories
had supported William by and large in his wars against
Louis XIV, but the financing of these wars had forced
the Tory landholder to dig deeply into his pockets to
provide the money, and there was always the suspicion
that the ultimate benefits derived from these wars had
gone either to William's Dutch subjects or to the Whiggish commercial interests at home who appeared to be
waxing fat from the war. There would be no more wars
unless it could be demonstrated that England's own interests were at stake. The Tories also meant, of course,
that it would have to be demonstrated that their own
landed interests were at stake as well. Of course, the
only way to guarantee this point was to have a majority
in the House of Commons, and it was not possible to
pass legislation that could provide such a guarantee.

The hope of the Tories for the future was in their
ability to portray an image of being the "patriotic"
party. Ever since 1640 they and their Royalist ancestors
had acquired the aura of being the party of divine-right
monarchy and upholders of the royal prerogatives. Their
adherence to the Bill of Rights and the Dutch accession had compromised this. Now they were on a new
tack. The thread that connects the modern Conservative party with its seventeenth-century ancestor is a
thread that comes much more clearly into focus with

the passage of the Act of Settlement than from any of the earlier decisions taken by the party. There is the beginning of the transformation from being the party of the crown to being the party of England.

Further evidences of the great change that was taking place in the Tory party are the provisions of the Act of Settlement relating to the role of the Privy Council and the forms through which advice was to be tendered to the king. All important matters of state—anything remotely within the competence of the Privy Council—was to be transacted there and nowhere else. The king was not to take advice from private persons or from councilors in private. All advice formally given was to be given in council and signed by all consenting members. No one not born a subject of the British crown was to be capable of holding any office under the crown or to be elected to the House of Commons or to receive gifts of land from the crown. This was another retroactive attack upon the habit of William to lean overly much upon his fellow Dutchmen for advice and to reward them with gifts. Even naturalized British subjects were to be barred from participation in the English government. A further provision, barring all holders of an office of trust or profit under the crown from sitting in the Commons, soon was to prove unworkable and the Whigs were to secure its effective repeal, excepting only a few token offices.

Even though the Act of Settlement came thirteen years after the flight of James II, it must be regarded as part of the Revolution settlement, and the last part. It was part of the settlement because the Bill of Rights and its provisions for the succession would have expired on Anne's death without it. On the other hand there has to be some point at which the conscious recognition of the unity of a particular era comes to a terminal point. What Dr. Plumb calls the era of political instability was not to end for another twenty-five years, but the era of constitutional instability was largely over with the passage of the Act of Settlement. The Hanoverian succession would be delayed until the death of Anne, but once the Act had been passed it was just a matter of time. The crucial decisions had been made and were to be irrevocable. The anti-Hanoverian risings in 1715 and 1745 were not only anticlimactic, they were the last gasps of a mere faction and represented a Scottish denial of the union of that kingdom with England far more than they represented a constitutional crisis for England itself.

A final résumé of the state of the parties in 1701 should suffice to put finis to our present study and to the constitutional crises that had made the seventeenth century the century of revolution. Many ingredients go to make up a truly modern political party. Among these the most important would seem to be the combination within each party of tendencies both for opposition and for governing. The Tory party, as the heirs of Civil War royalism, had all the necessary qualifications for a party of government. The reign of James II had begun to foster the growth of an opposition mentality within the Tory ranks. This new tendency was of sufficient importance to bring about a change of dynasty and to guarantee that it would be done peacefully and bloodlessly. The final proof of their conversion was the passage of the Act of Settlement. William III himself did not try to have the succession changed to provide for an heir of his own body, both because he knew his health was failing and because he was indeed a good enough patriot himself to realize that a Tory Act of Settlement was the surest way to guarantee the peace and safety of the kingdom. Even if it meant two generations in the political wilderness for the Tories, it was a price that they were willing to pay in 1701. William let them pay it, and the Act was passed. Anne was to do her best to keep the Church party in office during her reign, but the Tories were well on the way to becoming the Country party even before her accession and while the Tories were themselves in office.

The Whigs, on the other hand, had been the heirs

of the Civil War Parliamentarians. Even when in office in the reign of Charles II, the Whigs acted much more like a country opposition than they did a party of government. The Exclusion Crisis proved their undoing. Even though four of the immortal seven who invited William to England in 1688 were Whigs, the success of the Glorious Revolution depended much more upon the willingness of the Tories to participate. At least the Whigs allowed them to do so. It was this forbearance on their part that constituted their first grasping of the requirements of being a party of government. Even though the Whigs controlled the House of Commons in the Convention, they did not push their claims to dominate the settlement beyond the point where the Tories could not follow them. After 1694 the Whig junto formed the ministry under William III, and quickly came to appreciate the joys and the fruits of office. Even though they would be in the opposition during the last two years of William's reign and during much of Anne's reign, they were no longer a party that was trying to change the system. They were going to drop their republican baggage, just as the Tories were going to have to drop their Jacobite baggage. It was the Whigs who were going to repeal the ban on placemen (i.e., those appointed by the crown to an office of trust or profit) having seats in Commons. It was also the Whigs who were going to forget the need to force accountability upon the king's advisers, at least when they themselves were in office. By the death of William III both parties were willing and able to accept office and to make the system work, for their own and for the nation's interest.

The Glorious Revolution by no means ushered in an era of tranquillity, liberalism, or democracy, much less utopia. What it did usher in was the fundamental agreement in both parties that the role of crown was to make foreign policy and to further the commercial interests of the nation. Local government in turn was the province of the landed families and the oligarchies in the boroughs. Both knew that the fruits of ministerial office were worth having and were worth fighting for, even fighting viciously for. But both also realized that once in power there was little point in either enhancing the powers of the central government to the point where being in opposition would be intolerable, or in so restricting the benefits of office while in opposition that there would be no pleasure in enjoying the fruits of office when in power. The constitutional principles of both parties had reached such a stage by 1701 that Dr. Plumb's political stability could be achieved without the need to make any further drastic changes either in the system of government or in the basic principles of the parties.

The settlements in Scotland and in Ireland were necessary for England, but the England of 1700 was a far cry from the England of 1600. The combination of wealth, stability, and a determined will was sufficient to secure an easy acceptance of the new dynasty in the northern kingdom, and the most that the Catholic Irish could do was to determine the English and Dutch armies to go to the necessary lengths of force and cruelty to crush forever any opposition in Ireland that the English were not willing to tolerate for their own purposes. Beyond securing English hegemony in the British Isles, the events in the other two kingdoms were not crucial to the success of the revolution in England nor are they essential to our understanding of the revolution in England.

The revolution of 1688–89 was truly an English revolution and it was indeed glorious.

PART IV

Appendices

A. GODDEN V. HALES, KING'S BENCH
16 JUNE 1686

[*Arthur Godden, Sir Edward Hales's coachman, brought a collusive action against him for holding a colonel's commission without complying with the Test Act. On March 29 Hales was convicted at Rochester assizes, but he pleaded a dispensation under the Great Seal and appealed to the King's Bench, Lord Chief Justice Herbert presiding.*]

L.C.J. This is a case of great consequence, but of as little difficulty as ever any case was that raised so great an expectation, for if the King cannot dispense with this statute he cannot dispense with any penal law whatsoever. . . .

There is no law whatsoever but may be dispensed with by the supreme law-giver; as the laws of God may be dispensed with by God himself; as it appears by God's command to Abraham to offer up his son Isaac. So likewise the law of Man may be dispensed with by the legislator, for a law may either be too wide or too narrow, and there may be many cases which may be out of the conveniencies which did induce the law to be made; for it is impossible for the wisest law-maker to foresee all the cases that may be or are to be remedied, and therefore there must be a power somewhere, able to dispense with these laws. But as to the case of simony that is objected by the other side, that is against the laws of God, and a special offence, and therefore *malum in se*, which I do agree the King cannot dispense with. . . .

The case of the sheriff is a much stronger case than this, and comes up to it in every particular, for that statute doth disable the party to take and the King to grant; and there is also a clause in that statute which says that the patent shall be void notwithstanding any *non obstante* to the contrary, . . . and yet by the opinion of all the judges of England the King has a power of dispensing with that statute. . . .

[However, on the strained plea that this doubt about the statute of sheriffs affected the whole administration of justice, Herbert adjourned the case to take the opinion of the judges of common pleas and the barons of the Exchequer. Of the other eleven judges all but one fully concurred with him, and on 21 June, when the hearing was resumed, he so reported.]

. . . We think we may very well declare the opinion of the court to be that the King may dispense in this case; and the judges go upon these grounds:

1. That the Kings of England are sovereign princes.
2. That the laws of England are the King's laws.
3. That therefore 'tis an inseparable prerogative in the Kings of England to dispense with penal laws in particular cases, and upon particular necessary reasons.
4. That of those reasons and those necessities the King himself is sole judge. . . .
5. That this is not a trust invested in or granted to the King by the people, but the ancient remains of the sovereign power and prerogative of the Kings of England, which never yet was taken from them, nor can be. And therefore, such a dispensation appearing upon record to come time enough to save him from the forfeiture, judgement ought to be given for the defendant.

B. JAMES II'S DECLARATION FOR LIBERTY OF CONSCIENCE

APRIL 4, 1687

It having pleased Almighty God not only to bring us to the imperial crown of these kingdoms through the greatest difficulties but to preserve us by a more than ordinary providence upon the throne of our royal ancestors, there is nothing now that we so earnestly desire as to establish our government on such a foundation as may make our subjects happy, and unite them to us by inclination as well as duty; which we think can be done by no means so effectually as by granting to them the free exercise of their religion for the time to come, and add that to the perfect enjoyment of their property, which has never been in any case invaded by us since our coming to the Crown; which, being two things men value most, shall ever be preserved in these kingdoms during our reign over them as the truest methods of their peace and glory.

We cannot but heartily wish, as it will easily be believed, that all the people of our dominions were members of the Catholic Church. Yet we humbly thank God it is, and hath of long time been, our constant sense and opinion (which upon divers occasions we have declared) that conscience ought not to be constrained, nor people forced in matters of mere religion; it has ever been directly contrary to our inclination, as we think it is to the interest of government, which it destroys by spoiling trade, depopulating countries and discouraging strangers; and finally, that it never obtained the end for which it was employed . . .

We therefore, out of our princely care and affection for all our loving subjects, that they may live at ease and quiet, and for the increase of trade and encouragement of strangers, have thought fit by virtue of our royal prerogative to issue forth this our declaration of indulgence, making no doubt of the concurrence of our two Houses of Parliament when we shall think it convenient for them to meet.

In the first place we do declare that we will protect and maintain our archbishops, bishops and clergy, and all other our subjects of the Church of England in the free exercise of their religion as by law established, and in the quiet and full enjoyment of all their possessions, without any molestation or disturbance whatsoever.

We do likewise declare that it is our royal will and pleasure that from henceforth the execution of all and all manner of penal laws in matters ecclesiastical, for not coming to Church, or not receiving the sacrament, or for any other nonconformity to the religion established, or for by reason of the exercise of religion in any manner whatsoever, be immediately suspended; and the further execution of the said penal laws . . . is hereby suspended.

And to the end that by the liberty hereby granted the peace and security of our government in the practice thereof may not be endangered, we have thought fit, and do hereby straitly charge and command all our loving subjects, that we do freely give them leave to meet and serve God after their own way and manner, be it in private houses or places purposely hired or built for that use, so that they take especial care that nothing be preached or taught amongst them which may any ways tend to alienate the hearts of our people from us or our government; and that their meetings and assemblies be peaceable, openly and publicly held, and all persons freely admitted to them; and that they do signify and make known to some one or more of the next justices of the peace what place or places they set apart for those uses . . .

And forasmuch as we are desirous to have the benefit of the service of all our loving subjects, which by the law of nature is inseparably annexed to and inherent in our royal person, and that none of our subjects may for the future be under any discouragement or disability (who are otherwise well inclined and fit to serve us) by reason of some oaths or tests that have been usually administered on such occasions, we do hereby further declare that it is our royal will and pleasure that the oaths commonly called the oaths of supremacy and allegiance, and also the several tests and declarations mentioned in the acts of parliament made in the 25th and 30th years of the reign of our late royal brother King Charles II [i.e. the Test Acts of 1673 and 1678] shall not at any time hereafter be required to be taken, declared or subscribed by any person or persons whatsoever, who is or shall be employed in any office or place of trust, either civil or military, under us or in our government. And we do further declare it to be our pleasure and intention from time to time hereafter to grant our royal dispensation under our great seal to all our loving subjects so to be employed, who shall not take the said oaths, or subscribe or declare the said tests or declarations, in the above-mentioned acts and every of them . . .

C. A LETTER TO A DISSENTER
UPON OCCASION OF HIS MAJESTY, JAMES THE SECOND'S LATE GRACIOUS DECLARATION OF INDULGENCE OF THE 4TH OF APRIL, 1687

by George, Marquis of Halifax

SIR;—Since Addresses are in fashion, give me leave to make one to you. This is neither the effect of fear, interest, or resentment; therefore you may be sure it is sincere: and for that reason it may expect to be kindly received. Whether it will have power enough to convince, dependeth upon the reasons, of which you are to judge; and upon your preparation of mind, to be persuaded by truth, whenever it appeareth to you. It ought not to be the less welcome, for coming from a friendly hand, one whose kindness to you is not lessened by difference of opinion, and who will not let his thoughts for the public be so tyed or confined to this or that subdivision of Protestants as to stifle the charity, which besides all other arguments, is at this time become necessary to preserve us. I am neither surprized nor provoked, to see that in the condition you were put into by the laws, and the ill circumstances you lay under, by having the exclusion and rebellion laid to your charge, you were desirous to make yourselves less uneasy and obnoxious to authority. Men who are sore, run to the nearest remedy with too much haste, to consider all the consequences: grains of allowance are to be given, where nature giveth such strong influences. When to men under sufferings it offereth ease, the present pain will hardly allow time to examine the remedies: and the strongest reason can hardly gain a fair audience from our mind, whilst so possessed, till the smart is a little allayed. I do not know whether the warmth that naturally belongeth to new friendships, may not make it a harder task for me to persuade you. It is like telling lovers, in the beginning of their joys, that they will in a little time have an end. Such an unwelcome style doth not easily find credit: but I will suppose you are not so far gone in your new passion, but that you will hear still; and therefore I am under the less discouragement, when I offer to your consideration two things. The first is, the cause you have to suspect your new friends. The second, the duty incumbent upon you, in Christianity and prudence, not to hazard the public safety, neither by desire of ease, nor of revenge. To the first: consider that notwithstanding the smooth language which is now put on to engage you, these new friends did not make you their choice, but their refuge: they have ever made their first courtships to the Church of England, and when they were rejected there, they made their application to you in the second place. The instances of this, might be given in all times. I do not repeat them, because whatsoever is unnecessary, must be tedious, the truth of this assertion being so plain, as not to admit a dispute. You cannot therefore reasonably flatter yourselves, that there is any inclination to you. They never pretended to allow you any quarter, but to usher in liberty for themselves under that shelter. I refer you to Mr. Coleman's letters, and to the Journals of parliament, where you may be convinced, if you can be so mistaken as to doubt; nay, at this very hour, they can hardly forbear, in the height of their courtship, to let fall hard words of you. So little is nature to be restrained; it will start out sometimes, disdaining to submit to the usurpation of art and interest. This alliance, between liberty and infallibility, is bringing together the two most contrary things that are in the world. The Church of Rome doth not only dislike the allowing liberty, but by its principle it cannot do it. Wine is not more expressly forbidden to the Mahometans, than giving heretics liberty is to Papists: they are no more able to make good their vows to you, than men married before, and their wife alive, can confirm their contract with another. The continuance of their kindness, would be a habit of sin, of which they are to repent, and their absolution is to be had upon no other terms, than their promise to destroy you. You are therefore to be, hugged now, only that you may be the better squeezed at another time. There must be something extraordinary, when the Church of Rome setteth up bills, and offereth plaisters, for tender consciences; by all that hath hitherto appeared, her skill in chirurgery lieth chiefly in a quick hand, to cut off limbs; but she is the worst at healing, of any that ever pretended to it. To come so quick from another extreme, is such an unnatural motion, that you ought to be upon your guard; the other day you were sons of

Belial, now, you are angels of light. This is a violent change, and it will be fit for you to pause upon it, before you believe it: if your features are not altered, neither is their opinion of you, whatever may be pretended. Do you believe less than you did, that there is idolatry in the Church of Rome? Sure you do not. See then how they treat, both in words and writing, those who entertain that opinion. Conclude from hence, how inconsistent their favour is with this single article, except they give you a dispensation for this too, and by a Non Obstante, secure you, that they will not think the worse of you. Think a little how dangerous it is to build upon a foundation of paradoxes. Popery now is the only friend to liberty, and the known enemy to persecution: the men of Taunton and Tiverton, are above all other eminent for loyalty. The quakers from being declared by the Papists not to be Christians, are now made favourites, and taken into their particular protection; they are on a sudden grown the most accomplished men of the kingdom, in good breeding, and give thanks with the best grace, in double refined language. So that I should not wonder, though a man of that persuasion, in spite of his hat, should be master of the ceremonies. Not to say harsher words, these are such very new things, that it is impossible not to suspend our belief, till by a little more experience we may be informed whether they are realities or apparitions: we have been under shameful mistakes, if these opinions are true; but for the present, we are apt to be incredulous; except we could be convinced, that the priests words in this case too, are able to make such a sudden and effectual change; and that their power is not limited to the sacrament, but that it extendeth to alter the nature of all other things, as often as they are so disposed. Let me now speak of the instruments of your friendship, and then leave you to judge, whether they do not afford matter of suspicion. No sharpness is to be mingled where healing only is intended; so nothing will be said to expose particular men, how strong soever the temptation may be, or how clear the proofs to make it out. A word or two in general, for your better caution, shall suffice: suppose then, for argument's sake, that the mediators of this new alliance should be such, as have been formerly employed in treaties of the same kind, and there detected to have acted by order, and to have been impowered to give encouragements and rewards. Would not this be an argument to suspect them? If they should

plainly be under engagements to one side, their arguments to
the other, ought to be received accordingly; their fair pretences
are to be looked upon as part of their commission, which may
not improbably give them a dispensation in the case of truth,
when it may bring a prejudice upon the service of those by
whom they are employed. If there should be men who having
formerly had means and authority to persuade, by secular arguments, have in pursuance of that power, sprinkled money
amongst the dissenting ministers; and if those very men should
now have the same authority, practise the same methods, and
disburse, where they cannot otherwise persuade: it seemeth to
me to be rather an evidence than a presumption of the deceit.
If there should be ministers amongst you, who by having fallen
under temptations of this kind, are in some sort engaged to
continue their frailty, by the awe they are in, lest it should be
exposed: the persuasions of these unfortunate men must sure
have the less force; and their arguments, though never so specious, are to be suspected, when they come from men who
have mortgaged themselves to severe creditors, that expect a
rigorous observation of the contract, let it be never so unwar-
rantable. If these, or any others, should at this time preach
up anger and vengeance against the Church of England; may
it not without injustice be suspected, that a thing so plainly
out of season springeth rather from corruption than mistake;
and that those who act this cholerick part, do not believe
themselves, but only pursue higher directions, endeavour to
make good that part of their contract which obliged them,
upon a forfeiture, to make use of their inflaming eloquence?
They might apprehend their wages would be retrenched if they
should be moderate: and therefore, whilst violence is their
interest, those who have not the same arguments, have no
reason to follow such a partial example. If there should be
men, who by the load of their crimes against the government,
have been bowed down to comply with it against their conscience; who by incurring the want of a pardon, have drawn
upon themselves the necessity of an entire resignation: such
men are to be lamented, but not to be believed. Nay, they
themselves, when they have discharged their unwelcome task,
will be inwardly glad that their forced endeavours do not succeed, and are pleased when men resist their insinuations;
which are far from being voluntary or sincere, but are squeezed
out of them, by the weight of their being so obnoxious. If in

the height of this great dearness by comparing things, it should happen, that at this instant, there is much a surer friendship with those who are so far from allowing liberty, that they allow no living to a Protestant under them. Let the scene lie in what part of the world it will, the argument will come home, and sure it will afford sufficient ground to suspect. Apparent contradictions must strike us; neither nature nor reason can digest them: self-flattery, and the desire to deceive ourselves, to gratify a present appetite, with all their power, which is great, cannot get the better of such broad conviction, as some things carry along with them. Will you call these vain and empty suspicions? Have you been at all times so void of fears and jealousies, as to justify your being so unreasonably valiant, in having none upon this occasion? Such an extraordinary courage at this unseasonable time, to say no more, is too dangerous a virtue to be commended. If then for these and a thousand other reasons, there is cause to suspect, sure your new friends are not to dictate to you, or advise you; for instance, the addresses that fly abroad every week, and murther us with 'another to the same;' the first draughts are made by those who are not very proper to be secretaries to the Protestant Religion; and it is your part only to write them out fairer again. Strange! that you who have been formerly so much against set forms, should now be content the priests should indite for you. The nature of thanks is an unavoidable consequence of being pleased or obliged; they grow in the heart, and from thence show themselves either in looks, speech, writing or action: no man was ever thankful, because he was bid to be so, but because he had, or thought he had some reason for it. If then there is cause in this case to pay such extravagant acknowledgments, they will flow naturally, without taking such pains to procure them; and it is unkindly done, to tire all the post-horses with carrying circular letters, to sollicit that, which would be done without any trouble or constraint: if it is really in itself such a favour, what needeth so much pressing men to be thankful, and with such eager circumstances, that where persuasions cannot delude, threatnings are employed, to fright them into a compliance? Thanks must be voluntarily, not only unconstrained, but unsolicited, else they are either trifles or snares, they either signify nothing, or a great deal more than is intended by those that give them. If an inference should be made, that whosoever thanketh the king for his Declaration, is by that engaged to justify it in point of law; it is a greater stride, than I presume all those care to make who are persuaded to address: if it shall be supposed, that all the thankers will be repealers of the Test, whenever a parliament shall meet. Such an expectation is better prevented before, than disappointed afterwards; and the surest way to avoid the lying under such a scandal, is not to do any thing that may give a colour to the mistake: these bespoken thanks are little less improper than love letters that were solicited by the lady to whom they are to be directed; so that besides the little ground there is to give them, the manner of getting them, doth extremely lessen their value. It might be wished, that you would have suppressed your impatience, and have been content, for the sake of religion, to enjoy it within yourselves, without the liberty of a public exercise, till a parliament had allowed it; but since that could not be, and that the artificers of some amongst you have made use of the well meant zeal of the generality, to draw them into this mistake; I am so far from blaming you with that sharpness, which, perhaps the matter in strictness would bear, that I am ready to err on the side of the more gentle construction. There is a great difference between enjoying quietly the advantages of an act irregularly done by others, and the going about to support it against the laws in being: the law is so sacred, that no trespass against it is to be defended; yet frailties may in some measure be excused, when they cannot be justified. The desire of enjoying a liberty, from which men have been so long restrained, may be a temptation that their reason is not at all times able to resist. If in such a case, some objections are leapt over, indifferent men will be more inclined to lament the occasion, than to fall too hard upon the fault, whilst it is covered with the apology of a good intention; but where to rescue yourselves from the severity of one law, you give a blow to all the laws, by which your religion and liberty are to be protected; and instead of silently receiving the benefit of this indulgence, you set up for advocates to support it; you become voluntary aggressors, and look like counsel retained by the prerogative against your old friend Magna Charta, who hath done nothing to deserve her falling thus under your displeasure. If the case then should be, that the price expected from you for this liberty, is giving up your right in the laws, sure you will think twice, before you go any further in such a losing bargain. After giving thanks for the breach of one law, you lose the right of complaining of the breach of all the rest; you will not very well know how to defend yourselves, when you are pressed; and having given up the question, when it was for your advantage, you cannot recall it, when it shall be to your prejudice. If you will set up at one time a power to help you, which at another time by parity of reason shall be made use of to destroy you, you will neither be pitied, nor relieved against a mischief you draw upon yourselves, by being so unreasonably thankful. It is like calling in auxiliaries to help, who are strong enough to subdue you: in such a case your complaints will come too late to be heard, and your sufferings will raise mirth instead of compassion. If you think, for your excuse, to expound your thanks so as to restrain them to this particular case, others, for their ends, will extend them further; and in these differing interpretations, that which is backed by authority will be the most likely to prevail, especially when by the advantage you have given them, they have in truth the better of the argument, and that the inferences from your own concessions are very strong and express against you. This is so far from being a groundless supposition, that there was a late instance of it, the last session of parliament, in the house of lords, where the first thanks, though things of course, were interpreted to be the approbation of the king's whole speech, and a restraint from the further examination of any part of it, though never so much disliked; and it was with difficulty obtained, not to be excluded from the liberty of objecting to this mighty prerogative of dispensing, merely by this innocent and usual piece of good manners, by which no such thing could possibly be intended. This sheweth, that some bounds are to be put to your good breeding, and that the constitution of England is too valuable a thing to be ventured upon a compliment. Now that you have for some time enjoyed the benefit of the end, it is time for you to look into the danger of the means: the same reason that made you desirous to get liberty, must make you solicitous to preserve it: so that the next thought will naturally be, not to engage yourself beyond retreat, and to agree so far with the principles of all religions, as not to rely upon a death-bed repentance. There are certain periods of time, which being once past, make all cautions ineffectual, and all remedies desperate. Our understandings are apt to be hurried on by the first heats;

which, if not restrained in time, do not give us leave to look back, till it is too late. Consider this in the case of your anger against the Church of England, and take warning by their mistake in the same kind, when after the late king's restoration, they preserved so long the bitter taste of your rough usage to them in other times, that it made them forget their interest, and sacrifice it to their revenge. Either you will blame this proceeding in them, and for that reason not follow it, or if you allow it, you have no reason to be offended with them; so that you must either dismiss your anger, or lose your excuse; except you should argue more partially than will be supposed of men of your morality and understanding. If you had now to do with those rigid prelates, who made it a matter of conscience to give you the least indulgence; but kept you at an uncharitable distance, and even to your more reasonable scruples continued stiff and exorable, the argument might be fairer on your side; but since the common danger hath so laid open that mistake, that all the former haughtiness towards you is for ever extinguished, and that it hath turned the spirit of persecution, into a spirit of peace, charity and condescension; shall this happy change only affect the Church of England? And are you so in love with separation, as not to be moved by this example? It ought to be followed, were there no other reason than that it is a virtue; but when besides that, it is become necessary to your preservation, it is impossible to fail the having its effect upon you. If it should be said, that the Church of England is never humble, but when she is out of power, and therefore loseth the right of being believed when she pretendeth to it; the answer is, first, it would be an uncharitable objection, and very much mis-timed; an unseasonable triumph, not only ungenerous, but unsafe: so that in these respects it cannot be urged, without scandal, even though it could be said with truth. Secondly, this is not so in fact, and the argument must fall, being built upon a false foundation; for whatever may be told you, at this very hour, and in the heat and glare of your present sun-shine, the Church of England can in a moment bring clouds again; and turn the royal thunder upon your heads, blow you off the stage with a breath, if she would give but a smile or a kind word; the least glympse of her compliance, would throw you back into the state of suffering, and draw upon you all the arrears of severity, which have accrued during the time of this kindness to you; and yet the Church of England, with all her faults, will not allow herself to be rescued by such unjustifiable means, but choseth to bear the weight of power, rather than lie under the burthen of being criminal. It cannot be said, that she is unprovoked; books and letters come out every day, to call for answers, yet she will not be stirred. From the supposed authors and the stile, one would swear they were undertakers, and had made a contract to fall out with the Church of England. There are lashes in every address, challenges to draw the pen in every pamphlet; in short, the fairest occasions in the world given to quarrel; but she wisely distinguisheth between the body of dissenters, whom she will suppose to act, as they do, with no ill intent; and these small skirmishers picked and sent out to picqueer, and to begin a fray amongst the Protestants, for the entertainment, as well as the advantage of the Church of Rome. This conduct is so good, that it will be scandalous not to applaud it: it is not equal dealing, to blame our adversaries for doing ill, and not to commend them when they do well. To hate them because they persecuted, and not to be reconciled to them when they are ready to suffer, rather than receive all the advantages that can be gained by a criminal compliance, is a principle no sort of Christians can own, since it would give an objection to them never to be answered. Think a little, who they were that promoted your former persecutions, and then consider how it will look to be angry with the instruments, and at the same time to make a league with the authors of your sufferings. Have you enough considered what will be expected from you? Are you ready to stand in every borough by a virtue of a Conge d'elire, and instead of election, be satisfied if you are returned? Will you in parliament, justify the dispensing power, with all its consequences, and repeal the Test, by which you will make way for the repeal of all the laws, that were made to preserve your religion, and to enact others that shall destroy it? Are you disposed to change the liberty of debate, into the merit of obedience, and to be made instruments to repeal or enact laws, when the Roman Consistory are Lords of the Articles. Are you so linked with your new friends, as to reject any indulgence a parliament shall offer you, if it shall not be so comprehensive as to include the Papists in it. Consider that the implied conditions of your new treaty are no less, than that you are to do everything you are desired, without examining,

and that for this pretended liberty of conscience, your real
freedom is to be sacrificed: your former faults hang like chains
still about you, you are let loose only upon bail; the first act
of con-compliance, sendeth you to jail again. You may see that
the Papists themselves do not rely upon the legality of this
power, which you are to justify, since they being so very
earnest to get it established by a law, and the doing such very
hard things in order, as they think, to obtain it, is a clear
evidence, that they do not think that the single power of the
crown is in this case a good foundation; especially when this
is done under a prince, so very tender of all the rights of sovereignty, that he would think it a dimunition to his prerogative, where he conceiveth it strong enough to go alone, to call
in the legislative help to strengthen and support it. You have
formerly blamed the Church of England, and not without
reason, for going so far as they did in their compliance; and
yet as soon as they stopped, you see they are not only deserted, but prosecuted: conclude then from this example, that
you must either break off your friendship, or resolve to have
no bounds in it. If they do not succeed in their design, they
will leave you first; if they do, you must either leave them,
when it will be too late for your safety, or else after the
squeaziness of starting at a surplice, you must be forced to
swallow transubstantiation. Remember that the other day
those of the Church of England were Trimmers for enduring
you, and now by a sudden turn, you are become the favourites;
do not deceive yourselves, it is not the nature of lasting plants
thus to shoot up in a night; you may look gay and green for
a little time, but you want a root to give you a continuance.
It is not so long since, as to be forgotten, that the Maxim
was, 'It is impossible for a Dissenter not to be a Rebel. Consider at this time in France, even the new converts are so far
from being employed, that they are disarmed: their sudden
change maketh them still to be distrusted, notwithstanding
that they are reconciled: what are you to expect then from
your dear friends, to whom, whenever they shall think fit to
throw you off again, you have in other times given such arguments for their excuse? Besides all this, you act very unskil-
fully against your visible interest, if you throw away the advantages, of which you can hardly fail in the next probable
revolution. Things tend naturally to what you would have, if
you would let them alone, and not by an unseasonable activity

lose the influences of your good star, which promiseth you
every thing that is prosperous. The Church of England convinced of its error in being severe to you; the parliament whenever it meeteth, sure to be gentle to you; the next heir bred
in the country, which you have so often quoted for a pattern
of indulgence; a general agreement of all thinking men, that
we must no more cut ourselves off from the Protestants
abroad, but rather enlarge the foundations upon which we
are to build our defences against the common enemy; so that
in truth, all things seem to conspire to give you ease and satisfaction, if by too much haste to anticipate your good fortune,
you do not destroy it. The Protestants have but one article of
human strength, to oppose the power which is now against
them, and that is, not to lose the advantage of their numbers,
by being so unweary as to let themselves be divided. We all
agree in our duty to our prince, our objections to his belief,
do not hinder us from seeing his virtues; and our not complying with his religion, hath no effect upon our allegiance;
we are not to be laughed out of our passive obedience, and the
doctrine of non-resistance, though even those who perhaps
owe the best part of their security to that principle, are apt
to make a jest of it. So that if we give no advantage by the
fatal mistake of misapplying our anger, by the natural course
of things, this danger will pass away like a shower of hail; fair
weather will succeed, as lowering as the sky now looketh, and
all by this plain and easy receipt. Let us be still, quiet and
undivided, firm at the same time to our religion, our loyalty,
and our laws, and so long as we continue this method, it is
next to impossible, that the odds of two hundred to one
should lose the bett, except the Church of Rome, which hath
been so long barren of miracles, should now in her declining
age, be brought to bed of one that would out-do the best she
can brag of in her Legend. To conclude, the short question
will be, whether you will join with those who must in the end
run the same fate with you. If Protestants of all sorts, in their
behaviour to one another, have been to blame, they are upon
the more equal terms, and for that very reason it is fitter for
them now to be reconciled. Our dis-union is not only a re-
proach, but a danger to us; those who believe in modern miracles, have more right, or at least more excuse, to neglect all
secular cautions; but for us, it is as justifiable to have no re-

ligion, as wilfully to throw away the human means of preserving it. I am, dear sir, your most affectionate humble servant.

D.   THE PETITION OF THE SEVEN BISHOPS

MAY 18, 1688

The humble petition of William archbishop of Canterbury [Sancroft] and of divers suffragan bishops of that province [St. Asaph, Bath and Wells, Bristol, Chichester, Ely, and Peterborough] now present with him, in behalf of themselves and others of their absent brethren, and of the clergy of their respective dioceses,
  Humbly sheweth,

That the great averseness they find in themselves to the distributing and publishing in all their churches your Majesty's late declaration for liberty of conscience proceedeth neither from any want of duty and obedience to your Majesty, our Holy Mother, the Church of England, being both in her principles and constant practice unquestionably loyal nor yet from any want or due tenderness to dissenters, in relation to whom they are willing to come to such a temper as shall be thought fit when that matter shall be considered and settled in parliament and Convocation, but among many other considerations from this especially, because that declaration is founded upon such a dispensing power as hath often been declared illegal in parliament, and particularly in the years 1662, 1672, and in the beginning of your Majesty's reign, and is a matter of so great moment and consequence to the whole nation, both in Church and State, that your petitioners cannot in prudence, honour or conscience so far make themselves parties to it as the distribution of it all over the nations, and the solemn publication of it once and again even in God's house and in the time of His divine service, must amount to in common and reasonable construction.

Your petitioners therefore most humbly and earnestly beseech your Majesty that you will be graciously pleased not to insist upon their distributing and reading your Majesty's said declaration.

E. THE LETTER OF INVITATION FROM THE IMMORTAL SEVEN

JUNE 30, 1688

We have great satisfaction to find by Russell and since by M. Zuylestein that your Highness is so ready and willing to give us such assistance as they have related to us. We have great reason to believe we shall be every day in a worse condition than we are, and less able to defend ourselves, and therefore we do earnestly wish we might be so happy as to find a remedy before it be too late for us to contribute to our own deliverance; but although these be our wishes, yet we will by no means put your Highness into any expectations which might misguide your own councils in this matter; so that the best advice we can give is to inform your Highness truly both of the state of things here at this time and of the difficulties which appear to us.

As to the first, the people are so generally dissatisfied with the present conduct of the Government in relation to their religion, liberties and properties (all which have been greatly invaded), and they are in such expectation of their prospects being daily worse, that your Highness may be assured there are nineteen parts of twenty of the people throughout the kingdom who are desirous of a change and who, we believe, would willingly contribute to it, if they had such a protection to countenance their rising as would secure them from being destroyed before they could get to be in a posture to defend themselves. It is no less certain that much the greatest part of the nobility and gentry are as much dissatisfied, although it is not safe to speak to many of them beforehand; and there is no doubt but that some of the most considerable of them would venture themselves with your Highness at your first landing, whose interests would be able to draw great numbers to them whenever they could protect them and the raising and drawing of men together. And if such a strength could be landed as were able to defend itself and them till they could be got together into some order, we make no question but that strength would quickly be increased to a number double to the army here, although their army should remain firm to them; whereas we do upon very good grounds believe that their army then would be very much divided among themselves, many of the officers being so discontented that they continue in their service only for a subsistence (besides that some of their minds are known already) and very many of the common soldiers do daily show such an aversion to the popish religion that there is the greatest probability imaginable of great number of deserters which would come from them should there be such an occasion; and amongst the seamen it is almost certain there is not one in ten who would do them any service in such a war.

Besides all this, we do much doubt whether the present state of things will not yet be much changed to the worse before another year . . .

These considerations make us of the opinion that this is a season in which we may more probably contribute to our own safeties than hereafter. . . . We who subscribe this will not fail to attend your Highness upon your landing and to do all that lies in our power to prepare others to be in as much readiness as such an action is capable of, where there is so much danger in communicating an affair of such a nature till it be near the time of its being made public. But, as we have already told your Highness, we must also lay our difficulties before your Highness, which are chiefly that we know not what alarm your preparations for this expedition may give, or what notice it will be necessary for you to give the States beforehand, by either of which means their intelligence or suspicions here may be such as may cause us to be secure before your landing. And we must presume to inform your Highness that your compliment upon the birth of the child (which not one in a thousand here believes to be the Queen's) hath done you some injury . . .

If upon due consideration of all these circumstances your Highness shall think fit to adventure upon the attempt, or at least to make such preparations for it as are necessary (which we wish you may), there must be no more time lost in letting us know your resolution concerning it, and in what time we may depend that all the preparations can be so managed as not to give them warning here . . .

signed by Shrewsbury, Devonshire, Danby, Lumley,
the Bishop of London, Edward Russell and Henry Sidney.

F. PRINCE WILLIAM OF ORANGE'S DECLARATION

SEPTEMBER 30, 1688

. . . We cannot any longer forbear to declare that, to our great regret, we see that those counsellors who have now the chief credit with the King have overturned the religion, laws, and liberties of those realms and subjected them in all things relating to their consciences, liberties and properties to arbitrary government . . .

Those evil counsellors for the advancing and colouring this with some plausible pretexts did invent and set on foot the King's dispensing, power by virtue of which they pretend that, according to the law, he can suspend and dispense with the execution of the laws that have been enacted by the authority of the king and parliament for the security and happiness of the subject and so have rendered those laws of no effect . . .

Those evil counsellors, in order to the giving some credit to this strange and execrable maxim, have so conducted the matter, that they have obtained a sentence from the judges declaring that this dispensing power is a right belonging to the Crown; as if it were in the power of the twelve judges to offer up the laws, rights and liberties of the whole nation to the King, to be disposed of by him arbitrarily and at his pleasure . . .

It is likewise certain that there have been, at divers and sundry times, several laws enacted for the preservation of those rights and liberties, and of the Protestant religion; and, among other securities, it has been enacted that all persons whatsoever that are advanced to any ecclesiastical dignity, or to bear office in either university, as likewise all others that should be put into any employment civil or military should declare that they were not papists, but were of the Protestant religion, and that, by their taking of the oaths of allegiance and Supremacy, and the Test: yet those evil counsellors have, in effect, annulled and abolished all those laws, both with relation to ecclesiastical and civil employments . . .

[those evil counsellors] have not only without any colour of law, but against the express laws to the contrary, set up a commission of a certain number of persons, to whom they have committed the cognizance and direction of all ecclesiastical matters; in the which commission there has been, and still is, one of his Majesty's ministers of state, who makes now public profession of the Popish religion [Sunderland] . . . and those evil counsellors take care to raise none to any ecclesiastical dignities but persons that have no zeal for the Protestant religion, and that now hide their unconcernedness for it under the specious pretence of moderation . . .

The Declaration then instances the favouritism of papists, the pressures on the clergy and local government, the forfeiture of the charters and the trial of the seven bishops as grievances against the 'evil counsellors' of James II and continues:

Both We ourselves and our dearest and most entirely beloved Consort the Princess have endeavoured to signify in terms full of respect to the King the just and deep regret which all these proceedings have given us . . .

The last and great remedy for all those evils is the calling of a parliament, for securing the nation against the evil practices of those wicked counsellors; but this could not be yet compassed, nor can it be easily brought about: for those men apprehending that a lawful parliament being once assembled, they would be brought to an account for all their open violations of law, and for their plots and conspiracies against the Protestant religion, and the lives and liberties of the subjects, they have endeavoured, under the specious pretence of liberty of conscience, first to sow divisions amongst Protestants, between those of the Church of England and the dissenters. . . . They have also required all the persons in the several counties of England that either were in any employment, or were in any considerable esteem, to declare beforehand that they would concur in the repeal of the Test and penal laws; and that they would give their voices in the elections to parliament only for such as would concur in it . . .

But, to crown all, there are great and violent presumptions inducing us to believe that those evil counsellors, in order to the carrying on of their evil designs, and to the gaining to themselves the more time for effecting of them, for the encouraging of their complices, and for the discouraging of all good subjects, have published that the Queen hath brought forth a son; though there hath appeared both during the

Queen's pretended bigness, and in the manner in which the birth was managed, so many just and visible grounds of suspicion that not only we ourselves, but all the good subjects of those kingdoms, do vehemently suspect that the pretended Prince of Wales was not born by the Queen . . .

And since our dearest and most entirely beloved Consort the Princess, and likewise ourselves, have so great an interest in this matter, and such a right, as all the world knows, to the succession to the Crown . . . and since the English nation has ever testified a most particular affection and esteem both to our dearest Consort the Princess and to ourselves, we cannot excuse ourselves from espousing their interests in a matter of such high consequences; and from contributing all that lies in us for the maintaining both of the Protestant religion and of the laws and liberties of those kingdoms; and for the securing to them the continual enjoyments of all their just rights: to the doing of which we are most earnestly solicited by a great many lords, both spiritual and temporal and by many gentlemen and other subjects of all ranks.

Therefore it is that we have thought fit to go over to England and to carry with us a force sufficient, by the blessing of God, to defend us from the violence of those evil counsellors; and we, being desirous that our intention in this may be rightly understood, have, for this end, prepared this declaration, in which we have hitherto given a true account of the reasons inducing us to it: so we now think fit to declare that this our expedition is intended for no other design but to have a free and lawful parliament assembled as soon as possible . . .

We do, in the last place, invite and require all persons whatsoever, all the peers of the realm, both spiritual and temporal, all lords lieutenants, deputy lieutenants, and all gentlemen, citizens, and other commons of all ranks, to come and assist us, in order to the executing of this our design, against all such as shall endeavour to oppose us, that so we may prevent all those miseries which must needs follow upon the nation's being kept under arbitrary government and slavery, and that all violences and disorders, which may have overturned the whole Constitution of the English government, may be fully redressed in a free and legal parliament . . .

G. THE DECLARATION OF RIGHTS
FEBRUARY 13, 1689

Whereas the late King James the Second, by the assistance of divers evil counsellors, judges, and ministers employed by him, did endeavour to subvert and extirpate the Protestant religion and the laws and liberties of the kingdom.

1. By assuming and exercising a power of dispensing with and suspending of laws, and the execution of laws, without the consent of parliament.
2. By committing and prosecuting divers worthy prelates for humbly petitioning to be excused concurring to the said assumed power.
3. By issuing and causing to be executed a commission under the Great Seal for erecting a court called the Court of Commissioners for Ecclesiastical Causes.
4. By levying money for and to the use of the Crown by pretence of prerogative, for other time and in other manner than the same was granted by parliament.
5. By raising and keeping a standing army within this kingdom in time of peace without the consent of parliament and quartering soldiers contrary to the law.
6. By causing several good subjects, being Protestants, to be disarmed at the same time when papists were both armed and employed contrary to the law.
7. By violating the freedom of election by members to serve in parliament.
8. By prosecutions in the Court of King's Bench for matters and causes cognizable only in parliament; and by divers other arbitrary and illegal courses.
9. And whereas of late years, partial, corrupt, and unqualified persons have been returned and served on juries in trials, and particularly divers jurors in trials for high treason, which were not freeholders.
10. Excessive bail hath been required of persons committed in criminal cases, to elude the benefit of laws made for the liberty of the subjects.

11. And excessive fines have been imposed; and illegal and cruel punishments inflicted.
12. And several grants and promises made of fines and forfeitures, before any conviction or judgment against the persons, upon whom the same were to be levied.

All which are utterly and directly contrary to the known laws and statutes and freedom of this realm.

And whereas the said late King James the Second having abdicated the government, and the throne being thereby vacant, his Highness the Prince of Orange (whom it hath pleased Almighty God to make the glorious instrument of delivering this kingdom from popery and arbitrary power) did (by the advice of the lords spiritual and temporal, and divers principal persons of the Commons) cause letters to be written to the lords spiritual and temporal, being Protestants; and other letters to the several counties, cities, universities, boroughs, and Cinque Ports, for the choosing of such persons to represent them, as were of right to be sent to parliament, to meet and sit at Westminster upon January 22, 1689 . . .

And thereupon the said lords spiritual and temporal and Commons . . . do in the first place (as their ancestors in like case have usually done) for the vindicating and asserting their ancient rights and liberties, declare:

1. That the pretended power of suspending of laws, or the execution of laws, by regal authority, without consent of parliament, is illegal.
2. That the pretended power of dispensing with laws, or the execution of laws, by regal authority, as it hath been assumed and exercised of late, is illegal.
3. That the commission for erecting the late Courts of Commissioners for Ecclesiastical Causes and courts of like nature are illegal and pernicious.
4. That levying money for or to the use of the Crown, by pretence of prerogative, without grant of parliament, for longer time, or in other manner than the same is, or shall be granted, is illegal.
5. That it is the right of the subjects to petition the King, and all commitments and prosecutions for such petitioning are illegal.
6. That the raising or keeping a standing army within the kingdom in time of peace, unless it be with consent of parliament, is against law.

7. That the subjects which are Protestants may have arms for their defence suitable to their conditions and as allowed by law.

8. That election of members of parliament ought to be free.

9. That the freedom of speech and debates or proceedings in parliament ought not to be impeached or questioned in any court or place out of parliament.

10. That excessive bail ought not to be required, nor excessive fines imposed; nor cruel and unusual punishments inflicted.

11. That jurors ought to be duly impanelled and returned, and jurors which pass upon men in trials for high treason ought to be freeholders.

12. That all grants and promises of fines and forfeitures of particular persons before conviction are illegal and void.

13. And that for redress of all grievances, and for the amending, strengthening and preserving of the laws, parliaments ought to be frequently held.

And they do claim, demand, and insist upon all and singular the premisses, as their undoubted rights and liberties; and that no declaration, judgments, doings or proceedings, to the prejudice of the people in any of the said premisses, ought in any wise to be drawn hereafter into consequence of example.

To which demands of their rights they are particularly encouraged by the declaration of His Highness the Prince of Orange, as being the only means for obtaining a full redress and remedy therein.

Having therefore an entire confidence that his said Highness the Prince of Orange will perfect the deliverance so far advanced by him, and will still preserve them from the violation of their rights, which they have here asserted, and from all other attempts upon their religion, rights, and liberties.

The said Lords Spiritual and Temporal, and Commons, assembled at Westminster do resolve that William and Mary, Prince and Princess of Orange be, and be declared, King and Queen of England, France, and Ireland, and the dominions thereunto belonging, to hold the Crown and royal dignity of the said kingdoms and dominions to them the said Prince and Princess during their lives, and the life of the survivor of them; and that the sole and full exercise of regal power be only in, and executed by the said Prince of Orange, in the names of the said Prince and Princess, during their joint lives; and after their deceases, the said Crown and royal dignity of the said

Kingdoms and dominions to be to the heirs of the body of the said Princess; and for default of such issue to the Princess Anne of Denmark and the heirs of her body; and for default of such issue to the heirs of the body of the said Prince of Orange. And the Lords Spiritual and Temporal and the Commons do pray the said Prince and Princess to accept the same accordingly.

H.　ACT OF SETTLEMENT, 1701

AN ACT FOR THE FURTHER LIMITATION OF THE CROWN AND BETTER SECURING THE RIGHTS AND LIBERTIES OF THE SUBJECT

(12 & 13 Gul. III, cap. 2)

Whereas in the first year of the reign of your Majesty and of our late most gracious Sovereign Lady Queen Mary (of blessed memory) an Act of Parliament was made, entituled, *An Act for declaring the rights and liberties of the subject and for settling the succession of the crown,* wherein it was (amongst other things) enacted, established and declared, that the crown and regal government of the kingdoms of England, France and Ireland and the dominions thereunto belonging should be and continue to your Majesty and the said late queen during the joint lives of your Majesty and the said queen and to the survivor, and that after the decease of your Majesty and of the said queen and said crown and regal government should be and remain to the heirs of the body of the said late queen, and for default of such issue to her Royal Highness the Princess Anne of Denmark and the heirs of her body, and for default of such issue to the heirs of the body of your Majesty; and it was thereby further enacted, that all and every person and persons that then were or afterwards should be reconciled to or shall hold communion with the see or Church of Rome, or should profess the popish religion or marry a papist, should be excluded, and are by that Act made forever incapable to inherit, possess or enjoy the crown and government of this realm and Ireland and the dominions thereunto belonging or any part of the same, or to have, use or exercise any regal power, authority or jurisdiction within the same, and in all and every such case and cases the people of these realms shall be and are thereby absolved of their allegiance; and that the said crown and government shall from time to time descend to and be enjoyed by such person or persons being Protestants as should have inherited and enjoyed the same in case the said person or persons so reconciled, holding communion, professing or marrying as aforesaid were naturally dead; after the making of which statute and the settlement therein contained your Majesty's good subjects, who were restored to the full and free possession and enjoyment of their religion, rights and liberties by the providence of God giving success to your Majesty's just undertakings and unwearied endeavours for that purpose, had no greater temporal felicity to hope or wish for than to see a royal progeny descending from your Majesty, to whom (under God) they owe their tranquillity, and whose ancestors have for many years been principal assertors of the reformed religion and the liberties of Europe, and from our said most gracious sovereign lady, whose memory will always be precious to the subjects of these realms; and it having since pleased Almighty God to take away our said sovereign lady and also the most hopeful Prince William, duke of Gloucester (the only surviving issue of her Royal Highness the Princess Anne of Denmark), to the unspeakable grief and sorrow of your Majesty and your said good subjects, who under such losses being sensibly put in mind that it standeth wholly in the pleasure of Almighty God to prolong the lives of your Majesty and of her Royal Highness, and to grant to your Majesty or to her Royal Highness such issue as may be inheritable to the crown and regal government aforesaid by the respective limitations in the said recited Act contained, do constantly implore the divine mercy for those blessings, and your Majesty's said subjects having daily experience of your royal care and concern for the present and future welfare of these kingdoms, and particularly recommending from your throne a further provision to be made for the succession of the crown in the Protestant line for the happiness of the nation and the security of our religion, and it being absolutely necessary for the safety, peace and quiet of this realm to obviate all doubts and contentions in the same by reason of any pretended titles to the crown, and to maintain a certainty in the succession thereof to which your subjects may safely have recourse for their protection in case the limitations in the said recited Act should determine: therefore for a further provision of the succession of the crown in the Protestant line, we your Majesty's most dutiful and loyal subjects the Lords Spiritual and Temporal and Commons in this present Parliament assembled do beseech your Majesty that it may be enacted and declared, and be it enacted and declared by the king's most excellent Majesty, by and with the advice and consent of the Lords Spiritual and Temporal and Commons in this present Parliament assembled and by the authority of the same, that the most excellent Princess Sophia, electress and duchess dowager of Hanover, daughter of the most excellent Princess Elizabeth, late queen of Bohemia, daughter of our late Sovereign Lord King James the first of happy memory, be and is hereby declared to be the next in succession in the Protestant line to the imperial crown and dignity of the said realms of England, France and Ireland, with the dominions and territories thereunto belonging, after his Majesty and the Princess Anne of Denmark and in default of issue of the said Princess Anne and of his Majesty respectively, and that from and after the deceases of his said Majesty our now sovereign lord, and of her Royal Highness the Princess Anne of Denmark, and for default of issue of the said Princess Anne and of his Majesty respectively, the crown and regal government of the said kingdoms of England, France and Ireland and of the dominions thereunto belonging, with the royal state and dignity of the said realms, and all honours, styles, titles, regalities, prerogatives, powers, jurisdictions and authorities to the same belonging and appertaining, shall be, remain and continue to the said most excellent Princess Sophia and the heirs of her body being Protestants; and thereunto the said Lords Spiritual and Temporal and Commons shall and will in the name of all the people of this realm most humbly and faithfully submit themselves, their heirs and posterities, and do faithfully promise that after the deceases of his Majesty and her Royal Highness, and the failure of the heirs of their respective bodies, to stand to, maintain and defend the said Princess Sophia and the heirs of her body being Protestants, according to the limitation and succession of the crown in this Act specified and contained, to the utmost of their

powers with their lives and estates against all persons whatsoever that shall attempt anything to the contrary.

II. Provided always, and it is hereby enacted, that all and
every person and persons who shall or may take or inherit the
said crown by virtue of the limitation of this present Act, and
is, are or shall be reconciled to, or shall hold communion with,
the see or Church of Rome, or shall profess the popish religion
or shall marry a papist, shall be subject to such incapacities
as in such case or cases are by the said recited Act provided,
enacted and established; and that every king and queen of this
realm who shall come to and succeed in the imperial crown of
this kingdom by virtue of this Act shall have the coronation
oath administered to him, her or them at their respective coro-
nations, according to the Act of Parliament made in the first
year of the reign of his Majesty and the said late Queen Mary,
entituled, An Act for establishing the coronation oath, and
shall make, subscribe and repeat the declaration in the Act
first above recited, mentioned or referred to in the manner and
form thereby prescribed.

III. And whereas it is requisite and necessary that some
further provision be made for securing our religion, laws and
liberties from and after the death of his Majesty and the
Princess Anne of Denmark, and in default of issue of the body
of the said princess and of his Majesty respectively, be it enacted by the king's most excellent Majesty, by and with the
advice and consent of the Lords Spiritual and Temporal and
Commons in Parliament assembled and by the authority of
the same;

That whosoever shall hereafter come to the possession of
this crown shall join in communion with the Church of England as by law established.

That in case the crown and imperial dignity of this realm
shall hereafter come to any person not being a native of this
kingdom of England this nation be not obliged to engage in
any war for the defence of any dominions or territories which
do not belong to the crown of England without the consent
of Parliament.

That no person who shall hereafter come to the possession
of this crown shall go out of the dominions of England, Scotland or Ireland without consent of Parliament.

That from and after the time that the further limitation
by this Act shall take effect all matters and things relating to

the well governing of this kingdom which are properly cognizable in the Privy Council by the laws and customs of this realm shall be transacted there, and all resolutions taken thereupon shall be signed by such of the Privy Council as shall advise and consent to the same.

That after the said limitation shall take effect as aforesaid no person born out of the kingdoms of England, Scotland or Ireland, or the dominions thereunto belonging (although he be naturalized or made a denizen, except such as are born of English parents), shall be capable to be of the Privy Council, or a member of either House of Parliament, or to enjoy any office or place of trust either civil or military, or to have any grant of lands, tenements or hereditaments from the crown to himself or to any other or others in trust for him.

That no person who has an office or place of profit under the king, or receives a pension from the crown, shall be capable of serving as a member of the House of Commons.

That after the said limitation shall take effect as aforesaid judges' commissions be made *quam diu se bene gesserint*, and their salaries ascertained and established, but upon the address of both Houses of Parliament it may be lawful to remove them.

That no pardon under the great seal of England be pleadable to an impeachment by the Commons in Parliament.

IV. And whereas the laws of England are the birthright of the people thereof, and all the kings and queens who shall ascend the throne of this realm ought to administer the government of the same according to the said laws, and all their officers and ministers ought to serve them respectively according to the same, the said Lords Spiritual and Temporal and Commons do therefore further humbly pray that all the laws and statutes of this realm for securing the established religion and the rights and liberties of the people thereof, and all other laws and statutes of the same now in force, may be ratified and confirmed, and the same are by his Majesty, by and with the advice and consent of the said Lords Spiritual and Temporal and Commons, and by authority of the same, ratified and confirmed accordingly.

BIBLIOGRAPHY AND SUGGESTED READINGS

BOOKS

Ashley, Maurice. *John Wildman: Plotter and Postmaster*. New Haven, 1947.

Ashley, Maurice. *The Glorious Revolution of 1688*. New York, 1966.

Ashley, Maurice. *James II*. Minneapolis, 1977.

Baxter, Stephen. *William III*. London and New York, 1966.

Beloff, Max. *Public Order and Popular Disturbances, 1660–1714*. London, 1938.

Bloxam, J. R. *Magdalen College and King James II, 1686–1688*. Oxford, 1886.

Bosher, Robert S. *The Making of the Restoration Settlement: The Influence of the Laudians, 1649–1662*. New York, 1951.

Browning, Andrew. *Thomas Osborne, Earl of Danby, and Duke of Leeds, 1632–1712*. 3 vols. Glasgow, 1951.

Buranelli, Vincent. *The King and the Quaker*. Philadelphia, 1962.

Burnet, Bishop Gilbert. *A Supplement to Burnet's History of My Own Times*. Edited by H. C. Foxcroft. Oxford, 1902.

Burnet, Bishop Gilbert. [A] *History of His Own Times*. 6 vols. Oxford, 1833.

Burnet, Bishop Gilbert. [B] *History of His Own Times*. London, 1906.

Campbell, John, Lord. *The Lives of the Lord Chancellors of England*. 8 vols. London, 1845–69.

Carswell, John. *The Descent on England*. New York, 1969.

Childs, John. *The Army, James II, and the Glorious Revolution*. New York, 1980.

Churchill, Sir Winston S. *Marlborough: His Life and Times*. 4 vols. New York, 1933.

Clarke, Rev. J. S. *Life of James II*. 2 vols. London, 1816.

Cobbett, William. *Parliamentary History of England.* 36 vols. London, 1806–20.

Cragg, Gerald R. *Puritanism in the Period of the Great Persecution, 1660–1688.* Cambridge, 1957.

Dalrymple, Sir John. *Memoirs of Great Britain and Ireland.* Appendix. London and Edinburgh, 1771–73.

Daly, James. *Sir Robert Filmer and English Political Thought.* Toronto, 1979.

Davies, Godfrey. *The Restoration of Charles II.* London, 1955.

Dictionary of National Biography. (DNB)

Duckett, Sir George. *Penal Laws and Test Act.* London, 1883.

Earle, Peter. *Monmouth's Rebels: The Road to Sedgemoor.* New York, 1977.

Echard, Laurence. *The History of England.* 3d ed. London, 1718.

Evelyn, John. *Diary.* Edited by William Bray. London, n.d.

Feiling, Sir Keith. *A History of the Tory Party, 1640–1714.* Oxford, 1924.

Filmer, Sir Robert. *Patriarcha, or the Natural Power of Kings.* London, 1680.

Foxcroft, H. C. *A Character of a Trimmer.* Cambridge, 1946.

Franklin, Julian H. *John Locke and the Theory of Sovereignty: Mixed Monarchy and the Right of Resistance in the Political Thought of the English Revolution.* New York, 1978.

Haley, K. H. D. *The First Earl of Shaftesbury.* Oxford, 1968.

Halifax, George Savile, Marquis of. "Letter to a Dissenter . . . ," Somers Tracts. Vol. 9. 1809.

Halifax, George Savile, Marquis of. *Maxims of State.* New York, 1935.

Helm, P. J. *Jeffreys.* London, 1966.

Hill, B. W. *The Growth of Parliamentary Parties, 1689–1742.* Hamden, Conn., 1976.

Holdsworth, Sir William. *A History of English Law.* London, 1937.

Holmes, Geoffrey. *British Politics in the Age of Anne.* London, 1967.

Holmes, Geoffrey. *Britain after the Glorious Revolution, 1689–1714.* New York, 1969.

Hosford, David H. *Nottingham, Nobles, and the North: Aspects of the Revolution of 1688.* Hamden, Conn., 1976.

Hutton, William Holden. *The English Church from the Accession of Charles I to the Death of Anne (1625–1714).* London, 1903.

Jones, J. R. *The First Whigs: The Politics of the Exclusion Crisis, 1678–1683.* London, 1961.

Jones, J. R. *The Revolution of 1688 in England*. New York, 1972.

Jones, J. R. *Country and Court: England, 1658–1714*. Cambridge, Mass., 1977.

Jones, J. R., ed. *The Restored Monarchy, 1660–1688*. Totowa, N.J., 1979.

Journals of the House of Commons.

Keir, Sir David Lindsay. *The Constitutional History of Modern Britain Since 1485*. London, 1966.

Kenyon, J. P. *Robert Spencer, Earl of Sunderland, 1641–1702*. London, 1958.

Kenyon, J. P. *The Stuart Constitution: Documents and Commentary*. Cambridge, 1966.

Kenyon, J. P. *Revolution Principles: The Politics of Party: 1689–1720*. New York, 1977.

Lacey, Douglas R. *Dissent and Parliamentary Politics in England, 1661–1689*. New Brunswick, N.J., 1969.

Lee, Maurice, Jr. *The Cabal*. Urbana, Ill., 1965.

Lever, Sir Tresham, Bt. *Godolphin: His Life and Times*. London, 1952.

Levin, Jennifer. *The Charter Controversy in the City of London, 1660–1688., and Its Consequences*. London, 1969.

Locke, John. *Second Treatise on Government*. Edited by J. W. Gough. New York, 1966.

Macaulay, T. B. *The History of England from the Accession of James the Second*. 5 vols. Chicago, 1888.

Miller, John. *Popery and Politics in England, 1660–1688*. New York, 1973.

Nenner, Howard. *By Colour of Law: Legal Culture and Constitutional Politics in England, 1660–1689*. Chicago, 1977.

Ogg, David. *England in the Reign of Charles II*. 2 vols. Oxford, 1934.

Ogg, David. *England in the Reigns of James II and William III*. Oxford, 1955.

Pinkham, Lucile. *William III and the Respectable Revolution*. Cambridge, Mass., 1954.

Plum, Harry Grant. *Restoration Puritanism: A Study of the Growth of English Liberty*. Chapel Hill, 1943.

Plumb, J. H. *The Growth of Political Stability in England, 1675–1725*. London, 1967.

Pocock, J. G. A., ed. *Three British Revolutions: 1641, 1688, 1776*. Princeton, 1980.

Powley, Edward B. *The English Navy in the Revolution of 1688*. Cambridge, 1928.

Powley, Edward B. *The Naval Side of King William's War. 16th/26th November 1688–14th June 1690.* Hamden, Conn., 1972.

Prall, Stuart E. *The Agitation for Law Reform during the Puritan Revolution, 1640–1660.* The Hague, 1966.

Ranke, Leopold von. *History of England Principally in the Seventeenth Century.* 6 vols. Oxford, 1875.

Reresby, Sir John. *Memoirs.* Edited by Andrew Browning. Glasgow, 1936.

Roberts, Clayton. *The Growth of Responsible Government in Stuart England.* Cambridge, 1966.

Rubini, Dennis. *Court and Country, 1688–1702.* London, 1967.

Schwoerer, Lois. *The Declaration of Rights, 1689.* Baltimore, 1981.

State Trials. Edited by T. B. Howell. 21 vols. London, 1816.

Straka, Gerald. *Anglican Reaction to the Revolution of 1688.* Madison, Wis., 1962.

Sykes, Norman. *From Sheldon to Secker: Aspects of English Church History, 1660–1768.* Cambridge, 1959.

Tanner, J. R. *English Constitutional Conflicts of the Seventeenth Century, 1603–1689.* Cambridge, 1928.

Trevelyan, G. M. *The English Revolution, 1688–1689.* London, 1938.

Turner, F. C. *James II.* London, 1948.

Van der Zee, Henri, and Barbara, Van der Zee. *William and Mary.* New York, 1973.

Ward, R. Plumer. *An Historical Essay on the real Character and Amount of Precedent of the Revolution of 1688.* 2 vols. London, 1838.

Western, J. R. *Monarchy and Revolution: The English State in the 1680's.* Totowa, N.J., 1972.

Weston, Corinne Comstock, and Janelle Renfrow Greenberg. *Subjects and Sovereigns: The Grand Controversy over Legal Sovereignty in Stuart England.* New York, 1981.

Whiting, C. E. *Studies in English Puritanism from the Restoration to the Revolution, 1660–1688.* London, 1931.

Wolfe, John B. *Toward a European Balance of Power, 1620–1715.* Chicago, 1970.

ARTICLES

Beddard, Robert. "The Commission for Ecclesiastical Promotions, 1681–84." *Historical Journal* 10 (1967): 11–40.

Behrens, B. "The Whig Theory of the Constitution in the Reign of Charles II." *The Cambridge Historical Journal* 7 (1941): 42–71.

Cherry, George L. "The Legal and Philosophical Position of the Jacobites." *Journal of Modern History* 22 (1950): 309–21.

Haley, K. H. D. "A List of the English Peers, c. May, 1687." *English Historical Review* 69 (April 1954): 302–6.

Jones, J. R. "James II's Whig Collaborators." *Historical Journal* 3 (1960): 65–73.

Jones, J. R. "Political Groups and Tactics in the Convention of 1660." *Historical Journal* 6 (1963): 159–77.

Kenyon, J. P. "The Earl of Sunderland and the Revolution of 1688." *The Cambridge Historical Journal* 11 (1955): 272–96.

Kenyon, J. P. "The Nobility in the Revolution of 1688." *University of Hull Publications* (1963), Inaugural Lecture.

Laslett, Peter. "The English Revolution and Locke's 'Two Treatises of Government.'" *The Cambridge Historical Journal* 12 (1956): 40–55.

Mullett, Charles. "Religion, Politics, and Oaths in the Glorious Revolution." *Review of Politics* 10 (1948): 462–74.

Plumb, J. H. "The Elections to the Convention Parliament of 1689." *The Cambridge Historical Journal* 5 (1937): 235–54.

Sachse, W. L. "The Mob and the Revolution of 1688." *Journal of British Studies* 4 (November 1964): 23–40.

INDEX

Addled Parliament (1614), 250

Anglican Reaction to the Revolution of 1688 (Straka), xiii–xiv

Anglicans (Anglican Church, Anglicanism), xiv, 24, 25–39, 40–85 passim, 251, 255 (*see also* Church of England; Established Church; specific aspects, developments, individuals); Charles II and, 24, 25 ff., 40–85 passim; and Exclusion Crisis, 40–85 passim; James II and, 89, 90–91, 96 ff., 104, 106, 112, 113, 128–58 passim, 170, 177, 179, 180, 182, 183, 184–92 ff., 218; revolution settlement and, 160–65, 170, 203, 245–77 passim, 281–83; William III and, 160–65, 170, 203, 245–77 passim, 281–83

Anglicans/Tories, and William III and revolution settlement, 245–77 passim, 288–93

Anglo-Dutch wars, 31–34

Anne, Princess (*later* Queen Anne), 46, 133, 173, 207, 211, 230, 231, 276, 287–88, 290–91, 321–24

Anti-Catholicism (*see also* Catholics; specific Acts, aspects, developments, events, individuals): Charles II and, 47 ff., 53 ff., 62 ff., 66 ff., 70 ff., 74; James II and, 112, 125–26, 132, 141, 143–44; William III and, 178, 212, 239–40

Aquinas, St. Thomas, 254

Argyll, Archibald Campbell, Earl of, 95–96, 103

Aristocracy (aristocrats), 5, 233, 250–51, 256 (*see also* specific aspects, developments, groups); and invasion by William III, 205–6, 219

Aristotle, 254

Arlington, Henry Bennet, 1st Earl of, 34. *See also* Cabal, the

Army, Dutch (*see also* Anglo-Dutch wars): and William III and invasion of England, 206, 214–15, 216, 225–26, 231, 232, 258

Army, English, 275, 284; Charles II and, 28–29; James II and, 107–12, 117, 118–19, 122, 129, 133, 135, 151, 176–78, 201, 206, 215, 219, 227, 229–33, 237–38; revolution settlement and, 275, 284; standing army issue and, 28–29, 275, 284; William III and invasion of England and, 215, 219, 227, 229–33, 237–38

Army, French, 207, 217

Ashley, Maurice, xii–xiii, 119, 128, 143, 233

Ashley Cooper, Anthony. *See* Shaftesbury, Anthony Ashley Cooper, 1st Earl of

"Association" (declaration), and invasion by William III, 226

Augsburg, League of, 216–17

Austria, 10, 84

Baber, Sir John, 139–40

Baptists, 141, 142, 143, 144–45

Barillon, Paul, 93–95, 103, 107, 110, 112, 127–28, 131, 133, 179,

Library of Congress Cataloging-in-Publication Data
Prall, Stuart E.
The bloodless revolution.
Reprint. Originally published:
Garden City, N.Y., 1972.
Bibliography: pp. 326–330.
Includes index.
1. Great Britain—Politics and government—1660–1688.
2. Great Britain—Politics and government—Revolution of
1688. 3. Great Britain—Politics and government—1689–
1702. I. Title.
DA435.P7   1985   942.06′7   85-40377
ISBN 0-299-10294-7